FRANCE, ALGERIA AND THE MOVING IMAGE
SCREENING HISTORIES OF VIOLENCE 1963–2010

LEGENDA

LEGENDA is the Modern Humanities Research Association's book imprint for new research in the Humanities. Founded in 1995 by Malcolm Bowie and others within the University of Oxford, Legenda has always been a collaborative publishing enterprise, directly governed by scholars. The Modern Humanities Research Association (MHRA) joined this collaboration in 1998, became half-owner in 2004, in partnership with Maney Publishing and then Routledge, and has since 2016 been sole owner. Titles range from medieval texts to contemporary cinema and form a widely comparative view of the modern humanities, including works on Arabic, Catalan, English, French, German, Greek, Italian, Portuguese, Russian, Spanish, and Yiddish literature. Editorial boards and committees of more than 60 leading academic specialists work in collaboration with bodies such as the Society for French Studies, the British Comparative Literature Association and the Association of Hispanists of Great Britain & Ireland.

The MHRA encourages and promotes advanced study and research in the field of the modern humanities, especially modern European languages and literature, including English, and also cinema. It aims to break down the barriers between scholars working in different disciplines and to maintain the unity of humanistic scholarship. The Association fulfils this purpose through the publication of journals, bibliographies, monographs, critical editions, and the MHRA Style Guide, and by making grants in support of research. Membership is open to all who work in the Humanities, whether independent or in a University post, and the participation of younger colleagues entering the field is especially welcomed.

ALSO PUBLISHED BY THE ASSOCIATION

Critical Texts
Tudor and Stuart Translations • *New Translations* • *European Translations*
MHRA Library of Medieval Welsh Literature

MHRA Bibliographies
Publications of the Modern Humanities Research Association

The Annual Bibliography of English Language & Literature
Austrian Studies
Modern Language Review
Portuguese Studies
The Slavonic and East European Review
Working Papers in the Humanities
The Yearbook of English Studies

www.mhra.org.uk
www.legendabooks.com

RESEARCH MONOGRAPHS IN FRENCH STUDIES

The *Research Monographs in French Studies* (RMFS) form a separate series within the Legenda programme and are published in association with the Society for French Studies. Individual members of the Society are entitled to purchase all RMFS titles at a discount.

The series seeks to publish the best new work in all areas of the literature, thought, theory, culture, film and language of the French-speaking world. Its distinctiveness lies in the relative brevity of its publications (50,000–60,000 words). As innovation is a priority of the series, volumes should predominantly consist of new material, although, subject to appropriate modification, previously published research may form up to one third of the whole. Proposals may include critical editions as well as critical studies. They should be sent with one or two sample chapters for consideration to Professor Diana Knight, Department of French and Francophone Studies, University of Nottingham, University Park, Nottingham NG7 2RD.

❖

Editorial Committee
Diana Knight, University of Nottingham (General Editor)
Robert Blackwood (University of Liverpool)
Jane Gilbert, University College London
Shirley Jordan, Newcastle University
Neil Kenny, All Souls College, Oxford
Max Silverman, University of Leeds

Advisory Committee
Wendy Ayres-Bennett, Murray Edwards College, Cambridge
Celia Britton, University College London
Ann Jefferson, New College, Oxford
Sarah Kay, New York University
Michael Moriarty, University of Cambridge
Keith Reader, University of Glasgow

PUBLISHED IN THIS SERIES

20. *Selfless Cinema? Ethics and French Documentary* by Sarah Cooper

21. *Poisoned Words: Slander and Satire in Early Modern France* by Emily Butterworth

22. *France/China: Intercultural Imaginings* by Alex Hughes

23. *Biography in Early Modern France 1540–1630* by Katherine MacDonald

24. *Balzac and the Model of Painting* by Diana Knight

25. *Exotic Subversions in Nineteenth-Century French Literature* by Jennifer Yee

26. *The Syllables of Time: Proust and the History of Reading* by Teresa Whitington

27. *Personal Effects: Reading the 'Journal' of Marie Bashkirtseff* by Sonia Wilson

28. *The Choreography of Modernism in France* by Julie Townsend

29. *Voices and Veils* by Anna Kemp

30. *Syntactic Borrowing in Contemporary French,* by Mairi McLaughlin

31. *Dreams of Lovers and Lies of Poets:*
Poetry, Knowledge, and Desire in the 'Roman de la Rose' by Sylvia Huot

32. *Maryse Condé and the Space of Literature* by Eva Sansavior

33. *The Livres-Souvenirs of Colette: Genre and the Telling of Time* by Anne Freadman

34. *Furetière's* Roman bourgeois *and the Problem of Exchange* by Craig Moyes

35. *The Subversive Poetics of Alfred Jarry,* by Marieke Dubbelboer

36. *Echo's Voice: The Theatres of Sarraute, Duras, Cixous and Renaude,* by Mary Noonan

37. *Stendhal's Less-Loved Heroines: Fiction, Freedom, and the Female,* by Maria C. Scott

38. *Marie NDiaye: Inhospitable Fictions,* by Shirley Jordan

39. *Dada as Text, Thought and Theory,* by Stephen Forcer

40. *Variation and Change in French Morphosyntax,* by Anna Tristram

41. *Postcolonial Criticism and Representations of African Dictatorship,* by Cécile Bishop

42. *Regarding Manneken Pis: Culture, Celebration and Conflict in Brussels,*
by Catherine Emerson

43. *The French Art Novel 1900-1930,* by Katherine Shingler

44. *Accent, Rhythm and Meaning in French Verse,* by Roger Pensom

45. *Baudelaire and Photography: Finding the Painter of Modern Life,* by Timothy Raser

46. *Broken Glass, Broken World: Glass in French Culture in the Aftermath of 1870,*
by Hannah Scott

47. *Southern Regional French,* by Damien Mooney

48. *Pascal Quignard: Towards the Vanishing Point,* by Léa Vuong

49. *France, Algeria and the Moving Image,* by Maria Flood

50. *Genet's Genres of Politics,* by Mairéad Hanrahan

51. *Jean-François Vilar: Theatres Of Crime,* by Margaret Atack

52. *Balzac's Love Letters: Correspondence and the Literary Imagination,* by Ewa Szypula

53. *Saints and Monsters in Medieval French and Occitan Literature,* by Huw Grange

54. *Laforgue, Philosophy, and Ideas of Otherness,* by Sam Bootle

55. *Theorizing Medieval Race: Saracen Representations in Old French Literature,*
by Victoria Turner

www.rmfs.mhra.org.uk

France, Algeria and the Moving Image

Screening Histories of Violence 1963–2010

❖

MARIA FLOOD

l

LEGENDA

Research Monographs in French Studies 49
Modern Humanities Research Association
2017

Published by Legenda
an imprint of the Modern Humanities Research Association
Salisbury House, Station Road, Cambridge CB1 2LA

ISBN 978-1-78188-692-2 (HB)
ISBN 978-1-78188-387-7 (PB)

First published 2017

Copy-Editor: Priscilla Sheringham

CONTENTS

❖

Acknowledgements   ix

Introduction   1

PART I: HISTORIES OF VIOLENCE: FRANCE

1   Blinding Visions: *Caché* and the 17 October 1961 Massacre   10

2   Stumbling over *Muriel*: Screening Torture in Post-War France   35

PART II: HISTORIES OF VIOLENCE: ALGERIA

3   Deep Wounds: Personal and Collective Histories in Assia Djebar's *La Nouba des femmes du Mont Chenoua*   58

4   Algiers as Heterotopia: Mothers and Whores in *Viva Laldjérie*   81

PART III: FRENCH HISTORIES, ALGERIAN VIOLENCE

5   Of Gods and Terrorists: *Des hommes et des dieux*   104

Conclusion   133

Bibliography   137

Filmography   147

Index   149

To my parents, Mary and Seán

ACKNOWLEDGEMENTS

❖

My first debt of gratitude is to Emma Wilson. Our conversations and her insight have been invaluable and her knowledge, generosity, and kindness unstinting. The attention to detail and patience offered by my editor Diana Knight was extraordinary, and I am also grateful to Graham Nelson, Priscilla Sheringham, and the rest of the team at Legenda. I would also like to express my thanks to Laura McMahon, whose eye for detail, encouragement, and friendship were so important to this project, particularly in the early stages. I thank Jenny Chamarette who has offered generous guidance at important stages, and Mariangela Pallidino, who has been a supportive mentor and friend. The initial research for the project was completed with the support of an AHRC Doctoral Scholarship, the Jebb Fund, and St. John's College, Cambridge, and I am grateful for their assistance. The Society for the Humanities at Cornell University and the Andrew Mellon Foundation also provided me with the material support required to complete this book, and particular thanks goes to Timothy Murray for his ebullient encouragement. I am also grateful to the Studies in French Cinema Research Bursary, which provided a grant that allowed me to obtain copyright for the cover image of this book. Part of Chapter 2 appeared in a different form in my 'Brutal Visibility: Framing Majid's Suicide in Michael Haneke's *Caché* (2005)', *Nottingham French Studies*, 56:1 (2017), 82–97, and I thank the editors of *NFS* for their advice in the writing of that paper. Many conversations have helped me along the way, and I would like to thank particularly: Jessica Eley, Francesca Hardy, Guy Austin, Timothy Lustig, Miguel Ángel Hernández Navarro, Joseph McGill, Adina Mocanu, Stacy Ndlovu, Melissa White, Emma Tobin, Hannah Scally, Rebecca Wanzo, Ida Dominijanni, Ricardo A. Wilson, and my colleagues at Keele University. For their continued friendship at all stages of this project, I would like to express my warmest gratitude to: Fiona Flood, Paula Flood, Kate Flood, Anna Flood, Zoë Foley, Damien Mooney, Jan Zylicz, Jérémie Le Pen, and Elizabeth Rush. Particular appreciation goes to my partner, Alan Russell, for his enduring patience, love, and proof reading skills. Finally, I would like to dedicate this book, with love and gratitude, to my parents.

M.F., Keele, December 2017

INTRODUCTION

❖

In the aftermath of the 17 October 1961 massacre, when thousands of peacefully protesting Algerians were pushed by police into the River Seine in Paris, an almost blanket ban on representations of the massacre was issued, both officially and unofficially, by the French state. A protest against the violence was organized by the 'Comité pour la paix en Algérie du Quartier Seine-Buci', a communist collective, which had originally started out as a theatrical troupe. One November day, several weeks after the massacre, Claude Angeli, a member of the group and a journalist working for the communist newspaper *L'Avant garde*, went out in the early hours of the Paris dawn to paint the slogan, 'Ici on noie les Algériens' [Here We Drown Algerians], on the banks of the Seine opposite the Institut Français, the fortress of hegemonic French culture. Later that morning, he returned with his colleague, journalist and amateur photographer Jean Texier, to take a photograph, dodging the armed guards who were already in position around the site of the slogan. Texier's photograph, reproduced as the cover image of this book, is devoid of human presence; it does not depict violence directly, or even apportion blame, yet the image becomes a form of testimony that marks the scene as a site of violence, and pays testament to the intimate connections between French and Algerian histories of violence in the late twentieth and early twenty-first centuries.[1]

In 2011, Algerian filmmaker Yasmina Adi released a commemorative documentary entitled *Ici on noie les Algériens* to mark the 50th anniversary of the Parisian massacre. Using Texier's image as the publicity still for the film, *Ici on noie les Algériens* is a memorial act designed to appeal to a wide audience, a collation and a summation of the main events and instances that occurred before, during, and after the massacre. In contrast to the absence evoked in Texier's image, Adi offers a new perspective on the massacre and aims to fill in forgotten historical threads: the deportation of hundreds of Algerian men, transported back to Algeria in the days following the massacre, and the women's protest, which took place on 19 October and resulted in multiple incarcerations. Adi also refers to Texier's photograph aesthetically, by drawing on the imagery of the river, counterpointing victim testimonies with shots of the dark, churning, but empty waters of the Seine.

From a fleeting expression of French left-wing insurrection against an oppressive state, to achieving the status of an iconic photograph, and finally gaining renown as the title of a popular, widely distributed documentary by an Algerian filmmaker, the trajectory of this phrase illustrates the profound interweaving of the aesthetic and the political in French and Algerian histories in the decades following decolonization. This book is an exploration of the interconnections between French and Algerian histories and lives, but it also asks how moving image art interacts with specific political, historical, and cultural moments to produce reflections of the past, as well as engaging with the material and ongoing ideological effects of historical violence. Each chapter examines one film, and my approach aims to interrogate the historical, political, and aesthetic dimensions of the film in question through the use of secondary historical sources, filmic and literary intertexts, political theory, and aesthetic theory. Each of the films in my corpus is based around a particular historical event that was subject to controversy, state suppression, or memorial or historical obfuscation. I consider Michael Haneke's *Caché* [*Hidden*] (2005) in order to examine the intersecting personal and political results of the 17 October 1961 massacre and its memorialization within contemporary French society. Alain Resnais's *Muriel ou le temps d'un retour* [*Muriel or the time of return*] (1963) treats the emerging historical narratives of female torture during the Algerian War, while embedding this traumatic past within the context of a troubled French society in the 1960s. Assia Djebar's *La Nouba des femmes du Mont Chenoua* [*The Nouba of the Women of Mount Chenoua*] (1978) gives a forum to the unrecognized roles of the rural women of the Chenoua region during the Algerian War. Nadir Moknèche's *Viva Laldjérie* [*Viva Algeria*] (2004), although set and made in the immediate aftermath of the Algerian Civil War of the 1990s, creates a semi-real, semi-fictional world of sexual and social freedom for women, where political danger lurks on the margins of the narrative. The final film of my corpus, Xavier Beauvois's *Des hommes et des dieux* [*Of Gods and Men*] (2010), is an outlier in a sense, because the film appears to be a rather self-evident historical drama about the kidnapping and murder of seven French monks by terrorists in Algeria during the Civil War. However, I read the film against its own purported aims, not as historical but rather as heritage drama in order to consider the role that colonial nostalgia plays in contemporary French cinema.

My aim in incorporating this historical material is not to engage in a compare and contrast exercise, naively imposing historical truth onto the films in question, nor is it to point out historical or filmic inaccuracies and inconsistencies with the aim of denigrating films for their lack of historical realism or verisimilitude. Rather, I seek to illuminate the intersections between the historical, the political and the aesthetic in the works in question, in order to highlight the significance of particular representational choices. To this end, I offer a series of detailed close readings, positioning the films within trends and movements in film studies, namely European cinema and the auteur in *Caché*, the French New Wave in *Muriel*, the *cinéma moudjahid* [freedom-fighter cinema] and the *cinéma de l'urgence* [cinema of crisis] movements with reference to *La Nouba des femmes du Mont Chenoua* and *Viva Laldjérie* respectively, and the heritage film in conjunction with *Des hommes et des dieux*. I am not a historian, and this is not a work of history, nor is this book an attempt to argue, in historian Robert Rosenstone's words, 'for an acceptance of the dramatic feature film — and the visual media in general — as a legitimate way of doing history'.[2] Some films can certainly 'do' history, as Rosenstone suggests, and many cinematic works are undoubtedly valuable historical documents, either for what they depict, or for the conditions of reception and production that surround their creation. One such film, Gillo Pontecorvo's *La Bataille d'Alger* [*The Battle of Algiers*] (1966) is a valuable historical resource for several reasons: as an instance of Italian and Algerian co-production; for the authenticity of its settings and actors; for the historical moment of global decolonization it captures; and as an iteration of politically inspired left-wing 'Third Cinema'. Perhaps most importantly it captures the tactical operations of the French military and the Algerian rebels. Indeed, the conflict between an Islamic guerrilla group and a powerful militarized Western state has resulted in the film's screening in the Pentagon, as well as rumoured screenings among the Black Panthers and the IRA.[3]

Other films can be considered to 'do' history by virtue of the impact they have on the national historical narrative. This was the case with Rachid Bouchareb's *Indigènes* [*Days of Glory*] (2006), a film which dramatized the lives of African soldiers who fought in World War II for the French, and had their contribution ignored, both historically and materially, following the conflict. The film brought to light the lack of reparations for African soldiers, and instigated material change: in 2006, Jacques Chirac increased the level of pensions paid to veteran African soldiers, bringing them into line with those of their French counterparts. Bouchareb's next film, *Hors la loi* [*Outside the Law*] (2010), the second in what he calls a Franco-Algerian trilogy, covered the decolonization of Algeria and the 17 October 1961 massacre. Unlike its predecessor, the film inspired huge controversy at Cannes, having provoked negative reactions among right wing and *pied-noir* groups and state representatives, with the most vocal detractor being Lionnel Luca, UMP Deputy in the National Assembly.

Rosenstone suggests that history on film might be studied in the following groupings, which mix generic and thematic concerns: 'innovative' drama, biographical film, documentary, single director, single topic drama (the Holocaust, for example), and mainstream drama, which includes big-budget Hollywood productions of historical spectacle, such as Steven Spielberg's *Saving Private Ryan* (1998). Yet *La Bataille d'Alger*, might be studied under several of those categories as a topic film (decolonization, the Algerian War), a director film (Pontecorvo as *auteur*), a mainstream drama because of its brisk, relentless rhythm, or an 'innovative' drama, for the revolutionary faux-documentary techniques it employs. The fact that one film can fall so easily into several categories, and even contradictory categories (mainstream versus innovative), thus undermines the simplicity of Rosenstone's classifications, and exposes the slippery nature of historical representation. Indeed, another class that might well have been added to Rosenstone's inventory is that of the 'counter-narrative', reconsiderations of the official version of an event that set out to fill a perceived historiographical void in the national collective memory. Films like *Indigènes* and *Hors la loi* function as counter-narratives, in that they emphasize their rootedness in historical research, and explicitly aim to resurrect or fill in forgotten or neglected historical narratives. Counter-narratives aim to increase public awareness of an under-represented or misrepresented historical event, a process based on the assumption that knowledge and recognition of this omission can effect social and political change.

The omission of iconic texts like *The Battle of Algiers* from my corpus, as well as self-evidently important works of the cultural zeitgeist like *Hors la loi* and *Indigènes*, relates to my desire to avoid focusing on the explicitly 'historical' film, the counter-narrative, or the mainstream historical spectacle. Instead, I look for what the films do not necessarily yield in explicit terms, due to the creation of a deliberate aesthetic of ambiguity, biographical limitations and self-representation, form and funding concerns, ethical and aesthetic choices, or insidious ideological agendas. I seek to make explicit the nascent historical impetus that lies behind many works, while also underscoring how a film interacts with the past it depicts and the present in which it was received. To this end, information around the creation and reception of the films is incorporated, for example, the climate of censorship in France when *Muriel* was released, the memorial furore around the 17 October 1961 massacre when *Caché* was made, and the repression of women's narratives in 1970s Algeria. I have also included details surrounding spectator and critical response where relevant in order to highlight the film's political impact. Particulars about the director's biography, personal and political objectives and their relation to French and Algerian histories have also been included where pertinent, to further ground the works in a concrete socio-political forum. Thus, I aim to show how films that are not explicitly 'historical' treat the question of history, and how films that purport to represent history can become vehicles for a particular ideology.

My work here has been informed by many of the productive examinations of the processes of history, memory, and culture that have taken place within the context of French studies and memory studies, particularly the work of Michael Rothberg and Mireille Rosello.[4] Rothberg's consideration of the dynamics of multidirectional memory, whereby the memory of the Holocaust unleashes or opens a memorial space for the emergence of colonial histories in the public sphere, offers one model for the analysis of intersecting histories. I share the basic premise of Rothberg's work, that the memorialization of one historic trauma does not necessarily block others from view, and in many respects, my tripartite research methodology, which brings into focus the historical, political and aesthetic components of a work, reflects his interdisciplinary approach. Rosello's work also aligns the political with the representational, and her 2010 text, *The Reparative in Narratives*, discusses the notion that memorialization and cultural recognition of historical trauma may not be enough: there is a remainder, what she calls the 'reparative' in narratives, a form of cultural and social recognition still present after a text has been worked through the public sphere. Yet Rothberg's focus on the intersections of Holocaust and colonial narratives assumes a pre-existing separation, a distinction that, in the case of the Franco-Algerian histories examined in the present work, cannot be assumed. Indeed, while there are analyses of French cinema about the Algerian conflict (Austin 2007; Sharpe 2020), Franco-Algerian and émigré filmmaking (Tarr 2005; Higbee 2007), as well as a few works on Algerian and Maghrebi cinema (Martin 2011; Austin 2012), this is the first book-length study to consider the parallel, and occasionally intersecting, representations of French and Algerian histories in cinema.[5] Moreover, while Rosello emphasizes the memorialization of cultural trauma in relation to French colonial histories, I focus on how the historicization process itself reflects and interacts with aesthetic choices.

The book has been divided into three sections, with sections one and two treating the geographical and historical terrain of France and Algeria respectively, while section three examines *Des hommes et des dieux* as an instance of French history writ large within the context of a specifically Algerian conflict. Part I examines *Caché* and *Muriel*, films that are grounded in France and in a French perspective on historical traumas, namely the 17 October 1961 massacre and the torture of women during the Algerian War. Algeria has often been figured, politically and aesthetically, as absence in the French imaginary. Pierre Nora's seminal project *Les Lieux de mémoire* [*Sites of Memory*] (1984, 1986, 1992) has been criticized by Richard Derderian and others for its failure to include colonial sites of memory.[6] Indeed, the Algerian War itself has been designated a 'guerre sans nom' [the war without a name] by Patrick Rotman and Bernard Tavernier, due to the use of metaphors of absence to refer to the war, including 'la situation en Algérie' [the situation in Algeria], or 'l'affaire algérienne' [the Algerian affair]. Rotman and Tavernier note that 'officiellement, l'Algérie n'était pas une guerre; une partie de la France ne pouvait se battre contre une autre' [officially, France was not at war; one part of France could not fight another part].[7] In a similar sense, the 17 October 1961 massacre was only named a massacre in February 1999, when a French court recognized Jean-Luc Einaudi's right to use the word, and French torture was called 'la question' [the question].[8] The obfuscation of Algeria from a French imaginary is reflected aesthetically in both *Caché* and *Muriel*, which use sound and image disjunctions and visual and verbal gaps to highlight historical exclusions. Moreover, these films open the question of how one responds to the pain and suffering of another — neither Haneke nor Resnais has personal connections to Algeria, or French-Algerian history. In this section, I also chart changes over time in the historical narrative: 17 October 1961 moves from near exclusion to becoming a huge topic of cultural and memorial debate, while the torture of women during the Algerian War was recognized in a number of high profile cases, most notably that of Djamila Boupacha, but not fully historicized in testimonial narratives until the 1990s.

Rather than reflecting upon an absence of historical representation through aesthetic techniques, as is the case with *Caché* and *Muriel*, the films examined in Part II, *La Nouba des femmes du Mont Chenoua* and *Viva Laldjérie*, instead return to the image as a means of restoring not only lost histories, but also marginalized personal narratives. It is worth noting that both of the Algerian filmmakers I have selected are francophone, and beyond this, they insist upon their dual identities as Algerian and francophone and the importance of their linguistic heritage. In Djebar's case, this linguistic heritage situates her in a position of privilege in relation to her Algerian compatriots, the women who she films using a documentary technique, and how she negotiates this liminal site, as well as her status as a postcolonial and feminist representative, will be interrogated. Similarly, the cinematic conditions surrounding postcolonial and Maghrebi cultural production in the present day are pertinent to an examination of *Viva Laldjérie*, where academic and popular detractors have raised many critiques of the film's supposed lack of historical or cultural realism. Both Djebar and Moknèche must navigate a representational space between fiction and reality, and both seek to undermine an image of an Algeria trapped in ongoing and relentless cycles of conflict.

Benjamin Stora disparages the 'clichéd' pronouncements of an Algeria condemned to endless reiterations of violence: 'les clichés nous replongent dans l'obscurité d'un pays voué à un drame éternel. Pourquoi cette vision d'une Algérie toujours emportée dans la malédiction, guidée par un crescendo morbide?' [Clichés take us back to the darkness of a country doomed to never-ending disaster. Why present this vision of a perpetually accursed Algeria, driven by a morbid escalating force?].[9] This is a vision that plays out in stark terms in *Des hommes et des dieux*, the focus of Part III of this book, which brings some of these debates about historical representation, politics, and aesthetics into the present day. The film offers a visually opulent Algerian stage for what is essentially a French tragedy. Based on revelations in the public sphere regarding the death of the monks, this film presents itself somewhat disingenuously as a historical drama, one that paints a morally unambiguous universe where the lines between good and evil, and French and Algerian, are clearly drawn. Unlike the other works in my corpus, which were all received in polemical terms by specific factions, *Des hommes et des dieux* was a resounding popular and critical success. Yet I read the film as a nostalgic ideological vehicle of universalist, republican, Christian, and profoundly French values, set in the proto-colonial space of contemporary Algeria.

This is not an explicitly comparative work: my aim here is not to point to the overlapping aspects of French and Algerian histories, but rather to highlight their inextricability. Within the context of ongoing debates about terrorism, migration, history, and memory, Joseph McGonagle and Edward Welch suggest that 'perhaps now more than ever, we need to think through France and Algeria together'.[10] Yet I would argue that it has never been fully possible to think of them separately, because of the profound and ongoing impact of their shared histories. French and Algerian histories are still interwoven into collective life and collective imaginaries in both countries, and as Saïd Bouamama notes of the 17 October 1961 massacre, 'dans la vie collective, les silences sont mortelles' [in collective life, silences are deadly].[11] This study looks at how films can address shared historical silences, or partially recreate them. In this sense, my work here can be aligned with Rancière's conception of the role of cinema in the historical process, when he argues that 'le cinéma n'enregistre pas simplement l'événement historique mais crée cet événement' [cinema not only recorded that historic event but created that event].[12] Cinema crafts images that move and exist across space and time, generating their own histories and speaking to audiences at diverse historical moments. Within the context of French and Algerian narrations, this book argues that the moving image itself can become its own kind of historical event, generating aesthetic, political, and cultural meaning for different groups at diverse temporal moments.

Notes to the Introduction

1. Vincent Lemaire et Yann Potin describe the double valence of the slogan, as designating the massacre but also as a marker of the deliberate erasure of its occurence: 'Le slogan [...] ne désigne pas seulement un acte de répression mais bien une politique de disparition systématique. Les noyades sont dénoncées à la fois comme instrument de terreur et comme stratégie de dissimulation de la terreur. [The slogan, "Here we drown Algerians", refers not only to an act of repression, but also to a politics of systematic extermination. The drownings are denounced both as an instrument of terror, and as a strategy to cover up that terror]. Vincent Lemaire and Yann Potin, ' "Ici on noie les Algériens": Fabriques documentaires, avatars politiques et mémoires partagées d'une icône militante (1961–2001)', *Genèses* 49 (2002), 140–62, (p. 143). This is my translation, and all translations hereafter are my own unless otherwise indicated.
2. Robert Rosenstone, *History on Film: Film on History* (London: Routledge, 2006), p. xviii.
3. Mark Parker, 'The Battle of Algiers (La battaglia di Algeri)', *Film Quarterly*, 60:4 (2007), 62–66.
4. Mireille Rosello, *Reparative in Narratives: Works of Mourning in Progress* (Liverpool: Liverpool University Press, 2010) and Michael Rothberg, *Multidirectional Memory: Remembering the Holocaust in the Age of Decolonization* (Stanford: Stanford University Press, 2009).
5. Guy Austin, *Algerian National Cinema* (Manchester: Manchester University Press, 2012); Guy Austin, 'Representing the Algerian War in Algerian Cinema: *Le Vent des Aurès*', *French Studies*, 61:2 (2007), 182–95; Will Higbee, 'Locating the Postcolonial in Transnational Cinema: The Place of Algerian Émigré Directors in Contemporary French Film', *Modern and Contemporary France*, 15:1 (2007), 51–64; Florence Martin, *Screens and Veils: Maghrebi Women's Cinema* (Bloomington: Indiana University Press, 2011); Mani Sharpe (forthcoming, 2020), *Screening the Algerian War in French Cinema* (Edinburgh: Edinburgh University Press); Carrie Tarr, *Reframing Difference: Beur and Banlieue Filmmaking in France* (Manchester: Manchester University Press, 2005).
6. Richard L. Derderian, 'Algeria as a *lieu de mémoire*: Ethnic Minority Memory and National Identity in Contemporary France', *Radical History Review*, 83 (2002), 28–43 and Stephen Legg, 'Contesting and Surviving Memory: Space, Nation, and Nostalgia in *Les Lieux de mémoire*', *Environment and Planning D: Society and Space*, 23:4 (2005), 481–504.
7. Pierre Nora, *Les Lieux de mémoire: Vol. 1, La République* (Paris: Gallimard, 1984); *Vol. 2, La Nation* (Paris: Gallimard, 1986); *Vol. 3, Les France* (Paris: Gallimard, 1992); Patrick Rotman and Bertrand Tavernier, *La Guerre sans nom: les appelés d'Algérie (1954 — 1962)* (Paris: Seuil, 1992), p. 109.
8. Cole, Joshua, 'Entering History: The Memory of Police Violence in Paris, October 1961', in *Algeria & France, 1800–2000: Identity, Memory, Nostalgia*, ed. by Patricia M. E. Lorcin (Syracuse: Syracuse University Press, 2006), pp. 117–34 (p. 121). The euphemistic nomination of torture as 'la question' gained notoriety with the publication of Henri Alleg's account entitled *La Question* (Paris: Les Éditions de Minuit, 1958).
9. Benjamin Stora, *La Guerre invisible: Algérie, années 90* (Paris: Presses de Sciences Po, 2001), p. 10.
10. Joseph McGonagle and Edward Welch, 'Untying the Knot? France and Algeria in Contemporary Visual Culture', *Modern and Contemporary France*, 19:2 (2011), 123–28, (p. 124).
11. Bouamama, speaking in Daniel Kupferstein, *17 Octobre 1961: Dissimulation d'un massacre* (2001).
12. Jacques Rancière, *Figures de l'histoire* (Paris: Presses Universitaires de France, 2012), p. 32; Jacques Rancière, *Figures of History*, trans. Julie Rose (Cambridge: Polity Press, 2014), p. 30.

PART I

❖

Histories of Violence:
France

CHAPTER 1

❖

Blinding Visions: *Caché* and the 17 October 1961 Massacre

'Je n'ai rien à cacher' [I have nothing to hide], protests the central protagonist Georges (Daniel Auteuil) in Michael Haneke's *Caché*. Yet Georges, like the film itself, equivocates: they both contain hidden elements that are personal and political, aesthetic and historical. *Caché* tells the story of the bourgeois Parisian couple Anne (Juliette Binoche) and Georges Laurent, whose materially comfortable existence is disturbed by the advent of a series of anonymous videotapes, drawings, and phone calls. The videotapes depict the exterior of their house in central Paris using surveillance, CCTV-style footage, while the drawings show crude, childish sketches of both human and chicken heads, with violent streaks of red, blood-like splatters across the white pages. Having initially feigned ignorance to his wife of the origin of the videos and drawings, Georges gradually reveals that he believes the source to be a childhood playfellow named Majid (Maurice Bénichou). Majid's parents were Algerian workers on Georges's family farm, and they travelled to Paris to take part in the 17 October 1961 protests led by the FLN (Front de Libération Nationale [National Liberation Front]) against the French government. They never returned, and Georges's parents considered adopting the orphaned Majid. However, the six-year old Georges told a series of lies about the boy, including that he beheaded a cockerel, which resulted in Majid's expulsion from the Laurent family home. Although Majid, and later his son, disclaim any knowledge of the videotapes, following an increasingly fraught series of events, including the apparent abduction of their son Pierrot (Lester Makedonsky), Georges and Anne have Majid and his son interned in jail overnight. Upon their release, Majid invites Georges to his apartment, where, without apparent cause, he takes his own life, leaving Georges reeling from the psychological consequences of this spectacle of self-violence.

   Caché touches on a wide range of themes, and the film poses a series of complex questions without offering any definitive answers. At one point, Georges accuses Anne of inventing mystery and drama after reading too many 'polars' [thrillers]. *Caché* itself starts as a kind of 'polar', a 'whodunnit' with elements of the socio-political thriller, and it morphs into a quasi-allegorical tale that leaves behind disquiet and uncertainty, far from the satisfying conclusion of a formally stable thriller. Haneke discusses his own uneasiness with film genres, describing the disjunction between the individual's experience of life and its portrayal on film: 'I do think that our perception of reality is fragmentary, [...] but genre films always pretend that reality is transportable, which means that it is explicable'.[1] Narrative ambiguity and a lack of causality, combined with a strong sense of creeping, everyday violence feature in *Caché*, and this aesthetic resonates across Haneke's œuvre. Beginning his career in television in Austria in the 1970s, Haneke has written and directed twelve films, touching on the themes of interpersonal conflict, television and media, immigration and inequality, European bourgeois hypocrisy, death, and aging. Profiting from the generous state and non-state funding resources available to filmmakers in France, including the CNC (Centre national du cinéma et de l'image animée), Canal+ and ARTE, many of Haneke's films are set in France or in the French language, including *Code Inconnu* [*Code Unknown* (2000)], *La Pianiste* [*The Piano Teacher* (2001)], *Le Temps du Loup* [*Time of the Wolf* (2003)], *Amour* (2012), and of course, *Caché*. A major success on the festival circuit, *Caché* was followed by another acclaimed socio-historical fable set in Germany in the 1910s, *The White Ribbon*, which was nominated for a Foreign Language Oscar in 2009.

Haneke has explicitly stated his desire to work outside the Hollywood system, refusing the teleological, cause-and-effect driven, and character-motivated narratives of the blockbuster style. Contrasting his aesthetic with that of popular genre filmmaking, he writes, 'my films [...] are an appeal for a cinema of insistent questions instead of false (because too quick) answers, for clarifying distance in place of violating closeness, for provocation and dialogue instead of consumption and consensus'.[2] The insistence on spectator engagement and the refusal to offer closed and cohesive narratives are, according to Thomas Elsaesser, characteristics of European cinema. Moreover, Haneke's control over his work, the reappearance of consistent aesthetic and thematic concerns, and his appeal on an art-house and festival circuit position him as a quintessential European *auteur*.[3] If, as Andrew Sarris suggests, the *auteur* can be distinguished by a single, overarching 'interior meaning' or '*élan* [impulse] of the soul', Haneke's impulse moves him towards the question of how to represent violence: interpersonal, physical, political, and symbolic acts, which violate or destroy emotional and bodily integrity.[4] In *Caché*, the entire narrative is structured around a single act of historical violence: the 17 October 1961 massacre of peaceful Algerian protestors by French police. Yet this history barely features in the film, and instead Haneke weaves a moral fable in which various forms of violence intersect: the violence resulting in segregation along ethnic and social lines; the violence of lies, and their consequences; the violence on televised media, whereby images of destruction are carried into the domestic sphere unbidden on a daily basis; and finally, physical violence in the form of extreme self-harm.

The themes and issues raised in *Caché* straddle several disciplinary frameworks, and for this reason, academic criticism of the film in the fields of film studies, French, and postcolonial studies has been abundant. Few critics have failed to remark upon Haneke's evocation of an unseen and unspecified element in the narrative regime of *Caché*, an unknown menace that generates consistent spectator discomfort. Catherine Wheatley opens her 2012 BFI monograph on *Caché* with a personal reflection on the feelings of uneasiness Haneke's cinema has aroused in her, while Ranjana Khanna evokes the Freudian uncanny in relation to Haneke's mise-en-scène (2007). Other criticism of *Caché* has variously touched on drawing and trauma (Austin), registers of image (Beugnet), psychoanalysis and trauma (Croombs), sight and concealment (Ezra and Sillars), grief and loss (Flood), urban geography and space (McNeill), proximity, distance and suffering (Saxton), and colonial imagery (Silverman).[5] In intervening in this debate, I situate the film within its historical context, in order to highlight the issues of space and visibility that played out in the massacre, and are refigured in *Caché*. I then consider the economic and social distinctions drawn between Majid and Georges, and the spectator's identification with the latter. My discussion pays close attention to the interface between form and content in Haneke's cinema, an interaction that is particularly relevant to a consideration of Majid's suicide. Described by Austin as the most traumatizing but least discussed sequence, and condemned by Paul Gilroy, a close reading of this scene according to the aesthetic theory of the grotesque illuminates the intersecting aesthetic and political issues raised by Haneke's work.[6]

17 October 1961: Historical Forgetting and Cultural Memorialization

On the night of 17 October 1961, 30,000 Algerians gathered for a demonstration that took them from suburbs like Nanterre and Gennevilliers on the outskirts of Paris towards the centre, in protest against a recently imposed curfew that prohibited the movement of Algerians between the hours of 8:30PM and 5:30AM.[7] Despite the fact that 11,538 people were arrested on that evening alone (and by the end of the week that figure had reached more than 14,000), and despite fatalities due to police violence that range in estimate from 30 to 335, the event more or less disappeared from public consciousness for several decades.[8] Although Paulette Péju published an account of the massacre in 1961, and historian Pierre Vidal-Naquet continued limited research on the events throughout the 1970s and the 1980s, French government censorship made publication difficult, and public ignorance of the massacre continued in France until the early 1990s.[9] In Algeria, the 17 October became the 'Journée Nationale de l'Immigration' [National Immigration Day], yet this designation was not explicitly related to the 17 October 1961 massacre, and Jim House and Neil Macmaster suggest that it rather came to stand more broadly for French colonial and postcolonial violence, and for the social and economic hardships of Algerian immigrants in France.[10]

The reliance on testimonial accounts of the 17 October 1961 massacre may be due to the historical uncertainties that surrounded the violence, and that to some extent still persist: it was, and is, impossible to definitively determine the number of deaths. As Joshua Cole writes, 'uncertainty about this question [...] has been deftly translated by irresponsible commentators, beginning with Maurice Papon himself, into an uncertainty about the event as a whole'.[11] The trial of Maurice Papon for his role in the deportation of Jews from Bordeaux to Auschwitz eventually took place in October 1997, after fourteen years of legal wrangling. It concomitantly brought to light his actions as police chief in Paris in 1961. Jean-Luc Einaudi, a historian and journalist, gave evidence at Papon's trial, highlighting the systematic and deliberate manner in which the massacre was not only perpetrated but also distorted and camouflaged by Papon's control of the press, producing what René Dazy describes as 'un véritable festival de mensonge, d'erreur, et d'intoxication dans la presse et ceci était très bien organisé' [a staggering display of lies, errors, and poison in the press, all very well organized].[12] On the night of 17 October, there were 'quelques images rassurantes' [a few reassuring images] on television, but by 24 October, the French media no longer reported on the event.[13] According to Einaudi, a full-scale cover-up was effectuated, and thus the emergence of a more complete picture was delayed by over two decades.[14]

Papon's report following the event claimed that just three people had died: two killed by police acting in self-defence, and one due to cardiac arrest. Papon's defence also implied that the police were unprepared; however, not only did he know from a captured document that the protest was going to be entirely peaceful, but he had also gained experience in organizing police operations at short notice in the so-called 'Algiers putsch' of 13 May 1958.[15] The FLN wanted a peaceful demonstration and individuals were searched for weapons upon leaving the *bidonvilles* [shantytowns].[16] Hocine Amor, a resident of the Nanterre shantytown and not an FLN member, recalls: 'le responsable du FLN nous a dit: "vous allez sortir, vous manifestez sans violence, même pas un couteau sur vous"' [you must go out, protest without violence, without even a knife on you].[17]

From the 1990s onwards, a plethora of historical and cultural memorial endeavours in relation to the 17 October 1961 incidents began to emerge. Einaudi was an important figure in this respect. However, because he was not a professionally trained historian he was denied access to police archives, and his book, *La Bataille de Paris* [*The Battle of Paris*] (1991), documents the event exclusively through eyewitness testimony. Until the mid-1990s, Einaudi's account seemed poised to become the standard and accepted version of events, until the *préfecture de police* in Paris granted Jean-Paul Brunet, a professional historian with posts at both the École Normale Supérieure and the Université de Paris, access to their archives. Despite Brunet's claim that, in contrast to Einaudi, he wishes to separate history from politics, the title of his book, *Police contre FLN: Le drame d'octobre 1961* [*Police against FLN: The Drama of October 1961*] immediately evokes a politicized rhetoric of confrontation. Einaudi calls the event a massacre; for Brunet it is a 'drama'.[18] Furthermore, the direct antagonism implied in Brunet's title between the police and the FLN is misleading; although many of the Algerians protesting might have been FLN members, this was a peaceful protest, which included many women and children. The discrepancy between Brunet's estimate of 30–50 deaths and Einaudi's figure of 335 may relate to their source material: police archives on the one hand, and witness testimony on the other. Yet Cole notes that Brunet treats testimonial material differently depending on its source and whether or not it props up his theory of police self-defence: 'with witness testimony that tends to support his larger argument about the FLN's responsibility, Brunet is more indulgent'.[19]

In the field of cultural memorialization, the massacre, and particularly its suppression, has become a huge topic of debate, with multiple fictional, quasi-fictional, and documentary works addressing the violence. Cultural acts which participated in this resurgence around the 17 October 1961 massacre abound, and span a period from the mid-1980s to the present day. These include: two literary works, Didier Daeninckx's *Meurtres pour mémoire* [*Murder in Memoriam*] (1983) and Leila Sebbar's novella *La Seine était rouge* [*The Seine was Red*] (1999); three fictional films, Bourlem Guerdjou's *Vivre au paradis* [*Living in Paradise*] (1998), Alain Tasma's *Nuit noire* [*Black Night*] (2004) and Rachid Bouchareb's *Hors la loi* [*Outside the Law*] (2010); Daeninckx and Mako's collaboration on the *bande déssinée* [comic book], *Octobre noir* [*Black October*] (2011); five documentaries, *Le Silence du fleuve* [*The Silence of the River*] (Agnès Denis, 1991), the Channel 4 co-production, *Une journée portée disparue* [*Secret History: Drowning by Bullets*] by Philip Brooks and Alan Hayling (1992), Daniel Kupferstein's *Dissimulation d'un massacre* [*Covering Up a Massacre*] (2001), Yasmina Adi's commemorative documentary *Ici on noie les Algériens* [*Here We Drown Algerians*] (2010), and Mehdi Lallaoui's *À propos d'octobre* (2011); and two online interactive documentaries, *Le Monde*'s *La Nuit oubliée* [*The Forgotten Night*] and *17.10.61*, by the Raspouteam collective.[20]

Mireille Rosello's distinction between historical eras and moments of memory illuminates some of the stakes in the memorial furore that surrounded the massacre from the 1990s onwards. Rosello distinguishes between a historical period as a demarcated era with concrete temporal parameters that are imposed in the historicization process of the following decades or centuries, and a 'moment of memory', when a traumatic occurrence from a historical period returns to public consciousness, sometimes decades later. Moments of memory designate and create what is perceived as acceptable discourse around a particular issue: 'the moment of memory is not reducible to one story, but opens up a scene of production and reception, it delineates the contours of a specific public during a specific time and place'.[21] Moments of memory act as a frame that delineates what is visible or invisible within the context of a historical debate. Rosello uses the term 'event of memory' to refer to cultural and social acts (books, films, paintings, installation art, comic books) that participate in this moment, by contributing to or creating public awareness about a past event. For Rosello, this cultural and historical resurgence is what makes the work 'legible, [...] the conduit of what we recognise as facts, without evidence to the contrary'.[22] Haneke remarks that he conceived *Caché* having watched in 2001 Kupferstein's *Dissimulation d'un massacre* on ARTE, a Franco-German arts channel with wide public distribution. *Caché* may thus be considered as an event of memory participating in the moment of memory around the 17 October 1961 massacre. However, it treats the history and the historicization of the massacre rather differently: by scarcely referring to it overtly, and refusing visual evidence, the film foregrounds the colonial and postcolonial concerns around space, power, and visibility that the massacre raises in the present day.

These issues around visibility and identity are central to Jacques Rancière's discussion of the massacre and its impact on French society. For Rancière, the brutality of the state response to the protest brought to light the fundamental hypocrisy of the French colonial system: for what could be more democratic, more expressive of the French *épistème* of *liberté*, *égalité*, *fraternité* than an entirely peaceful protest at a perceived social injustice? Rancière writes: 'cette journée, avec son double aspect manifeste et caché, a en effet été un point tournant, un moment où les apories éthiques du rapport entre le mien et l'autre se sont transformées en subjectivation politique' [That day, with its dual aspect, both overt and hidden, was, in effect, a turning point, a moment when the ethical aporias around the relationship between the self and the other were transformed into a kind of political subjectification].[23] These words draw attention to the dual aspects of the massacre, vacillating between excesses of visibility and invisibility. Indeed, it was the very presence of Algerian protestors in the centre of Paris that sparked the extreme brutality of the police. Roger Chaix, former director of the Direction générale de la sécurité intérieure [General Directorate for Internal Security], underlines this: 'nous ne voulions pas donner le spectacle d'une ville de Paris sous le coup du FLN [...] ça nous ne pouvons pas accepter' [We didn't want to show images of Paris under the control of the FLN... we just couldn't allow that].[24] Rancière argues that it was the very emergence of Algerians into public space as political subjects that led to the violent reprisals, attempts to render them invisible through censorship, or more disturbingly, death. Writing about the October 1961 massacre specifically, and about political protests more generally, he notes: 'une manifestation est politique non parce qu'elle a tel lieu et porte sur tel objet mais parce que sa forme est celle d'un affrontement entre deux partages du sensible [...] ainsi [...] ses sujets sont toujours précaires' [A demonstration is political not because it occurs in a particular place and bears upon a particular object but rather because its form is that of a clash between two partitions of the sensible [...] therefore [...] its subjects are always precarious].[25] The precariousness of the Algerian subjects who took part in the 17 October 1961 march was brutally underscored by the violence of the repression, and Rancière further suggests that the political protest represents not only a clash between two opposing groups or even ideologies, but more fundamentally, between divergent modes of regulating what can be seen and not seen in public space, and by prescribing what individuals and groups are visible, audible and participate in political life.

The power of the 17 October 1961 march lay in the movement of otherwise socially isolated individuals from the geographical fringes of Paris to the centre, and the rendering visible of a collective that had been disregarded in political life. There is evidence to suggest that the movement of these ethnically-distinguished immigrants from the margins to the centre was not well received: on 18 October 1961, *Le Parisien libéré* described the protest as a 'flot d'Algériens' [flood of Algerians] who 'déferlent vers le centre de la capitale en multipliant les exactions et les cris hostiles' [pour into the capital, their shouting becoming increasingly hostile and their actions more brutal].[26] There were also reports of a 'champs lexicale d'animalité' [bestial language] in the press, further dehumanizing the protesters, using a zoomorphic imagery that is evoked in *Caché*.[27] In the following sections, I discuss the play of power, space and vision in *Caché*, delineating the significance of the distinctions between Georges and Majid in terms of the situation and mise-en-scène of living space, linking this to wider socio-cultural inequities.

Space and Power: The Uncomfortable World of *Caché*

Caché participates in the memorial resurgence around the massacre, but only obliquely references the key historical event that inspired its creation. The film assumes a degree of audience familiarity with the 17 October 1961 repression, and only verbally references it once. This allusion occurs as Georges tries to explain and justify to Anne his connections with Majid, following a series of lies that have been exposed by the visual evidence of one of the anonymous videotapes:

> En octobre soixante et un, le FLN a appelé les Algériens à manifester. Ils sont allés à Paris. 17 Octobre soixante et un. Je ne te fais pas un dessin. Papon. Massacre policier. Ils ont noyés à peu près deux cent Arabes dans la Seine. Il semble que les parents de Majid étaient de ceux-là. En tout cas ils ne sont jamais revenus.

> [In October 1961, the FLN called Algerians to protest. They went to Paris. 17 October 1961. I won't spell it out for you. Papon. Police massacre. They drowned about 200 Arabs in the Seine. It seems that Majid's parents were among them. In any case, they never came back.]

Georges's account presumes prior knowledge: it is sufficient to say the words 'Papon' and 'massacre policier' for Anne to understand, and Georges cites the higher figure of 200 deaths, associated with Einaudi's testimonial, left-leaning account.[28] Georges's refusal to offer a visual image, 'je ne te fais pas un dessin', references the drawings that have served as reminders of his own childhood transgressions, but also evokes an element of invisibility regarding the number of deaths. This play between vision and a refusal to see is central to *Caché*, and it evokes the double aspect of the massacre, as an event that happened in the centre of Paris yet remained suppressed for decades. It also references the fact that at the time, the massacre was largely without visual representation: apart from a few photographs by Elie Kagan, and a censored film by Jacques Panijel, *Octobre à Paris* (1961), all other visual documents were censored or destroyed.[29]

As Georges notes, Majid's parents travelled to Paris and never returned, and when Georges's father goes to search for them, he is summarily dismissed, told that he should be grateful to be rid of a couple of *bougnoules* (a racist term designating a person of Arab or North African origin). These words highlight the hierarchies of social status that exist between the French farmer and his Algerian workers, and from the outset of the film, Haneke emphasizes the intergenerational aspect of this social order. The director employs space and settings, mise-en-scène, characterization, and audience identification to underscore the cultural and social differentiation of Majid and Georges.[30] This is, first of all, inscribed in the geographical positioning and symbolic valences of Majid's apartment in relation to Georges's home. While Georges's house is located in the *13ème arrondissement*, a relatively affluent area, Majid lives almost 14 kilometres away, beyond the *périphérique*, the ring road constructed by Papon, the police chief in charge at the time of the 17 October 1961 massacre. Majid's physical distance from the centre of Paris, the centre that Georges inhabits so comfortably, is also reflected in the names of the streets where they live. As Ezra and Sillars have noted, the camera that captures Georges's home is placed on Rue des Iris, Iris being a Goddess who carries messages to humans from the divine realm, thus already evoking the spectral aspect of the anonymous tapes, and positioning Majid as an other-worldly, opaque figure.[31] Moreover, while Majid lives on the communist inspired Avenue Lénine, the road that Georges actually lives on is Rue Brillat-Savarin. This appellation links Georges to an intrinsically French lineage of gastronomy, manners, and good taste, as Jean Anthelme Brillat-Savarin was a late 18th century epicure and gastronome who wrote a book entitled *Physiologie du goût* (The Physiology of Taste).

At one point, Majid even refers to Georges's childhood farmhouse as a 'domaine' [estate], a word associated with old world vineyards, rustic luxury, and inherited legacies. This positing of Georges as a classically French bourgeois figure is intentional, and represents another instance of Haneke's frequent treatment of manners and mores of the upper middle-class family.[32] Georges's first suspicion as to the identity of the sender of the videotapes is that it is one of his son's friends, 'un de ces abrutis qui veut se moquer des parents bobos de leur pote' [one of those morons who wants to get at their mate's trendy middle-class parents]. 'Bobo', or 'bourgeois bohémian', suggests both wealth as well as a cultural and artistic lifestyle, confirmed by the bookshelves that form the backdrop to many domestic scenes in the film, as well as the tasteful and muted décor, its browns, creams, and beiges blending with the monochrome tones of the family's clothing. The Laurent costumes are excessively drab: they all wear loose, shapeless garments in black, navy, grey, or beige, clothes that are clearly of high quality materials, but that leave no room for the expression of individuality. The mise-en-scène of the books can even become oppressive: in every scene in which Georges and Anne speak, they are fenced in by a floor to ceiling backdrop of books, a framing which is reiterated in shots of them at work, Anne in a publishing house and Georges on his literary television show [Figures 1.1 and 1.2]. Indeed, in several scenes, the books are reflected in the dining room mirrors behind Anne as she speaks, and this omnipresence of the physical object is contrasted with a lack of use: we never see a single adult character reading. Haneke uses this contrast to point to the insincerity of the bourgeois lifestyle and Georges's role as a literary television star in particular. Georges's boss even comments on this hypocrisy, remarking that he has not read the newest sensation from Anne's publishing house, because 'vous savez ce que c'est, on n'a le temps de rien' [you know what it's like, we don't have time to do anything].

The spatial configuration of Georges's home can be connected to an affect of distance and emotional coldness that he exhibits throughout the film. The first shot of the film is an image of the exterior of Georges and Anne's home [Figure 1.3]. Set back from the pavement, the house is shielded by successive layers of exterior barriers: first a fence, then a hedge, then an overhang, and there are no large windows, only a set of small, frosted squares set in the exterior wall. Georges's house is embedded in the surrounding architecture like the centre of a spiral, and to the left and right of the foreground, the walls of buildings encompass the image, and behind, six separate layers of apartment blocks ascend upwards. There is no patch of sky: Georges's home is surrounded on all sides. Inside, there is a long,

FIGS. 1.1 and 1.2. Books. *Caché*, dir. by Michael Haneke (2005).

FIG. 1.3. Closed exterior, closed interiors. *Caché*, dir. by Michael Haneke (2005).

FIG. 1.4. Constructed conviviality — The Dinner Party.
Caché, dir. by Michael Haneke (2005).

dark corridor (complete with the requisite bookshelves) that must be traversed before one accesses the main living room: it is not easy to accede to the heart of this family. This is clearly the home of an individual who values privacy, but in Haneke's characterization of Georges, this privacy extends to a lack of emotional warmth or empathy. In this first sequence of the meal, Georges, Anne, and Pierrot observe all the rituals of the familial repast and sit down to a classically French supper, with delicately poured, moderately sized glasses of wine. Yet strangely, this meal lacks any emotional depth, in spite of the fact that Anne and Georges have just received the first of the anonymous videotapes. The couple snap at each other, and seem incapable of communicating productively about who might have sent the tape. The conversation seems stilted, excessively formal for a gathering of intimate family members. They speak almost in monosyllables, and the only exchange is a cold interrogation of Pierrot's tardiness.

The dinner party sequence also connects space, power, and emotional detachment, but broadens it beyond the world of the Laurent family into a wider social milieu. This sequence opens with an establishing shot of the Laurent dining table at which three heterosexual couples in their forties are in the middle of a meal, with male and female guests seated alternately according to gender [Figure 1.4]. The camera is positioned from the perspective of one corner of the table, between Georges and Mathilde (Nathalie Richard), the wife of Anne's boss, Pierre (Daniel Duval). The scene is filmed using a high angle shot, as if the spectator occupied the ghostly position of a semi-welcome guest standing at the table, both inside and outside the gathering. A male guest recounts what appears to be a personal anecdote, about meeting an elderly woman in a café who claims he reminds her of a figure from her past — this turns out to be her beloved dog, who apparently died in a car accident on the day the storyteller was born. The tale ends with surprise and raucous laughter, as the man says he has a scar behind his ear in the place where the dog was hit by a car. This story, and the sequence overall, serve several important functions. Firstly, through the positioning of the camera, it draws the spectator into the scene, and by extension, the world of the film: we know as much as the guests, and are carried along with the ambiguous tale. Secondly, the man gives an account of a living being, not quite human, who comes back to life and is reincarnated in another form — much like Majid, who returns in an other-worldly fashion to haunt Georges, whether it is through the tapes or the manner of his death. Like the massacre of the 17 October 1961 itself, the past reappears in the present, and old injuries can take on new life through the processes of memorialization, often through the form of storytelling. Finally, the female partner of the man telling the story asks, 'mais c'est vrai ou non?' [but is it true?], highlighting uncertainty and disbelief, and symbolically underscoring both the unreliability of Haneke's narrative techniques, and the incredulity that initially greeted testimonial accounts of the 17 October 1961 events. This woman is considerably younger than her companion and marked as somewhat naïve by this question that the others brush aside. She is also black, thus adding a comforting image of diversity in the midst of the Laurent's privilege, and again marking them as liberal, tolerant, and open-minded, at least in their own self-image. After the story, the camera angle switches abruptly to an almost violating closeness with individual characters: Mathilde and Pierre describe a sick woman who has separated from her partner and was once their mutual friend. This woman has not coped successfully with the separation and she does not fit in to the neat couplings that characterize this scene. Mention of her incites an abrupt change in conversation, and this emphasizes the fragility of the friendships here displayed so convivially: the film hints that Pierre and Anne may be having an affair, and the fact that Mathilde is telling this story of the spurned ex-wife underscores her own vulnerability to exclusion from the group.

Haneke asks, with reference to the almost excessive disaffection displayed by Georges throughout the film, 'est-ce que cette froideur vient de tout ce qu'on a mis sous le tapis?' [Does this coldness come from everything that they have swept under the carpet?].[33] He thus explicitly connects the hidden and the invisible to Georges's psychological state. Significantly, the two spaces that incite a partial or total loss of control in Georges, his family home in the country and Majid's apartment in the suburbs, are removed from the comfortable centre of his existence in the heart of Paris. The first time Georges dreams of Majid is when he visits his mother on their country estate: violent visions of Majid beheading the cockerel return in the form of nightmares, even if he manages to maintain a calm exterior during the day. In contrast to the cavernous stillness and dispassionate tonalities of the Laurent home, Majid's apartment is a small but brightly lit space, cluttered with a variety of coloured objects. The groomed and narrow residential streets of Georges's home give way to the wide concrete avenues and boulevards of peripheral Paris, ceding to the dark and ominous hallway that leads to Majid's studio. Once the action is removed from the centre, from Georges's terrain as it were, the constraints of his rigidly self-possessed world seem to collapse, and he threatens Majid with physical violence: 'c'est étrange, hein? Je ne me suis pas battu une seule fois depuis que je suis adulte, je trouve ça répugnant. Et là, je...' [It's strange, isn't it? Since I've been an adult, I haven't once been in a fight, I find it repulsive. And now, I...].

This rupture in Georges's civil and composed public persona recalls imperial fears of the collapse of civilisation in the colonies, depicted in literary texts like Gustave Flaubert's *Voyage en Orient* [Voyage to the Orient] (1849–1851), Gérard de Nerval's *Les Filles du feu* [*Daughters of Fire*] (1854), Ernest Feydeau's *Alger: Etude* [*Algiers: A Study*] (1862), Joseph Conrad's *The Heart of Darkness* (1899), and later, Julien Duvivier's film *Pépé le moko* (1937).[34] Haneke alludes to French stereotypes of Algerians and Muslims in the film, and Max Silverman has pointed out that the depiction of Majid echoes Frantz Fanon's description in *Les Damnés de la terre* [*The Wretched of the Earth*] (1961) of French typecasting of Algerian Muslims, including knives, suicide, and throat-slitting. As Silverman notes, 'uncannily, the image of the Algerian which returns to haunt Georges's mind is composed of the same elements'.[35] Indeed, it is Georges's semi-conscious, childhood cognizance of the normative prejudices of his culture (Arabs are violent and carry infection) that allows him to manipulate his domestic situation and have Majid removed. Majid's suicide also echoes the *égorgeurs* [throat-cutters], FLN soldiers who cut the throats of dissenting Algerians, recorded in the book of the same title by Benoît Rey (1961).[36] Throat cutting is also associated in a French imaginary of North Africans with the Islamic practice of cutting the throats of sheep and goats to produce halal meat. Ranjana Khanna reiterates this link to animality, associating Majid's death with the death of the cockerel: 'the animal becomes the trace of the non-human and the foreigner [...] the inhuman, as the trace of the animal, is dropped into the film again and again'.[37]

Geographical positioning in relation to a centre, the mise-en-scène of living space, and the evocation of specifically Algerian colonial prejudices like animality and primitivism suggest that Haneke is deliberately evoking both French and European stereotypes of postcolonial immigrants and outsiders. The social and cultural frameworks within which Georges and Majid are placed function according to fairly conventional evocations of a *Français de souche* (a 'pure-blooded' French person) and a French-Algerian. These stereotypes appear to exist latently in the Laurents' minds, in spite of their liberal, bookish politics, and their racially diverse friends. When Georges describes his father's sadness that Majid's parents did not return to the farm, he notes, 'Papa les aimait bien, ça devait être de bons ouvriers' [Dad liked them a lot, they must have been good workers]. It seems Georges cannot conceive of any affection for, or attachment to, the Algerian workers beyond their capacity for labour and the production of money for their employers. This gives the viewer an insight into how Georges perceives the world and his position in it — one in which life is valuable and worth preserving only in so far as it produces benefit for him.

Yet in spite of Georges's hypocritical and self-interested outlook, on many occasions throughout the film, the spectator is invited or compelled to share his point of view. The opening shot of the film, an image of Georges's house, turns out to be footage played from one of the videotapes in the Laurent's cassette player: we have been watching precisely what they are watching, and our introduction to the story of Majid is synchronized with their own. Georges also mediates the spectator's knowledge of the action in the film. Even when he withholds some information about Majid from Anne, the viewer is offered a window into this story through his nightmares. There are also several switches throughout the film where the perspective of the tapes merges with Georges's vision, with the most important instance of this overlap being the dark hallway that leads to Majid's studio. First depicted on the tape and filmed as a tracking shot at eye-level, this shot is repeated when Georges visits Majid's apartment for the first time — as if the perspective of the tape emerged from Georges's own consciousness. Moreover, at several moments throughout the film when Georges is interacting with other characters, and particularly Majid, his head is positioned in the centre, or slightly left or right of centre in the frame, so that the viewer's perspective is almost (if not completely) aligned with that of the central character.[38]

Haneke has spoken of his desire to create a kind of 'productive unease' in the spectator, to jar them out of easy assumptions about the significance of images and narratives.[39] Part of the unease that is generated in *Caché* relates to the audience's identification with Georges and perhaps Anne, through the camera techniques outlined above, but also through their behaviour and social status. Haneke's audiences are art-house, ergo middle-class and reasonably moneyed, and he wants to expose their fallibilities and inconsistencies, revealing the prejudices and nastier affects that lurk underneath. As Tarja Laine notes, 'the mirror that Haneke's cinema holds in front of Georges is also held in front of his target audience of liberal, European intellectuals'.[40] Mark Cousins goes further, suggesting that Haneke targets the self-delusions of European chattering classes, and that his films shock and disturb them with the intensity of unpleasant identifications, but masochistically, they enjoy it: '*Caché* held a mirror up to such socio-intellectual networks and showed them anxieties which, to them, were unexpected, clever and stimulating'.[41]

The fact that Haneke invites identification with Georges and Anne, and assumes a socio-economically proximate spectator, means that we share the Laurents' assumptions about the guilt of Majid and his son regarding the tapes and drawings. This is despite the fact that Haneke is at pains to construct an audio-visual world of ambiguity of inference. The opening shot itself establishes a consistent rapport with what remains outside of the visual frame: when Anne and Georges's disembodied voices eventually appear on the soundtrack, the first words they speak are 'Alors?... Rien' [So?...Nothing].[42] The footage that we see of Georges's home might in fact be CCTV footage, banal surveillance of the most quotidian kind, which we either take for granted or assume is there for our own protection. The opening scene establishes the diegetic camera itself as an unreliable image source within the context of the film: the tape that has been made of Georges's house does not correspond to any workable angle, because he walked straight past the point where the tape should have been taken from, and did not see it. In this case, we are presented with both a failure to see on Georges's part, and a fundamental ambiguity about what has been seen. From the outset Haneke emphasizes impossible spaces of enunciation: the tape exists, but how or why remains uncertain.

This notion of anxiety resonates with the fundamental uncertainty regarding inference and interpretation that surfaces and resurfaces consistently throughout

Caché. A dispute in the street between Georges and a young male cyclist who nearly knocks him over is a conflict about the ambiguities of sight, and the power hierarchies that are inscribed in the occupation of particular city spaces. Having just received another anonymous postcard, Georges goes to report this incident to the police. As he leaves the precinct, sandwiched protectively between two large police vehicles, he steps out onto the road without looking and is nearly hit by a cyclist, a young black man wearing a hooded sweatshirt and tracksuit pants. Georges shouts 'connard' [moron] after the man, who spins around menacingly, as the two begin to exchange verbal threats. This scene is a clear example of the subtleties of Haneke's construction of audience identification with Georges: the camera is positioned behind Georges's left shoulder, with Anne to his right, and the cyclist in the left middle ground of the image [Figure 1.5]. The audience faces the empty space of the road, situated between Georges and the cyclist, but looking at the young man from George's perspective. There is no shot-reverse-shot in this sequence, which would allow us to see Georges from the man's point of view: rather, our gaze remains almost, but not completely, aligned with that of Georges, a hostile, aggressive but *familiar* character.

FIG. 1.5. The Cyclist. *Caché*, dir. by Michael Haneke (2005).

Georges insists that the cyclist was mistaken because he was travelling in the wrong direction down a one-way street, while the young man shouts that Georges stepped into the street without looking. Anne manages to diffuse the situation by suggesting that they were both at fault because neither 'paid attention': 'tu n'as pas fais attention, et nous n'avons pas fait attention, ok?' [you didn't pay attention, and we didn't pay attention either, ok?]. The scene emphasizes Georges's inability to see a situation from the perspective of another person. It also suggests that right and wrong are not helpful concepts in resolving a dispute, just as the fact of Georges's childhood ignorance does not alter the reality of Majid's life in care homes and transient dwellings following his expulsion from the Laurent estate. The publicity posters for the cinematic release of *Caché* use a still from this scene, with the Parisian backdrop of the sequence and the cyclist edited out, replaced with a vacuum of hazy darkness. In the poster, Georges's stretched-out arm assumes the quality of a searching and fearful indeterminacy, yet in the narrative context of the film this is a motion of overt hostility. The ambiguity of this gesture and its meaning underlines the notion that fear and aggression towards a perceived outsider go hand in hand: Georges's anger again arises from the desire to control and appropriate a space that he believes he possesses, or has a greater right to possess. This anger can tip into fear and violent retribution. The incident further indicates an underlying distinction between forms of vision: it is not only a question of looking, but also of seeing. Georges can look at the tapes as much as he wants, but that does not mean that he will see their meaning, just as 17 October 1961 happened in plain sight, and yet went unseen by juridical authorities and media commentators for several decades.

This dispute also highlights the links between visibility and power, and the occupation of public space. It echoes Chaix's insistence that the 'spectacle' of Algerians in the centre of Paris could not be tolerated: their domain is invisibility, both physical and discursive, in the suburbs and away from the heart of French society. In *Caché*, Georges assumes a visual and spatial prerogative, and while he seems oblivious to his own often violent and aggressive intrusions into Majid's home, he fully resents any incursion into his own dominion. Georges's life in Paris before the introduction of Majid is presented as a series of seamless transitions from his comfortable home to dinner parties, the picturesque *ruelles* [little streets] he inhabits and his glossy television studio. The structures of Georges's life exclude Majid and others like him and keep Georges safely couched in the world of dinner parties and literary reviews. The videotapes and the drawings arrive as intrusions of an outside threat that progressively encroaches upon the carefully constructed core of Georges's life. It is particularly pertinent that the method chosen to torment a television star is video surveillance and visual images. We watch Georges watching himself; Anne and their friends meet to view his show, as do his aunt and mother; we discover that he has many captive fans; and Majid first encounters him through the medium of television. The crucial difference between these 'watchings' is the control that Georges exerts over his image; while he personally edits and reconfigures his own images in his television show, the videotapes disrupt the frames through which he wishes to perceive his life and he cannot alter or manipulate their content. Georges's loss may thus be conceived as a loss of a scopic privilege, the right to look but not necessarily be looked at, unless the image viewed is a controlled projection.

Seeing is not only dependent on what is inside the frame or even awareness of what may be beyond it, but also on knowing how to look, and how to interpret what has been seen. Majid's character offers the most troubling challenge to interpretation, because his actions defy the expectations and presuppositions of both Georges and the spectator: his benign politeness, the tears he cries on the videotape that is sent to Anne, and his apparently truthful insistence that he is not responsible for the tapes. The culmination of the unease and confusion that Majid's character provokes is his suicide. In a film that consistently highlights the unreliable nature of the image, and the links between spatial control, visibility and power, Majid's death is made conspicuous by its violent and unambiguous visibility. In the following section, I offer a close reading of the brutal spectacle of self-violence in *Caché*, drawing on theories of the grotesque as an aesthetic that creates shock and forces an uncomfortable confrontation between the spectator and an image.

Grotesque Visions: Majid's suicide

The suicide of an Algerian man in a film about the memorialization and consequences of the 17 October 1961 massacre has invoked criticisms of the auto-destructive impulse of the outsider, his wilful self-annihilation. Paul Gilroy argues that the suicide generates a fantasy realm in which immigrants are no longer punished and contained by the powers of the state, but are removed violently at their own hands. Gilroy argues that 'getting the Arabs to do away with themselves is a timely fantasy in the context of today's pervasive Islamophobia'. Interpreting Majid's suicide as 'an exclusively aesthetic event', Gilroy reads it within the context of the colonial imagery and the stereotypes of barbarism and primitivism evoked in *Caché*. He argues that the audience views Majid's death with a 'deep if guilty pleasure' because European, bourgeois spectators secretly hope to rid Europe of its migrant populations, 'by any means possible', including suicide.[43] Gilroy's argument raises many important issues around this scene, which Haneke characterized as 'the most important shot of the film'.[44] Yet Majid's suicide scene can carry both aesthetic and political ramifications and affects, and their interaction relates precisely to Haneke's cinematic style and aims. As he notes, 'the *form* of representation determines the *effect* of the content', and in the scene of Majid's suicide, the manner in which it is depicted to the viewer directly impacts on how we receive its message.[45] If we feel pleasure in this scene, therefore, I argue that it is tied to the insertion of a grotesque element into the narrative, which breaks filmic rhythm, generates shock, and produces aesthetic symmetry in visual composition. Indeed, in 18th century German Romanticism, the act of suicide itself was linked to a surplus of feeling that sometimes tipped into the extremes of the grotesque, what Rudolph Binion describes as 'an excess of spirit which overflows form'.[46]

The grotesque operates as an aesthetic mode that privileges shock, suddenness, and according to Bernard McElroy, the 'physical, predominantly visual' in art.[47] Majid's suicide offers a deeply visceral depiction of physical violence, and it is potentially the only sequence in the film where vision is unambiguous: we know what we are looking at, even if we do not expect it. For Rancière, blatant visuality, the concrete manifestation of a fear that cannot be immediately denied or explained away, constitutes a movement towards the grotesque in representational art. He writes of the grotesque that 'la figuration graphique des monstres [...] rompt brutalement ce compromis entre le *faire voir* et le *ne pas faire voir* de la parole' [the graphic representation of monsters...brutally undoes this tacit compromise in speech between *making visible* and *not making visible*].[48] Rancière is speaking specifically of the power of words to imaginatively evoke images that never manifest themselves concretely, a pact between the reader and the text that the visibility of the grotesque ruptures. A parallel can be found in Haneke's deployment of filmic rhythm. Until the moment of Majid's death, Haneke has teased the viewer with an irregular narrative pattern that poses minor, although disturbing, threats (such as the drawings, Georges's dreams or Pierrot's disappearance) which are directly alleviated by the return to the slow, banal, if tense pulsations of everyday life. As spectators, we have been conditioned to believe that each posited, real peril (le *faire voir*) will ultimately be anti-climactic, and we can retreat once again into the quotidian, where the danger hovers on the margins, but remains unseen (le *ne pas faire voir*).

McElroy links the modern grotesque to Western fears about the collapse of civilization, and the return of primitive, animistic impulses that have been repressed in industrial societies. He describes the grotesque as 'an assault upon the idea of a rational world; it is an assault upon the reader himself, upon his sensibilities, upon his ideals, upon his feeling of living in a friendly, familiar world or his desire to live in one'.[49] The anonymous sender becomes a kind of ghostly spectre, and the relegation of the disruptive menace represented by the drawings and the tapes to a non-verbalised and non-visualised 'presence' means that the sudden and visceral manifestation of violence is even more shocking. The representational rupture that Majid's death constitutes within the context of the film's narrative also reflects a shattering of familiarity and expectation; his act evokes for both Georges and the spectator a realm of unpredictable and violent actions, where the buffers of civilisation no longer suffice to repel the unacceptable, the horrible, and the inexplicable.

The scene of Majid's death begins in the by now familiar hallway leading to Majid's door: light blue doors and doorframes, and a narrow, weakly lit corridor with white walls and brown floors. Georges's first visit to Majid's home was depicted using a multitude of shifting camera angles and perspectives and a series of altering shot-reverse-shots that allowed the spectator to discern various objects and to be positioned within the space. The apartment is composed of a single room: living quarters, kitchen, bedroom, and storage area in one. A large window illuminates a wall covered with different patterns of faded wallpaper, and a cramped kitchen bench, hob, and sink. There is a small kitchen table, with two chairs placed at a perpendicular angle, and to the right, a storage area where boxes, files, and clothes are stacked in loose and transitory piles, highlighting the impermanent and insecure nature of Majid's accommodation.[50] In the sequence depicting Majid's suicide, however, the spectator is not offered any spatial orientation. When Georges and Majid move into the inner room, the scene remains in a fixed long shot and a long take, and Majid faces outwards in the centre left of the image and Georges, with his back turned to the spectator, in the centre right. The extremely precise mise-en-scène and framing of this sequence lends it an air of immediacy and theatricality. The frame of the image might be the rectangular construction of the proscenium arch; the spectator is positioned as front row audience members at a play might be, neither close to nor distant from the action [Figure 1.6].

The grotesque is not a genre; rather, McElroy states, it is an aesthetic element 'used to expose in [...] exaggerated terms what has been implicit all along'.[51] The considered and detailed mise-en-scène echoes the ethnic and cultural stereotypes

FIG. 1.6. Majid's Suicide. *Caché*, dir. by Michael Haneke (2005).

previously mentioned, like throat-slitting, but also previous visual and narrative strands within the film, drawing our attention to the familiar elements of the scene's formal construction. As the men face each other, Majid rapidly and unexpectedly slits his throat with a knife. His body falls to the floor, as spurts of bright red blood erupt from his throat and streak the wall behind him. The triangular composition (Georges is stage left, Majid centre stage, and a gap stage right) echoes the triangular shape of the blood, both on the wall and in the drawings. The large spatter of blood recalls previous images of Majid beheading the chicken, and like the chicken, whose body jerks on the floor of the barn, Majid's body spasms as he dies. Like the Freudian uncanny, defined as 'that species of the frightening that goes back to what was once well known and had long been familiar', the grotesque is neither the wholly other nor the fully recognizable.[52] It must contain identifiable elements that tie it to comfortably familiar objects and people, and yet remain sufficiently removed from reality to disturb us. This is what Philip Thomson calls 'the ambivalently abnormal' quality of the grotesque, a confusion between real and unreal, absence and presence, and ultimately, life and death.[53] Seconds before he commits suicide, Majid's words hint at this interaction between presence and absence. He says to Georges, 'je voulais que tu sois présente' [I wanted you to be present], before absenting himself in the most fatal way possible. The lines between life and death are blurred in this scene, through the skin-crawling sound of air passing through Majid's artery, which is all the more remarkable in a film where, as Michel Chion points out, there is no music, so every sound becomes a potential menace.[54] In contrast to the cyclist's rebuke, in this scene, Georges has no choice: he must pay attention, be present to Majid's final moments. However, George's 'presence' is a questionable, transitory thing: a witness to Majid's death, his subsequent movements suggest that physically, mentally, and emotionally he cannot grasp the full portent of what he has seen. He literally absents himself from its reality by escaping into the cinema, later hiding from his friends, returning from work early, and going to bed in the middle of the day with a *cachet*, a sleeping pill.

Haneke writes that in depicting violence, the question he asks is not ' "How do I show violence?" but rather: "How do I show the viewer his own position vis-à-vis violence and its portrayal?" '.[55] Majid's body lies across the door, blocking Georges's escape, but like Georges, the spectator feels trapped by the image, stunned into immobility by shock.[56] The grotesque is fundamentally tied to viewer or reader response: what frightens, appals, and attracts the spectator of the grotesque is not necessarily the image itself, but our relation to it, what it recalls to us about our society and ourselves. As Elisheva Rosen argues, 'le grotesque n'est pas un effet induit par certains types de représentations, mais bien par la relation que nous entretenons avec ces représentations' [the grotesque is not an effect produced by certain types of representations, but rather the relationship that we have with these representations].[57] Majid's suicide elicits complex moral responses, and the position of the spectator in this sequence is worth considering, in the light of the discussion of audience identification with Georges, and the middle-class, European values he represents. There is a switch in perspective in this scene that points towards a slow process of spectator de-identification with Georges. Unlike previous depictions of Georges's advance to Majid's apartment, the spectator sees Georges approaching head on, rather than in a point of view shot or from over his shoulder: the camera is statically placed at Majid's door, as Georges walks towards the centre of the frame. Moreover, after the death, Georges wanders out of the frame to the right, and we see his shadow cast on the wall over Majid's body, a metaphorical figuration of the shadow Georges's actions have cast over the dead man's life. This small movement reminds us of our own stasis in front of the screen, but it also separates the viewer from Georges the character. During the two-minute sequence, there is no close-up of either Majid or Georges, which would have encouraged empathic identification and drawn the viewer into the emotional world of the characters. Susan Sontag has questioned our ability to ignore and politically disengage from images of suffering, suggesting that it may be the physical or affective distance from the sufferer that fails to move us. She writes: 'perhaps the only people with the right to look at images of suffering of this extreme order are those who could do something to alleviate it'.[58] Underscoring Sontag's assertion is the notion that proximity to extreme physical pain, whether through an image or actual presence, can produce the desire to assuage it. By refusing to allow us to see Georges's reaction, or indeed, Majid's face in close-up when he dies, Haneke turns viewers into voyeuristic witnesses of a suffering which they cannot alleviate. He describes this position as a kind of 'guiltless complicity': guiltless, in the sense that we have not contributed directly to Majid's pain, but complicit because of the intimacy implied in watching a human being die without intervening.[59]

This strategy of distanced spectatorship, which simultaneously refuses proximity to Majid but also creates distance from Georges, recalls Rancière's evocation of impossible identification with what he calls 'la cause de l'autre' [the other's cause] — the political struggles of those who are not part of one's own particular national, ethnic or religious community.[60] Rancière advocates a form of dis-identification with the agents of violence, or with the violence itself. In relation to the 17 October

1961 massacre, he writes: 'nous ne pouvions pas nous identifier à ces Algériens mais nous pouvions mettre en question notre identification avec le "peuple français" au nom duquel ils avaient été mis à mort' [We could not identify with those Algerians, but we could call into question our identification with the notion of a 'French people' in whose name they had been put to death].[61] Although we may not be able to identify with Majid in the film, his suicide shocks us into the realization that there is an unexplained void in his character, part of the story of his life that remains unseen and unspoken.

The suicide, as an instance of the grotesque as defined by McElroy, 'transforms the world from what we "know" it to be to what we fear it might be. It distorts or exaggerates the surface of reality in order to tell a qualitative truth about it'.[62] Although Majid's act may not exactly be characterised as inexplicable, it appears to be a distorted or exaggerated reaction to the reality of the events that touch his life as they have been portrayed. His death fractures the constructed reality of the film, and from this point onwards the question of who has created the tapes and the drawings becomes increasingly diminished in importance, and ultimately remains unsolved. The element of extremity in Majid's action serves to highlight a qualitative truth about the uncertainty of a posited reality, and of our presuppositions. The revulsion or distaste we feel may apply not only to the horror of Majid's action, but also to our realization of the extent to which we have underestimated and misunderstood his character: the rather easy terrorized/terrorist dialectic that the film has constructed no longer holds. Once Majid is introduced into the narrative, it is almost impossible not to assume that either he or his son is the creator of the tapes because we follow the story from Georges's perspective. This is despite Haneke's frequent insistence upon the unreliability of the narrative he appears to be constructing through the switches between diegetic and non-diegetic filmic space. This scene makes us aware as spectators of our own presumptions about victimizer and victimized. Indeed, the theatricality, the associations with animality, primitivism, and contemporary tropes relating the Muslim and the immigrant that Haneke plays on in this scene may serve to deepen our sense of discomfort in the spectator's previous assumptions regarding Majid and his son's guilt.

Geoffrey Galt Harpham characterizes the grotesque as 'a defence against silence when other words have failed'.[63] The idea that Majid's death is a border between silence and speech, the last resort of expression for an otherwise invisible or unheard person of event, can be linked to a phrase Anne uses, when describing how she felt when Pierrot disappeared. With typical Laurent reticence, she says that 'on était mort d'angoisse...bon, peut-être pas mort, mais on faisait un sang d'encre' [We were worried to death...well, maybe not to death, but we were freaked out]. The phrase 'sang d'encre', literally translating as 'a blood of ink', ties blood to ink and writing as a form of expression. Anne uses this phrase to express anxiety about being a parent who thinks she has lost a child: an inverse echo of Majid, who lost two sets of parents, biological and adoptive. Majid's trauma would have remained unexpressed (although it remains unexplained) because Georges, and to a certain extent the viewer, have failed to draw the necessary conclusions from what was presented in the drawings and the videotapes. When we fail to see, Majid's suicide forces a consideration of our presuppositions, becoming evidence of a life and of an existence that we have lost the opportunity to understand.

Majid's life and the manner of his death echoes the unknowability of the experiences and individuals lost in the 17 October 1961 massacre, while at the same time returning a visibility to death and loss that these historical victims were denied. Suppressed for many decades, the 17 October 1961 massacre can be characterized as an event that attempts a double annihilation, what Rancière calls a *vernichtung* [annihilation]: 'réduction à rien, c'est-à-dire anéantissement mais aussi anéantissement de cet anéantissement, disparition de ses traces, disparition de son nom même' [reduction to nothing, in other words, annihilation, but also annihilation of that annihilation, the disappearance of its traces, the disappearance of its very name].[64] Not only does the event itself affect an erasure, through the elimination of 'dissenting' individuals, but its representation is also subject to attempted eradication. In a similar sense, not only does Georges expunge Majid from his life, he also tries to erase any memory or recognition of his actions, and the effect they have had on the other's future. Even if Georges cannot be blamed for his actions as a child, his awareness of his family and society's stereotyping and prejudices about Algerians allows him to rid himself of the foreigner Majid. He refuses to denounce these prejudices as an adult, or to accept the consequences these actions have had for Majid. Although his 'bobo' lifestyle, left-wing views, and ethically diverse friendships seem to characterize him as a tolerant and open-minded individual, these practices are easily disrupted when he feels threatened and his behaviour towards Majid demonstrates that his sense of superiority and entitlement lies just below the surface of this polished, liberal exterior.

Although Georges rattles off the facts surrounding the circumstances of the massacre, the prejudices that led to the social exclusion of minority groups have not disappeared: the hierarchical geographical and social relations between the margin and the centre hold. *Caché* thus interrogates the potential failure of memorial practices and asks what, precisely, cultural commemoration of forgotten historical trauma can achieve: reparations, political or financial in nature; social recognition and mourning for lives lost; the assumption of responsibility and public apologies, recrimination and justice; or a shared national dialogue to promote inter-community and intergenerational communication? *Caché* suggests that an affirmation in the public sphere does not always lead to concrete socio-political improvement. The fear of the ethnically, religiously, and racially marked other who encroaches on the hidden centre of one's existence finds an echo in recent thinking of the European migrant crisis, the subject of Haneke's most recent film, *Happy End* (2017). Haneke spoke of this film at its premiere in Cannes, situating its themes within the wider context of his œuvre:

> I try to give clues to the spectators and leave the work in the hearts of the spectators. I hope that I go through life with open eyes. And we cannot talk about today's society without mentioning the blindness in which we live.[65]

Unlike Georges, who retreats into the cinema in order to escape his emotions following Majid's death, Haneke's film offers no safe haven for the negation of responsibility and the refusal to see. In *Caché*, the uncertainty generated by the rhythm of threat and alleviation makes the brutal visibility of the suicide scene, with its deployment of a grotesque aesthetic form, even more shocking. The initial 'whodunnit' narrative that partially aligns the viewer with Georges is ruptured in this sequence, as Majid's suicide forces the spectator to confront their own interpretative deficiencies. In this way, Haneke's cinema works against the violence inflicted by historical and interpersonal blindness, instead highlighting hidden histories and concealed prejudices and evoking a haunting sense of broader social and political exclusions and misconceptions.

Notes to Chapter 1

1. Quoted in Lawrence Chua, 'Michael Haneke', *BOMB*, (Summer 2002) <http://bombsite.com/issues/80/articles/2489> [Accessed 28 May 2013].
2. Quoted in Mattias Frey, 'Haneke's Film Theory and Digital Praxis', in *On Michael Haneke*, ed. by Brian Price and John David Rhodes (Michigan: Wayne State University Press, 2010), pp. 153–66, (p. 155).
3. Thomas Elsaesser, *European Cinema: Face to Face with Hollywood* (Amsterdam: Amsterdam UP, 2003), pp. 485–513. For more on the characteristics of European cinema and the contemporary European *auteur*, see Rosalind Galt, *The New European Cinema: Redrawing the Map* (New York: Columbia University Press, 2006) and Luisa Rivi, *European Cinema after 1989: Cultural Identity and Transnational Production* (Basingstoke/New York: Palgrave Macmillan, 2007).
4. Andrew Sarris, 'Notes on the "Auteur" Theory in 1962', in *Film Theory and Criticism: Introductory Readings,* 6th edn, ed. by Leo Braudy and Marshall Cohen (Oxford: Oxford University Press, 2004), pp. 400–03, (p. 402). See also André Bazin et al., 'Six Characters in Search of Auteurs: A Discussion about the French Cinema (1957)', in *The European Cinema Reader*, ed. by Catherine Fowler (Oxon: Routledge, 2002), pp. 64–72.
5. Guy Austin, 'Drawing Trauma: Visual Testimony in *Caché* and *J'ai 8 ans*', *Screen*, 48:4 (2007), 529 36; Martine Beugnet, 'Blind spot', *Screen*, 48:2 (2007), 227–31; Matthew Croombs, 'Algeria Deferred: The Logic of Trauma in *Muriel* and *Caché*', *Scope: An Online Journal of Film and Television Studies* 16 (2010); Elizabeth Ezra & Jane Sillars, 'Hidden in Plain Sight: Bringing Terror Home', *Screen*, 48:2 (2007), 215–21; Maria Flood, 'Brutal Visibility: Framing Majid's Suicide in Michael Haneke's *Caché* (2005)', *Nottingham French Studies*, 56:1 (2017), 82–97; Isabelle McNeill, *Memory and the Moving Image: French Film in the Digital Era* (Edinburgh: Edinburgh University Press, 2010); Ranjana Khanna, 'From Rue Morgue to Rue des Iris', *Screen*, 48:2 (2007), 237–44; Libby Saxton, 'Close Encounters with Distant Suffering: Michael Haneke's Disarming Visions', in *Five Directors: Auteurism from Assayas to Ozon*, ed. by Kate Ince (Manchester: Manchester University Press, 2008), pp. 84–111; Maxim Silverman (2007). 'The Empire Looks Back', *Screen*, 48:2 (2007), 245–49; Catherine Wheatley, *Caché [Hidden]: BFI Film Classics* (London: Palgrave Macmillan, 2011).
6. Austin, 'Drawing Trauma', p. 534; Paul Gilroy, 'Shooting crabs in a barrel', *Screen*, 48:2 (2007), 233–35.
7. I will designate the protesters as Algerians, for the sake of simplicity and also because the vast majority were first-generation immigrants, who by 1962 would be considered 'Algerian'. However, at this time they were officially considered French citizens, and designated 'Français musulmans d'Algérie' (see Einaudi, speaking in Mehdi Lallaoui's film, *À propos d'octobre*, 2011). Stora laconically refers to this slippery categorization, stating that the Algerian protestors occupied 'une certaine catégorie de "citoyen français"' [a particular category of "French citizen"]. Benjamin Stora, *La Gangrène et l'oubli: la mémoire de la guerre d'Algérie en France* (Paris: La Découverte, 1991), p. 94.

8. Jim House and Neil MacMaster, *Paris 1961: Algerians, State Terror, and Memory* (Oxford: Oxford University Press, 2006), pp. 161–67.

9. Vidal-Naquet published his research on the 17 October 1961 massacre in 2001, *Les crimes de l'armée française: Algérie, 1954–1962* (Paris: La Découverte). Paulette Péju's *Ratonnades à Paris, précédé de Les Harkis à Paris* both published by Éditions François Maspero in 1961, were censored upon release and reissued in 2000 with La Découverte.

10. House and MacMaster, p. 279.

11. Joshua Cole, 'Entering History: The Memory of Police Violence in Paris, October 1961', in *Algeria & France, 1800–2000: Identity, Memory, Nostalgia*, ed. by Patricia M. E. Lorcin (Syracuse: Syracuse University Press, 2006), pp. 117–34, (p. 119).

12. Dazy, quoted in *Dissimulation d'un massacre: 17 octobre 1961*, dir. by Daniel Kupferstein (2001).

13. *Une journée portée disparue: 17 Octobre 1961*, dir. by Philip Brooks and Alan Hayling (1991).

14. See Jean-Luc Einaudi, *La Bataille de Paris, 17 octobre 1961* (Paris: Seuil, 1991).

15. House and MacMaster, pp. 115–16.

16. Stora, *La Gangrène et l'oubli*, p. 94.

17. Jean-Luc Einaudi, *Scènes de la guerre d'Algérie en France* (Paris: le cherche midi, 2009), p. 198.

18. Jean-Paul Brunet, *Police contre FLN: le drame d'octobre 1961* (Paris: Flammarion, 1999).

19. Cole, 'Entering History', p. 131.

20. Didier Daeninckx, *Meurtres pour mémoire* (Paris: Gallimard, 1983); Leila Sebbar, *La Seine était rouge* (Paris: Actes Sud, 2009); Didier Daeninckx and Mako, *Octobre noir* (Paris: AD Libris, 2011); 'Le Monde', *La Nuit oubliée* <http://www.lemonde.fr/societe/visuel/2011/10/17/la-nuit-oubliee_1587567_3224.html> [Accessed 14 January 2015]; Collectif Raspouteam, *17.10.61* <http://www.politis.fr/17octobre1961/> [Accessed 14 January 2015].

21. Mireille Rosello, *Reparative in Narratives: Works of Mourning in Progress* (Liverpool: Liverpool University Press, 2010), p.106.

22. Ibid., p. 107. Resnais' *Muriel*, by contrast, might be considered to portray the beginning of one moment of memory relating to World War II, Algeria and the practice of torture by the French Army, which seems to be a history that is too recent to confront. As Rosello writes, 'the books and testimonies that denounced the use of torture in Algeria that were published in the 1960s belong to the moment of memory that started in the 1990s, and this seems paradoxical only if we do not distinguish between a historical period and a moment of memory'. Rosello, p. 107.

23. Jacques Rancière, *Aux bords du politique* (Paris: Gallimard, 1998), p. 210.

24. Chaix quoted in *Dissimulation d'un massacre*.

25. Rancière, *Aux bords du politique*, p. 245. Jacques Rancière, *Dissensus: On Politics and Aesthetics*, trans. Steven Corcoran, (New York: Bloomsbury Academic, 2010), p. 39.

26. Quoted in Stora, *La Gangrène et l'oubli*, p. 93.

27. Voiceover information in *Dissimulation d'un massacre*.

28. Einaudi first estimated the number of casualties to be 200, but following further interviews with witnesses, victims and FLN coordinators in the *bidonvilles*, revised this figure to produce a total of 325. See Paul Thibaud, 'Le 17 octobre 1961: Un moment de notre histoire', *Esprit*, 279 (2001), 6–19.

29. On censorship, see Maria Flood, 'Politics and the Police: Documenting the 17 October 1961 Massacre', *Contemporary French and Francophone Studies*, 20:4–5 (2016), 599–606. As Panijel notes of the relationship between the censorship of photographs and documents and the repression of the massacre itself in relation to *Octobre à Paris*, 'c'était normal que la police se précipite dessous, puisqu'on a voulu occulter l'événement [...] on a occulté le film. On a fait comme si ça n'existait pas' [It's normal that the police jumped on it, because they wanted to hide the event [...] they hid the film]. Quoted in Brooks and Hayling, *Une journée portée disparue*.

30. As McNeill writes, *Caché* presents an 'urban geography [...] incarnating in spatial terms the inequalities and injustices of the colonial system'. McNeill, *Memory and the Moving Image*, p. 154.

31. Ezra and Sillars, 'Hidden in Plain Sight', (p. 217).

32. See in particular *The Seventh Continent* (1989), *Funny Games* (1998) and *Amour* (2012).

33. Serge Toubiana, 'Entretien avec Michael Haneke', *Caché: DVD Extras* (Artificial Eye, Sony Pictures Classics, 2005).

34. For more on the collapse of the civility, morality, and sexual norms of the colonizer in the colony, particularly in relation to sexuality, see Victoria Thompson, 'I went Pale with Pleasure', in *Algeria & France, 1800–2000: Identity, Memory, Nostalgia*, ed. by P. M. E. Lorcin (Syracuse: Syracuse University Press, 2006), pp. 18–32, and the discussion of Flaubert and Nerval in Edward Saïd's *Orientalism* (London: Penguin Modern Classics [1978], 2003), pp. 179–94. On *Pépé le Moko* specifically, see David Henry Slavin, *Colonial Cinema and Imperial France, 1919–1939* (Baltimore, MD: The Johns Hopkins University Press, 2001).

35. Silverman, 'The Empire Looks Back', p. 246.

36. Benoît Rey, *Les Égorgeurs* (Paris: Editions de Minuit, 1961).

37. Khanna, 'From Rue Morgue', p. 239.

38. Silverman observes that Georges and the viewer are often misled in a similar way: 'the spectator and Georges are led to believe that the image we are watching hides something else, that the fixed image [...] contains its "blind spots" and that what is visible is haunted by what is off-screen and outside the frame'. Silverman, 'The Empire Looks Back', p. 133.

39. Michael Haneke, 'Violence and the Media', in *A Companion to Michael Haneke*, ed. by Roy Grundmann (Oxford: Wiley-Blackwell, 2010), pp. 247–55, (p. 576).

40. Tarja Laine, 'Hidden Shame Exposed: *Hidden* and the Spectator', in *The Cinema of Michael Haneke: Europe Utopia*, ed. by Ben McCann and David Sorfa (New York: Wallflower Press, 2011), p. 253. On Haneke's implied spectator, see also Alex Lykidis, 'Multicultural Encounters in Haneke's French-Language Cinema', in *A Companion to Michael Haneke*, ed. by Roy Grundmann (Oxford: Wiley-Blackwell, 2010), pp. 455–76 (p. 455).

41. Mark Cousins, 'After the end: word of mouth and *Caché*', *Screen*, 48:2, 223–26, (p. 224).

42. This negation in relation to the act of visualizing trauma recalls the opening sequences of Renais's *Hiroshima mon amour* (1959), which posited a similar trope of denial in the repeated refutation, 'tu n'as rien vu à Hiroshima' [You saw nothing in Hiroshima]. The words 'Alors Rien' are repeated many times throughout the interactions between Georges and Anne, underscoring both the failures of communication, and their lack of insight into the situation they are facing.

43. Gilroy, 'Shooting crabs in a barrel', p. 234.

44. Michael Haneke, quoted in Ipek A. Celik, '"I wanted you to be present": Guilt and the History of Violence in Michael Haneke's *Caché*', *Cinema Journal*, 50:1 (2010), 59–80 (p. 60).

45. Haneke, 'Violence and the Media', p. 578.

46. Rudolph Binion, *Past Impersonal* (Illinois: Northern University Press, 2005), p. 65–66.

47. Bernard McElroy, *Fiction of the Modern Grotesque* (London, The Macmillan Press, 1989), p. ix.

48. Jacques Rancière, *Le destin des images* (Paris: La Fabrique, 2003), p. 130. Jacques Rancière, *The Future of the Image*, trans. Gregory Elliott (London: Verso, 2007), p. 114.

49. McElroy, *Fiction of the Modern Grotesque*, p. 27.

50. Yamina Benguigui's *Inch Allah Dimanche* (2001) illustrates in detail the transience and impernance of the immigrant's lodgings, depicting a transitional space crammed with boxes and bags, even though the individuals in question have been in France for several decades.

51. McElroy, *Fiction of the Modern Grotesque*, p. x.

52. Sigmund Freud, *The Uncanny* (London: Penguin Books, 2003), p. 124.

53. Philip Thomson, *The Grotesque* (London: Matheur & Co., 1972), p. 27.

54. Michel Chion, 'Without Music: On Caché', in *A Companion to Michael Haneke*, ed. by Roy Grundmann (Oxford: Wiley-Blackwell, 2010), pp. 161–67.

55. Haneke, 'Violence and the Media', p. 579.

56. Students have described their reaction to the scene as a mixture of horror and fascination, with one student noting 'I wanted to look away but I couldn't'.

57. Elisheva Rosen, 'L'Étrange séduction du grotesque', in *À la recherche du grotesque*, ed. by Paul Gorcex (Paris: J & S Éditeur, 2003), p. 206.

58. Susan Sontag, *Regarding the Pain of Others* (NewYork: Farrer, Strauss & Giraux, 2001), p. 37.

59. Haneke, 'Violence and the Media', p. 576.

60. Jacques Rancière, 'La Cause de l'autre', *Lignes*, 1:30 (1997), pp. 36–49.

61. Rancière, *Aux bords du politique*, p. 120.

62. McElroy, *Fiction of the Modern Grotesque*, p. 5.
63. Geoffrey Galt Harpham, *On the Grotesque: Strategies of Contradiction in Art and Literature* (Princeton, NJ: Princeton University Press), p. 3.
64. Jacques Rancière, *Figures de l'histoire* (Paris: Presses Universitaires de France, 2012), p. 45. Jacques Rancière, *Figures of History*, trans. Julie Rose (Cambridge: Polity Press, 2014), p. 45.
65. Haneke quoted in Jordan Ruimy, 'Haneke talks "Happy End"'', *The Playlist*, (23 May 2017) <http://theplaylist.net/michael-haneke-talks-making-happy-end-wont-explain-film-cannes-20170523/> [Accessed 15 June 2017].

CHAPTER 2

❖

Stumbling over *Muriel*:
Screening Torture in Post-War France

Caché attempts to disrupt wilful blindness to the suffering of others, and to bring light to a hidden violence that lurks in everyday interactions and for the most part remains unseen. In a similar sense, Alain Resnais describes these commonplace hostilities as a driving force behind his 1963 film *Muriel, ou le temps d'un retour* [*Muriel, or the Time of Return*]: 'un des thèmes principaux était une haine de la violence qui peut être une chose très banale, très quotidienne' [one of the major themes was a hatred of violence which can be a very banal thing, a part of everyday life].[1] *Muriel* explores the practice of torture by the French army during the Algerian War. The film is set in in the northern region of Pas-de-Calais, in the 'ville martyre' [martyred town] of Boulogne-sur-Mer, a city that suffered devastating losses during World War II. *Muriel* treats the intersecting memories of World War II and the Algerian War, but at the heart of the film's narrative is the eponymous Muriel, a misnamed Algerian woman who was tortured and killed by a group of French soldiers during the conflict. This woman occupies a position of importance in the film's narrative, and as the title suggests, the return staged is her ghostly haunting of the main protagonist, Bernard (Jean-Baptiste Thierrée), a veteran of the Algerian War. Yet the viewer is denied visual access to this violence and to her interiority: Muriel never appears on the screen, nor is her torture visualized through the use of flashbacks. What limited knowledge spectators garner of her experience is mediated through one of the perpetrators, Bernard, who recounts his participation in the assault that leads to her death. Throughout the film, viewers may feel like Bernard, who upon first entering the room where Muriel was detained, records, 'D'abord, je ne l'ai pas vue. C'est en m'approchant de la table que j'ai buté sur elle' [At first, I didn't see her. It was as I approached the table that I stumbled over her].[2]

The verbal narration of Muriel's death is embedded within a filmic quasi-narrative that is disturbing, contradictory, and often physically wearying. Indeed, 'narrative' might be a generous term in a film that sets out, deliberately and consistently, to bemuse, mislead, and distress the viewer. The story concerns four central characters, their perambulations and ill-fated amorous liaisons as they circle the streets, cafés and alleys of Boulogne-sur-Mer. Hélène (Delphine Seyrig) is a soft-spoken, mentally scattered middle-aged antiques dealer, whose stepson Bernard has just returned from the Algerian War. A letter from her former lover

Alphonse (Jean-Pierre Kérien) disrupts Hélène's daily routine, and the film opens with his arrival from Paris in Boulogne-sur-Mer train station. Alphonse, who falsely states that he has just returned from Algeria, is accompanied by Françoise (Nita Klein), an articulate and attractive actress. Alphonse introduces the young woman as his niece, although in reality Françoise is his lover. Hélène struggles with a gambling addiction, which appears to be facilitated by a local businessman and her current lover, Le Smoke (Claude Sainval). In addition to this collection of largely unsympathetic characters, we are presented with Claudie (Laurence Badie), Hélène's middle-class friend who finances her gambling, Robert (Philippe Laudenbach), an unabashed veteran of the Algerian War who served with Bernard, and Marie-Dominique (Martine Vatel), Bernard's girlfriend who he calls Marie-Do, but also disturbingly refers to as 'Muriel'.

This description gives a sense of the intersecting falsehoods that structure the narrative of *Muriel*, and the moral ambiguity of the characters is reflected in the formal opacity of the film's techniques. *Muriel* is an experimental drama, and it incorporates many of the formal innovations that were current in the *Nouvelle Vague* [New Wave] movement of the 1950s and 1960s. Fragmented narration, jump cuts, nonlinear editing, and naturalistic settings and lighting are defining characteristics of *Nouvelle Vague* filmmaking, and all these techniques feature in *Muriel*. The *Nouvelle Vague* movement itself was broadly divided into two groups, designated according to the side of the River Seine in Paris on which they lived and worked. Jean-Luc Godard, François Truffaut, Jacques Rivette, Éric Rohmer and Claude Chabrol were among the *Rive Droite* [Right Bank] group of filmmakers, who wrote for the *Cahiers du cinéma* journal, founded by André Bazin. Resnais, along with Chris Marker and Agnès Varda, was part of the *Rive Gauche* [Left Bank] group. The *Rive Gauche* group often collaborated with authors in the *nouveau roman* [New Novel] movement, including Marguerite Duras, Alain Robbe-Grillet and Jean Cayrol, who wrote the screenplay of *Muriel*.

As Robert Farmer notes, the works of Godard, Truffaut and other members of the *Rive Droite* group frequently overshadowed the *Rive Gauche* filmmakers in the popular imagination, perhaps because Varda, Marker, and Resnais 'tended to be politically, aesthetically and intellectually demanding'.[3] Indeed, by the time he made *Muriel*, Resnais had gained recognition as a filmmaker who treated difficult and controversial political subjects: the destruction of African art by French colonialism in *Les Statues meurent aussi* [*Statues Also Die*, 1953] (a documentary collaboration with Marker), the Holocaust in *Nuit et Brouillard* [*Night and Fog*, 1955], and the bombing of Hiroshima by Allied forces in *Hiroshima mon amour* [*Hiroshima My Love*, 1959]. Yet unlike *Nuit et Brouillard* or *Hiroshima mon amour*, which were both filmed a decade or more after the events they depict, *Muriel* was filmed in the immediate aftermath of the Algerian War, and Resnais was a signatory of the *Manifeste des 121* [Manifesto of the 121], an open letter signed by 121 intellectuals in September 1960 against the Algerian War. Moreover, other cinematic representations of torture during the Algerian War did not emerge until years or sometimes decades later. Laurent Herbiet's *Mon colonel* (2006), Philippe Faucon's *La Trahison* [*The Betrayal*] (2005), and

Jean-Pierre Lledo's *Un rêve algérien* [*An Algerian Dream*] (2003) all appeared almost forty years after the war. Gillo Pontecorvo's 1966 *La Bataille d'Alger* [*The Battle of Algiers*] constitutes an exception, and it was an Italian-Algerian co-production, not of French provenance.

Within my corpus, *Muriel* is the most temporally proximate to the historical violence it depicts, as it was made one year after the official ceasefire in 1962. This alters the film's relation to historical accounts of female torture during the war, and in many ways, Resnais's film can be said to prefigure the historicization of the torture of women during the war through its focus on the underrepresentation of female victims. Recent readings of *Muriel* have focused on issues of the body, memory and trauma (Wilson: 2006), psychoanalysis (Croombs: 2014), and time and continental philosophy (McMahon: 2016).[4] My discussion intervenes in this debate by highlighting the historicization of torture during and after the Algerian War, and I draw on recent historiographical accounts of female torture during the war to illuminate the specifically gendered aspects of the female torture victim, particularly rape. I detail Resnais's use of visual and verbal disjunctions within the broader aesthetic framework of the film and connect these techniques to the account of Muriel's torture. I underscore the specifically sexual dimension of Muriel's torture by connecting Resnais's audio-visual asynchronous techniques, philosophical readings of the visual and verbal aspects of torture, and testimonial accounts, and by tying its omission to the suppression of the war in the consciousness of 1963 French society.

Gendered Violence: Torture and Denial

The use of torture in times of war is frequently justified by the need to obtain information: if the victim informed on collaborators, civilian lives could be saved. Paul Aussaresses, the French general who in 2000 defended the use of torture during the Algerian War and was stripped of his army rank, summarizes this position: 'Je n'ai jamais torturé personne parce que je voulais les punir, j'ai sauvé en interrogeant des gens, même avec brutalité, même jusqu'à leur mort, [...] j'ai sauvé un nombre considérable de vies humaines' [I never tortured anyone because I wanted to punish them, I saved lives by interrogating people, even brutally, even to death, [...] I saved a considerable number of human lives].[5] Jacques Massu, one of the army personnel upon whom the ambiguous figure of Colonel Mathieu in *La Bataille d'Alger* is based, echoes this claim, suggesting that 'il s'agissait d'obtenir le renseignement opérationnel urgent, dont dépendait la vie d'êtres innocents, délibérément sacrifiés par le F.L.N. à son objectif' [The lives of innocent people, deliberately sacrificed by the FLN for their aims, depended on obtaining this urgent operational information].[6] The statements of these military men are underpinned by a belief in a hierarchy of loss: there are 'innocent beings' whose lives must be saved, and there are those whose torture becomes incidental, because their lives are intrinsically less valuable. Ali-Yahia Abdennour, an ex-FLN member, lawyer, and human rights activist at the forefront of the campaign against torture in post-1988

Algeria, reiterates the dehumanizing element of torture: 'la torture [...] est un revers de la démocratie, la corruption ultime de l'être humain, la négation de l'humanité' [Torture [...] is a setback for democracy, the ultimate corruption of the human being, and the negation of humanity].[7] Florence Beaugé, a journalist with *Le Monde* who in 2005 undertook a detailed and widely disseminated consideration of torture during the Algerian War, suggests that the retrieval of key information is not the central purpose of torture, as military personnel suggest, but rather the emotional and moral degradation of the individual, the desire to assert dominance: 'la torture avait moins pour objet de faire parler que de faire entendre qui avait le pouvoir' [Torture was less about making people talk, more a way of making it clear who had power].[8] Moreover, Tzvetan Todorov points out that this defence is not borne out by experience; bombers are rarely caught before their bombs go off and despite the claims of military personnel like Colonel Roger Trinquier, that torture was 'the only way to win the war', France did not win, in spite of their use of torture.[9]

Torture in Algeria became a mechanism to attack and divide the entire community, and was as much an instrument of psychological assault as it was a means of inflicting physical pain. Former Algerian diplomat and UN representative Mohamed Lebjaoui notes that in Algeria torture was 'une entreprise de déshumanisation visant l'ensemble d'une communauté afin de la ramener par la violence au statut de dépendance. [...] elle est le colonialisme même, dépouillé de ses masques idéologiques' [A dehumanizing process, aimed at an entire community, designed to return it to a state of dependency through violence. [...] it is quite simply colonialism, with its ideological masks removed].[10] As Todorov writes, referring to torture during the war, and torture in a more general sense, 'the people I'm fighting, it is easy to paint them as less than human; in that way, I can legitimize my inhumane treatment of them'. Thus, degrees of humanity are central to the practice of torture, by which the people being tortured are somehow different, not quite the same kind of human being as 'we' are.[11]

Algerian women were marked as manifestly different, as both gendered and ethnic others, and they were subject to a sexualisation and forms of sexual violence that distinguishes their treatment from that of the male detainees. Raphaëlle Branche conceives of the Algerian War itself as a kind of figurative rape: 'symboliquement, cette guerre, de (re)conquête, est déjà un viol de la population' [symbolically, this war of (re)conquest is already a rape of the population].[12] The case of Djamila Boupacha brought to light the army's practices around the torture and rape of female detainees during the conflict and illustrates the sexualization of the Algerian conflict as a whole. Boupacha, a young Algerian woman who was arrested in 1960 for attempting to bomb a café in Algiers, was subsequently tortured and raped. In 1960, Boupacha brought suit against the French government, with French-Tunisian lawyer Gisèle Halimi serving as Boupacha's legal counsel. The trial brought widespread public attention to the practice of female torture, and an article by Simone de Beauvoir in *Le Monde* detailing Boupacha's violation furthered public knowledge about the army's practices.[13] However, the highly publicized nature of Boupacha's trial belies broader omissions and incredulity around the torture and rape of female detainees. Quite apart from politicians, veterans, and important military personnel with political and personal investments in the falsity of women's claims of having been tortured, even apparently impartial observers expressed doubt. In one of the earliest historical accounts of the war, written in 1977, Alistair Horne questions the veracity of women's testimonies, stating that 'rape, *if one is to believe Algerian sources,* assumed appalling proportions' [my italics].[14] Beaugé, in 2005, did not believe Algerian resistance fighter Louise Ighilahriz's account of torture and rape 'until it was confirmed to her by a veteran of the Algerian War'.[15]

This lack of credulity around women's narratives of violence may be because the project of gathering testimonial evidence from Algerian women who were victims of torture and rape, as well as from French veterans, has been a relatively recent phenomenon. While Patrick Rotman and Bertrand Tavernier's documentary *La Guerre sans nom: les appelés d'Algérie* (1992) addressed the silence of many French veterans regarding their deeds and experiences, sometimes citing acts of rape and torture, Branche's comprehensive work, *La Torture et l'Armée pendant la guerre d'Algérie*, was the first to address in extensive detail the specificities around the act of torture in relation to female victims.[16] What emerges from both of these critical studies is the extent to which the torture of women was explicitly differentiated by their sex. Branche remarks that 'soldiers came to see the [female] victims less as fellow human beings but instead as wholly different, i.e., women, Algerians and enemies'.[17] According to one veteran Branche interviewed, 'le problème des Algériennes c'est qu'elles étaient sales et voilées' [The problem with Algerian women was that they were dirty and veiled].[18] Highlighting the sexual nature of the act, the detainee Fatma Baichi records that in the centre where she was held, 'il y avait un tortionnaire, torse nu, qui torturait' [There was a torturer, bare-chested, torturing].[19] A veteran interviewed by Branche recalls an atmosphere of striptease, while another soldier remembers the proliferation of pornographic images pinned up and passed around army barracks. Some soldiers, many of them barely out of their teens and sexually inexperienced, even arrived in Algeria with badges announcing, 'Bon pour le service' [Good for Service], a phrase which interweaves the military and sexual connotations of 'service'.[20]

Unlike torture, rape was never officially sanctioned, but according to Marnia Lazreg, the army's policy of verifying the gender of a suspect by touching their genitals, ostensibly due to the utilization of the veil as a method of concealment by male FLN members, served as an 'incitement to rape' that led to rape becoming 'the ultimate test of sex identification'.[21] Drawing a distinction between rape and torture is rarely unproblematic in the context of war. Lazreg writes that some women used the word 'torture' as a code word for rape, 'as they continue to feel the trauma of having been violated but are unable to come to terms with it'.[22] The slippage between these terms is underscored by the words of M. Patin, President of the Committee of Public Safety and presiding magistrate at Boupacha's trial, who stated, 'il ne s'agit donc pas du véritable supplice' [it is not therefore a case of real torture], because unlike soldiers in Indochina, Boupacha had not been raped *per anum*.[23] This statement implies that only anal rape, committed against men as well as women, counts as real torture: vaginal rape does not. While it is important to recognize a distinction between the rape of the civilian population and that of the female (and to a lesser extent male) *maquisards* in terms of motivation, effect, and acknowledgment, both kinds of rape could be used to form bonds between the soldiers and to consolidate their identity in the face of an inassimilable other.[24] Branche concludes that rape served as a confirmation of a virile masculine identity and a means of subjugating the population by attacking one of its core values, the virtue of women: 'à travers la femme, bousculée, violentée, violée, le soldat atteint sa famille, son village, et tous les cercles auxquels elle appartient jusqu'au dernier: le peuple algérien' [Through the woman — battered, assaulted, raped — the soldier attacks her family, her village, and every sphere she belongs to, and finally, the Algerian population itself].[25]

The rape and torture of women constituted a form of symbolic violence, representing the penetration of Algerian territory and supremacy over the Algerian people. Ryan Kunkle even suggests that the Boupacha case 'illuminates the sexualization of the Algerian conflict as a whole'.[26] However, such an association between woman and territory can be detected even at the initial 1830 conquest of the country, when the Algerian woman, veiled or in the harem, came to represent the territory itself. The penetration of the geographical terrain of Algeria by French soldiers was bound up in an imaginary of unveiling, access to the harem, and the literal penetration of women through consensual sex, or rape. Eugène Delacroix's *Femmes d'Alger dans leur appartement* [*Women of Algiers in their Apartment*], painted in 1834, represents an early instance of the interweaving of female subjugation with political dominion. As Darcy Grimaldo Grigsby writes of this work, 'to wrest Algeria away from its ruler was to claim his harem, his property'.[27] The painter has penetrated the previously forbidden space of the Algerian harem, gained access to an enclosed and secret world of feminine intimacy and (apparent) sexual freedom and abandonment. Malek Alloula has also shown how colonial postcards, popular in the period from 1900 to 1930, operated in a similar manner. They depict images of naked or partially clad Algerian women in a variety of suggestive erotic or homoerotic poses and adorned with ethnically marked, exotic attire. For Alloula, these postcards suggest that 'these women, who were reputedly invisible or hidden, and, until now, beyond sight, are henceforth public [...] their intimacy can be broken into and violated'.[28] Posted by French colonists, merchants and tourists from Algeria to the *métropole*, the female bodies on the cards were visible, exposed, touched, as they passed from hand to hand for the duration of the journey. The cards were received in France as symbols of the power the colonizer held over the country and its people, rendered symbolically through the sexualized female form.

Within this imaginary of Algerian women as representative of the country itself, Resnais initially appears to replicate some of the problematic racial and sexual presumptions of previous representations. Like the women of Delacroix's painting and the postcards Alloula deconstructs, Muriel is voiceless, and her presence in the film is entirely mediated through the consciousness of a French man, who has physically abused her, and participated in her murder. For Algerian critic and novelist Rachid Boudjedra, in *Muriel*, 'l'Algérie [est] comme une pensée gênante que chacun cherche à oublier' [Algeria [is] like an embarrassing thought that everyone wants to forget].[29] At the core of this push towards obfuscation is the absent Algerian woman who stands in for the conflict itself, its attendant horrors, and its suppression in the consciousness of 1963 French society. However, although the characters, with the exception of Bernard, may want to forget Algeria, Resnais ensures that the viewer is recalled to the conflict with increasing intermittence as the film progresses. Moreover, if, as Fanon states, the dream of the colonizer is to tear away the veil that conceals the Algerian woman, Resnais leaves this covering firmly intact: the viewer is granted no visual access to Muriel's body.[30] The refusal to render Muriel visually while simultaneously constructing the narrative around her experience undergirds a wider play between the visual and the verbal in the film which plays out in the tension Resnais constructs between banality and horror, petty domesticity and acts of extreme violence.

Torture and Form: Visual and Verbal Disjunctions

The question of the filmic representation of torture is fraught with ethical and aesthetic limitations, but visual and verbal incongruities feature consistently in many representations of torture during the Algerian War, such as *La Bataille d'Alger*, *Mon colonel*, *La Trahison* and *Un rêve algérien*. These films refer to torture, and in each case, there is a refusal to offer a full audio–visual account of the act and a reluctance to employ the full formal scope of cinema as an audio–visual medium. By breaking the synchronous connection between image and sound, the viewer is momentarily lifted out of the narrative thread of the film, forced to pause and dwell in the horror of the act. *La Bataille d'Alger*, for example, offers alternating close-ups of victims and French soldiers, as well as of Algerian witnesses, while detailing visually each mode of torture used by the French — electrocution, water-boarding, and suspension from the wrists and elbows. However, although we are shown open mouths, wide and screaming with pain, Ennio Morricone's ecclesiastical organ score drowns out these cries of suffering. This increases the pathos of the close-ups of the tear-stained faces, frozen in horror, and because the screams stay silent, there is no solution, no release, and no easing of this pain. The torture scene in *Mon colonel* is again stylized, with a Christian classical music soundtrack and brief, rapidly edited images of the victims. Lledo's *Un rêve algérien* follows left-wing journalist Henri Alleg's journey back to Algeria, decades after his torture there at the hands of the French army, and therefore we are offered no visual images of the violence, only verbal accounts. Lledo's focus on the aftermath of torture underscores the degree to which torture is an act whose consequences go far beyond the time and place in which it originally took place. Godard's *Le Petit Soldat* [*The Little Soldier*] (1963) chooses to depict torture in a stylized manner, rendering it almost comic through the main character Bruno's farcical leap from a window to escape.

Visual and verbal disjunctions around the representation of torture may also relate to the frequently covert nature of the act, its shadowy legality. Darius Rejali argues that the monitoring of the actions of the state by the media and non-governmental organizations in twentieth and twenty-first century liberal democracies has moved towards clandestine and untraceable interrogation techniques, what he calls 'clean' torture. This form of torture leaves no long-term scars, and the techniques most often employed in this way include waterboarding, electrocution, sleep deprivation, static positioning, and torture using intermittent noises or relentless music. Torture in Pontecorvo's *La Bataille d'Alger*, for example, is overwhelmingly represented as 'clean', in that the torturers use techniques that leave little or no marks. In this film, torturers who seem experienced commit the act in a relatively public context, where soldiers seem both indifferent to the crime itself, as well as to the presence of witnesses. The torturers we see on screen are shown to 'successfully' deploy a variety of techniques in order to get the suspects to speak, particularly the combination of water techniques and electrocution, a style Rejali designates 'French modern'.[31]

The torture of Muriel, on the other hand, can be characterized as what Rejali terms 'dirty'. Bernard and the other soldiers must be inexperienced because they take the torture so far that the principal stated aim, the obtainment of information, is utterly negated: Muriel dies. As Rejali writes, 'Pain is not a constant, which they can simply increase. As the body is damaged, its ability to sense pain declines. More injury does not produce more pain, but its opposite'.[32] The torture of women was never officially sanctioned by the French Army, and the space in which it takes place, a disused shed, as well as the fact that Muriel remains anonymous, suggest that this was an event of highly questionable legality, even within the context of an already bitter, dirty, and divisive war. In *Muriel*, Resnais uses sound-image disjunctions to frame Bernard's account of torture, and to create a slippery audio-visual terrain that destabilizes a concrete interpretation of the plot, as he shifts between familiar characters and settings and de-familiarizing filmic techniques: editing, sound, music, dialogue, and setting. In this section, I discuss these techniques, the affective registers they generate, and how these formal structures serve to frame the 'dirty' act at the centre of the film: Muriel's torture.

The formal construction of *Muriel* creates a cleavage between sight and comprehension: as spectators, we may feel we are brought close to a kind of horror, and yet we cannot see or feel it concretely. Just as Bernard's kaleidoscope fragments the faces and objects he aims it at, distorting angles and colours, in *Muriel*, correlations between the audible and the visible are splintered and disfigured. Resnais's techniques in this film, the disconnection the spectator experiences as a result of the contrast between the familiar settings and natural lighting, and the disjunctive sound and editing, can be likened to the theatre of Bertolt Brecht. Tom Milne cites the German playwright in his review of *Muriel*: 'closely observe the behaviour of these people: consider it strange, although familiar'.[33] Brecht developed an aesthetic theory around what he called *verfremdung* [alienation], which Peter Brooker characterizes as the 'stripping the event of its self-evident, familiar, obvious quality and creating a sense of astonishment and curiosity'.[34] This aesthetic can be further connected to Resnais's work with Jean Cayrol on *Nuit et Brouillard*, and Resnais called this disjunction between the familiar and the unfamiliar a 'post-concentrationary aesthetic of dread', an 'art lazaréen' [art of Lazarus]. Cayrol had been interned at the Gusen concentration camp in 1943 for his participation in the French Resistance. Having escaped death during the war, he became fascinated with the biblical Lazarus, raised from the dead by Jesus, whom Cayrol associated with the survivors of the camps. This otherworldly figure, resurrected from death, resonates with Bernard's attempts to resuscitate the deceased Muriel through images, verbal recordings, and film.

Max Silverman notes that Cayrol's and Resnais's aesthetic in *Nuit et Brouillard* 'is dependent on a defamiliarisation and reinvention of the everyday through the shock of incomprehensible connections'.[35] *Muriel* also shuttles between effects of realism and experimentalism, creating a sense that the world portrayed has much of the ordinary about it, but like a familiar song played out of tune, something of the extraordinary resides in the everyday. The domestic and the urban settings represented in *Muriel* would have been intimately and unnervingly recognizable to the contemporary viewer because the film, with a hint of the grotesque, creates and reflects back the socio-political space of middle-class modernity in 1960s France. Following a sequence at a train station, the film moves through a series of familiar locations: cafés, bars, restaurants, department stores, and tobacconists, all features of modern, everyday life in 1960s France. This is a milieu maintained by what Resnais has called 'l'idée de Bonheur style "France-Dimanche", du petit Bonheur confortable à base de gueuletons et d'idées toutes faites' [An idea of Happiness in the style of 'France Dimanche', a comfortable little Happiness, based on lavish meals and preconceived ideas].[36] It is also worth noting that this is definitively not Paris: this is provincial France, and although a relatively urban area, culturally and socially, this is not the centre of metropolitan existence. As Françoise notes, 'on est au bout du monde' [we're at the end of the world].[37] The notion of a provincial France based on clichéd ideas and petty domesticity is echoed in the claustrophobic layout of Hélène's apartment, with its jarring proliferation of brown and beige objects. These items are in constant flux because of Hélène's work as an antique dealer who trades from home, thus reflecting the relentless nervous shifting and perambulations of Hélène herself. As Cayrol's script directions note of her apartment, 'rien n'est placé définitivement, tout est en transit' [nothing is placed definitively, everything is in transit].[38]

In the opening sequence of the film, the spectator's disorientation is established through the cinematography. The camera flits between the varied contemporaneous objects of the 1960s strewn about Hélène's apartment: telephones, coffee makers, crockery sets, ashtrays, vases, kitchen gadgets.[39] Resnais offers a series of close ups of these household objects, intercut with rapid shots of hands smoking cigarettes, gripping doors, and holding coffee pots, as well as brief, oblique close ups of Hélène and Bernard's faces. Overlaid above these images is the voice of a woman, who names items of furniture, with no apparent context: 'une commode', 'une commode d'un mètre vingt', 'une table suédoise...en bois de teck' [a chest of drawers, a chest of drawers one metre, twenty centimetres high, a Swedish table...in teak wood].[40] The word 'commode' will later be repeated by Alphonse when he expresses a desire to stay in the apartment, and its repetition, with the dual meaning of 'chest of drawers' and 'convenient' or 'practical', highlights one of the film's recurring themes: trivial domesticity, and the character's endless desire for bourgeois comfort, practicality and ease. In this sequence, the sounds of an urban area, traffic and honking horns hum in the background, and when the camera eventually turns on the woman who is speaking, she is depicted in a series of four consecutive, fast close ups, all taken from different angles. The rapid editing and close up shots of prosaic actions and items, the canted angles, and the incongruous magnification of these everyday items contribute to a sense of alienation and unease.

A sense of spectator familiarity with the settings and props of the film is enhanced by the use of natural lighting, which creates an effect of realism at odds with the film's insistence on its artificiality, through editing, dialogue, and music. Hans Werner Henze's soundtrack did contain songs that referred to the images, but Resnais felt that this distracted from the visual frames and so intentionally played the tracks backwards in order to make them unintelligible.[41] Perplexity can transmute into anxiety for the listener-viewer through the operatic soundtrack, sung by Rita Streich, whose sudden soaring and incomprehensible arias form a sharp contrast to the unremarkable activities of the characters. Resnais's editing techniques further disrupt any logic of contiguous space or time. The film contains more than 1000 shots, and reframing takes place through cuts rather than through tracking shots. Alyssa O'Brien has even identified what she terms the 'inverted jump cut', whereby shots are composed to give the illusion of continuity editing, whereas in fact they elide the passage of time. For example, Alphonse is seen striking a match, lighting a cigar and then stubbing out the cigar, a temporal elision that disquiets the viewer, but may not be consciously registered.[42]

Resnais gave specific instructions to cinematographer Sacha Vierny that no filters be used and that the film stock remain untreated and the lighting of both outdoor and indoor scenes was contingent upon the vagaries of the weather. Resnais's deployment of colour in the film also wavers between the realistic and the constructed. While filming in colour was perceived as being more naturalistic, the aesthetically disconcerting palate of brown, mustard, and beige tones that characterize the film are at once a marker of its artificiality, as well as a reference to the banal colour schemes of the modern city. The setting of the film, Boulogne-sur-Mer, mirrors this tension between familiarity and change, past and present, and tradition and modernity [Figures 2.1 and 2.2]. This martyred town has new apartment blocks that literally collapse into the sea, glossy neon-lighted casinos, and busy boulevards, as well as the crumbling walls of the old town, cliff face paths, and cobblestone streets. The tension between new and old constructions is played out in the town's train station: the film's narrative begins at the old depot with the arrival of Alphonse, but at the end of the film, a new structure has been built. It is also a town that, like the film, has no clearly recognisable centre. Watching *Muriel*, spectators frequently sense the disorientation of the man who asks 'Le centre, s'il vous plaît?' [Could you tell me the way to the town centre please?], only to be told, 'mais vous-y êtes' [But you are in it].[43]

FIG. 2.1. Boulogne-sur-Mer — the old and the new.
Muriel ou le temps d'un retour, dir. Alain Resnais (1963).

FIG. 2.2. Boulogne-sur-Mer — the old and the new.
Muriel ou le temps d'un retour, dir. Alain Resnais (1963).

Just as the old rubs up uncomfortably against the new in Boulogne-sur-Mer, the modern objects that clutter Hélène's apartment jostle for space with older pieces of furniture. As Bernard notes, 'on ne sait jamais quand on se réveille si c'est dans du Second Empire ou dans du rustique normand' [you never know whether you're going to wake up in a Second Empire décor or Normandy rustic].[44] However, because of the lack of spectator positioning within this space, we are never fully sure how large the apartment is, or where objects, rooms, and individuals are located. A panning shot of the apartment is only provided in the final sequence of the film. In the stage directions, Cayrol describes Hélène's apartment as a space that is 'un peu vide, malgré le nombre d'objets' [a bit empty, in spite of the number of objects].[45] This sense of emptiness at the heart of a film crowded with characters, objects, and locations is underscored by the frequent disjunctions between the dialogue and the associated images. Words in *Muriel* consistently bemuse, perplex, and mislead. Alphonse weaves a fabric of untruth around the time he claims to have spent in Algeria, and Hélène frequently equivocates about her gambling habit and often leaves sentences suspended, hanging in mid-air. On several occasions, Françoise, who possesses a youthful lucidity that is markedly absent in the other characters, implores people to say what they mean and to finish their sentences. She even shouts emphatically after Bernard on one occasion that she understands him, although what she could have garnered from their bemusing exchange remains unclear.

Confusion punctuates the characters' communications, and the viewer is compelled to partake in these misapprehensions: although the script is conceived in five chronological acts, within each act, the events are depicted out of synch. Even within the same conversation, Resnais omits blocks of words and phrases that might offer clarity, absences that are reflected in the many ellipses that punctuate the script and signalled to the watchful viewer by jerky editing, such as inverted jump cuts. Furthermore, exchanges that seem to carry some emotional importance and narrative illumination are almost always interrupted by an abrupt cut, a transition to another scene, or by other characters. In general, *Muriel* can be characterized by the dull a-political nature of the characters' interactions. Of course, this was precisely the milieu Resnais wanted to depict, that of the 'commode' and a 'Bonheur style "France-Dimanche"', and it is a world in which people speak about anything and everything, as long as it is insignificant. Again, an incongruity between image and word emerges: intimate close ups, often accompanied by creeping violin tones, lead to vociferations of the deadly dullest variety. In one sequence, a screeching violin score overlays a slow zoom into a close up of Claudie, and as the sound increases, the spectator waits for narrative revelation. Instead, erupting into an excess of surreal laughter, she says, 'avec une sauce moutarde!' [with a mustard sauce!]. Hélène even praises the comforting nature of the mundane and the commonplace, saying 'au fond c'est une histoire banale. Ça me rassure' [at the end of the day, it's a banal story. I find that reassuring].[46]

However, words in the form of written documents, depicted as visual images, do offer some narrative illumination, and point the viewer towards the story of Muriel. Muriel's spectral presence in the film is mediated and sustained by Bernard through the splintered narrative he attempts to construct of her life, or at least the end of her life, through photographs, letters, diary entries, and home-movie, newsreel-style footage of soldiers. The viewer is treated to lingering close ups of excerpts from Bernard's diary that point to the breakdown of modes of civilized behaviour in the context of the war, as well as drawing distinctions between civilian and soldierly existence: 'On est en guerre m'a dit enfin Petit Rouge. Quand tu seras civil tu pourras penser ce que tu voudras: pour la première fois j'ai remarqué qu'il ne se lavait plus les mains' [We're at war, Little Red said to me eventually. When you're a civilian you can think what you like: I noticed for the first time he no longer washed his hands] [Figure 2.3]. These written documents also point to Bernard's slow psychological disintegration following his participation in Muriel's torture: 'je suis fichu — je crois que j'ai envie de mourir, en tout cas je n'en ai plus peur, [...]

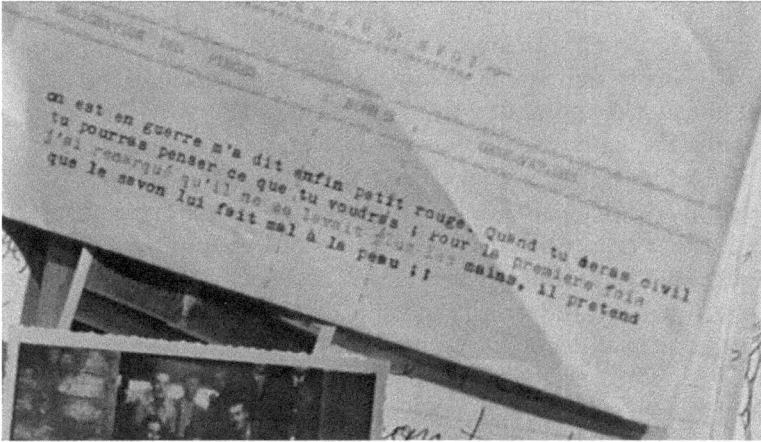

FIG. 2.3. Bernard's diary. *Muriel, ou le temps d'un retour*, dir. Alain Resnais (1963).

c'est avec Muriel que tout a commencé vraiment — que j'ai compris — c'est depuis Muriel que je ne vis plus vraiment' [I've had it — I think I want to die, at any rate, I'm no longer afraid of death. [...] Really, it all began with Muriel — when I understood — since Muriel I am no longer really living]. It is worth noting that there is little description of these documents in the script: Cayrol simply notes of the letters, 'dans ces phrases, le nom de Muriel revient souvent' [in these phrases, Muriel's name often reappears].[47] The detail appears to be Resnais's addition, and it is significant that this evidence of Bernard's connection to the dead woman is revealed in words. These words come to the viewer not in dialogue, a dialogue that has proved both limited in affect and unreliable in content, but in the form of images.

Seeing Absence: The Torture Sequence

In the sequence in which Bernard narrates Muriel's torture, the already brittle audio-visual frames of the film appear finally to crack, exposing (albeit verbally) the empty centre of the film, the gap of experience that organizes the entirety of what Suzanne Gauch has called the film's 'disappearing text': the Algerian War and the torture of Muriel.[48] On the one hand, this scene contrasts with the audio-visual disjunctions of the rest of the film outlined above, which confuse the viewer, who struggles to sequentially and spatially comprehend the action of the film. In a sense, the aesthetic properties of this scene contrast directly with the suicide scene in *Caché* where an excess of visual material was accompanied by little verbal explanation. Muriel's death as described in the torture sequence leaves little room for interpretative ambiguity, but at the same time, the images that overlay this narration initially appear to bear no relation to the actions they describe, and so words and images remain detached. The source of these images is still uncertain. According to François Thomas, Louis Malle at one point suggested that he made the recordings during his time as a soldier in Algeria and gave them to Resnais, but Resnais denied that this was the case. Thomas suggests that 'on ne peut pas exclure que Resnais n'ait pas gardé en mémoire la source et se trompe, ou que quelques plans aient été transmis à Resnais et son équipe de montage sans qu'ils en connaissent l'origine' [we cannot discount the possibility that Resnais forgot the source of the images, and has made a mistake, or that some shots were given to Resnais and his editing team without them knowing where they came from].[49]

The possibility that Resnais may have forgotten the source of the images highlights the slippery nature of recollection, a gap that is reflected in the incomplete nature of memories and accounts of torture. The act of torture itself may open a space between the visual and the verbal, and this cleavage is reflected in the responses to narrative accounts of torture. Scarry suggests that verbal descriptions of torture given by perpetrators can often obscure grim, physical realities that would be impossible to ignore if presented through a visual medium:

> Almost anyone looking at the physical act of torture would be immediately appalled and repulsed by the torturers. It is difficult to think of a human situation in which the lines of moral responsibility are more starkly or simply drawn, [...] yet as soon as the focus of attention shifts to the verbal aspect of torture, those lines have begun to waver and change their shape in the direction of accommodating and crediting the torturers.[50]

Scarry's analysis draws distinctions between the role of images and words in depicting a scene of torture, suggesting that if we witness torture, we cannot help but be moved to a moral condemnation of its horrors, whereas verbal rationalizations allow it to be perceived as a practice with potentially necessary political ends. The vocabulary that Scarry employs suggests a fundamental distinction between how visual and verbal representations of torture are approached: the sight of torture leaves the spectator 'appalled' and 'repulsed', terms that point towards a corporeal and moral outrage. On the other hand, verbal accounts, particularly those offered by perpetrators as justifications, lead to 'accommodation' and 'crediting', privileging a cognitive understanding of the act. If, as Scarry suggests, the torturer's justi-fication can obscure the visceral realities of the torture scene, Bernard's account of Muriel's death is unusual because the words of the perpetrator attempt to offer evidence that she was tortured and killed.

The sequence in which the torture of Muriel is described lies at the literal and thematic centre of Resnais's film (55 minutes into the 111-minute work), and as the sequence begins, the texture of the filmic image changes abruptly. Over-exposed, grainy Super-8 footage rolls, portraying what appear to be reasonably innocuous moving images of soldiers in Algeria. This footage contrasts with the immobile and numbed word-images that Bernard uses to describe both his own feelings and those he interprets in the voiceless Muriel. I quote the passage at length here, to give a sense of the tone and lexicon of the text:

> Personne n'avait connu cette femme avant. Je traversais le bureau où je travaillais [...].
> Le hangar était au fond, avec les munitions. D'abord, je ne l'ai pas vue. C'est en m'approchant de la table que j'ai buté sur elle. Elle avait l'air endormie,

mais elle tremblait de partout. On me dit qu'elle s'appelle Muriel. Je ne sais pas
pourquoi mais ça ne devait pas être son vrai nom. On était bien cinq autours
d'elle [...].

    Il fallait qu'elle parle avant la nuit.

    Robert s'est dressé, et l'a retournée. Muriel a gémi. Elle avait mis son bras
sur ses yeux. On la lâche, elle retombe comme un paquet.

    C'est alors que ça recommence. On la tire par les chevilles au milieu du
hangar pour mieux la voir. Robert lui donne des coups de pieds [dans les
hanches]. Il prend une lampe torche, la braque sur elle. Les lèvres sont gonflées,
pleines d'écume. On lui arrache ses vêtements. On essaie de l'asseoir, sur la
chaise, mais elle retombe. Un bras est comme tordu.

    Il faut en finir. Même si elle avait voulu parler elle n'aurait pas pu. Je m'y
suis mis aussi. Muriel geignait en recevant les gifles. La paume de mes mains
me brûlait. Muriel avait les cheveux tout mouillés.

    Robert allume une cigarette. Il s'approche d'elle. Elle hurle. Alors son regard
m'a fixé. Pourquoi moi? Elle a fermé les yeux, et elle s'est mise à vomir. Robert
a reculé, dégouté. Je les ai tous laissés.

    La nuit je suis revenue la voir. J'ai soulevé la bâche...

    Comme si elle avait séjournée longtemps dans l'eau...comme un sac de
pommes de terres éventré... avec du sang sur tout le corps, dans les cheveux...
des brûlures sur la poitrine. Les yeux de Muriel n'étaient pas fermés.

    Ça me faisait presque rien, peut-être même que cela ne me faisait rien du
tout.

    Le lendemain matin avant le salut aux couleurs, Robert l'avait fait
disparaître.[51]

[Nobody had seen this woman before. I walked through the office where I
worked [...]. The shed was at the back, with the ammunition. At first, I didn't
see her. It was as I approached the table that I stumbled over her. She seemed
to be asleep but she was trembling all over. I was told her name was Muriel. I
don't know why, but that can't have been her real name. There were five of us
around her [...]. We had to get her to speak before nightfall. Robert bent down
and turned her over. Muriel groaned. She had put her arm over her eyes. They
let go of her, she falls, lifeless. That's when it began again. They drag her by
her ankles into the middle of the shed to see her better. Robert kicks her [in
the hips]. He takes a torch and points it at her. Her lips are swollen, foaming.
They tear off her clothes. They try to sit her on a chair, but she falls off. One
of her arms seems to be broken. We have to bring this to an end. Even if she
had wanted to talk, she wouldn't have been able to. I started on her too. Muriel
groaned as she was beaten. The palms of my hands were burning. Muriel's hair
was all wet. Robert lights a cigarette. He goes up to her. She screams. Then
she stared at me. Why me? She closed her eyes, then began to vomit. Robert
recoiled, disgusted. I left them all. That night I came back to see her. I lifted
the tarpaulin. It was as if she had been underwater for a long time...Like a sack
of potatoes split open...she had blood all over her body and in her hair...burns
on her chest. Muriel 's eyes weren't closed. It had had very little effect on me,
perhaps no effect at all. The next morning, Robert had got rid of her].

Bernard's voice dominates the sequence, while Muriel's body is evoked in a series of
visceral verbs that highlight her physical condition: 'trembler', 'gémir', 'retomber',
'hurler', 'vomir' ['tremble', 'moan', 'fall again', 'scream', 'vomit'] as well as isolating

specific parts of her body, 'bras', 'yeux', 'chevilles', 'hanches', 'lèvres', 'cheveux', 'poitrine' ['arms', 'eyes', 'ankles', 'hips', 'lips', 'hair', 'chest']. The dominance of Bernard's voice and the emphasis on Muriel's body reflects Scarry's description of the torture scene: 'ultimate domination requires that the prisoner's ground become increasingly physical and the torturer's increasingly verbal, that the prisoner become a colossal body with no voice and the torturer a colossal voice [...] with no body'.[52] Muriel's body is broken, and therefore her voice, as a projection of the self that is dependent on the physical, is also silenced. She cannot even speak her own name — all that is left to Muriel are the non-verbal sounds of extreme pain. For a physical body that is so conspicuously absent from the visual world of the film, Muriel's corporality nonetheless occupies a significant space in Bernard's description. Her broken body also inspires a vocabulary of disgust: she is swollen, twisted, vomiting, and covered in scum. This disgust is implicitly gendered and it echoes the words of the veteran Branche interviewed, that Algerian women were 'dirty and veiled'.

It is not possible to ascertain whether Resnais and Cayrol imagined that the woman named 'Muriel' was raped as well as tortured, although there are several factors that indicate that this may have been the case. At the very least, such a reading of the scene would conform to the historiographical accounts outlined in the first section. In the overwhelming majority of testimonies where female insurgents were physically tortured, rape occurred as well, and according to Lazreg, 'although rape could take place without torture, torture seldom took place without rape'.[53] Moreover, the body parts listed in Bernard's narration further the fragmentation of Muriel's disintegrating, dying form, but also point towards a discrete sexualisation of her body. Apart from the arms, all other body parts can be considered secondary sexual characteristics, and it is worth noting that the words 'dans les hanches' [in the hips] do not appear in Cayrol's script: Resnais added them to the dialogue, as if to further emphasize the sexualisation implicit in the act. Indeed, the word 'hips' could serve as a euphemism for genitals: in Simone de Beauvoir's article on Djamila Boupacha's rape and torture for *Le Monde* on 2 June 1960, editors replaced the word 'vagin' [vagina] with 'ventre' [stomach], but as de Beauvoir points out, 'les lecteurs avaient compris' [readers understood], because it was the cornerstone of the exposé.[54] On formal and thematic levels, Celia Britton points to a consistent trope of intrusion in *Muriel*, for intrusion 'can be conceptualised in structural terms as an entity being broken *into* from the outside'.[55] Emma Wilson refers to the eroticism implicit in Bernard's attitude to Muriel, questioning Resnais's 'investment in (sexual) violence against women'. She further proposes that his account of Muriel might even function as a screen memory, 'a memory reworked to hide us from something still more disturbing'.[56]

If the story of 'Muriel' as Bernard recalls it might be characterized as a screen memory, it is possible that the memory that Bernard disavows can be read as his witnessing, or indeed participation in, Muriel's rape. When speaking to Hélène, Bernard names his girlfriend 'Muriel', rather than Marie-Do, the woman with whom he has a sexual and romantic relationship. This confusion between Muriel and Marie-Do at the very least points to a distorted emotional investment in the dead Algerian woman on the part of Bernard, and might even indicate a repressed memory of sexual contact. Such a complicated screening out of the trauma of rape would accord with Wilson's reading of *L'Année dernière à Marienbad [Last Year in Marienbad]* (1961), where she notes that Resnais excluded a rape scene from Alain Robbe-Grillet's script.[57] The repression of the memory of rape is not unusual, and Todorov cites the example of a soldier who firmly believed that he did not witness women being raped when in fact there was concrete evidence that he did. For Todorov, this 'transmutation of reality into fiction' came about because 'the reality was unbearable'. He continues:

> It is also within our capacity to treat acts that we have committed as fictions and feel as though we are standing apart from what we do, that we are watching 'from the outside' as a story unfolds in which we ourselves play no part.[58]

This highlights the dissociative aspect of the perpetrator's encounter with torture, which is explicitly visual: the torturer psychically detaches from sight at the scene, and disengages from their participation in the violent act. This disconnection between the event and one's participation is played out in Bernard's description of the scene of Muriel's torture: when he implicates himself in the scene, he speaks in the past tense but when he describes the actions of others, most of the narration switches to the present. Resnais refers to this dislocation between vision and comprehension in the perpetrator, noting in relation to Bernard: 'nous avons voulu montrer, dans *Muriel,* que [...] nous sommes tous capables de fréquenter l'horreur sans nous en apercevoir ou en faisant semblant de ne pas en apercevoir' [In *Muriel,* we wanted to show that [...] we are all capable of being confronted with horror, and not seeing it, or pretending not to see it].[59]

The centrality of Muriel's body to Bernard's description, and the absence of her voice, reflect Scarry's suggestion that the corporeal pain inflicted in torture is designed to inhibit the victim's capacity for speech: 'the goal of the torturer is to make the one, the body, emphatically and crushingly *present* by destroying it, and to make the other, the voice, *absent* by destroying it'.[60] Muriel's absent voice and her lack of image reflect the fact that the experience of torture is difficult to narrate, and images of the act are scarce. Torture is rarely sanctioned publicly, and visual evidence can be difficult to procure. Images of torture are profoundly shocking when they do emerge, in part, because of their rarity. This dearth of visual material leads to a reliance on testimonial accounts from victims or perpetrators, which further raises the question of proof. As Rejali asks, 'in the absence of visible wounds or photographs of actual torture, who is one to believe? [...] Torture breaks down the ability to communicate'.[61] *Muriel* even seems to deny the power of cinema itself to represent the historical trauma of torture. Bernard says, 'Je n'ai pas envie de faire du cinéma. J'accumule des preuves, c'est tout' [I don't want to make films. I'm gathering evidence, that's all].[62]

Yet the question of proof is extremely significant, and sections that draw attention to notions of truth and falsity, proof and belief frame the torture sequence. In the previous scene, Hélène and Alphonse sit in a car, discussing an unknown woman and an unknown event that occurred before their separation during World War II.

Hélène says, 'mais j'étais incapable' [But I wasn't able], evoking bodily or mental incapacitation, foreshadowing Muriel of whom, in the next scene, Bernard notes, 'même si elle avait voulu parler elle n'aurait pas pu' [Even if she had wanted to speak, she couldn't have]. Hélène also asks, 'Mais elle, vous l'avez crue?' [But did you believe her?], reflecting the incredulity that surrounded both Algerian and French civilian accounts of the war, particularly women's account of torture and rape.[63] The scene that follows the torture sequence also depicts Hélène and Alphonse, as the latter spins the lies that suggest he spent time in Algeria, highlighting one of the film's central concerns — Algeria and perceptions of what happened there — as both actual and illusory, terribly real and frighteningly distant.

The story of Muriel's torture, of which all tangible evidence has been lost because 'Robert l'avait fait disparaître' [Robert had got rid of her], is counterpointed by the documentary-style war images in the sequence: soldiers smiling at the camera, shooting at wooden targets, eating, resting, tinkering with guns [Figure 2.4]. As the sequence progresses, the images on screen alter, becoming less predictable; we see soldiers dancing somewhat ludicrously, shots of mosques, and Algerian women in burkas, and as the story reaches its close, the images are edited rapidly, intercut at speeds that inhibit us from reading them as a coherent narrative. By placing the images within the context of the voiceover, their semantic references are altered and they slowly draw our attention in rather ominous fashion to their ideological designs as what Judith Butler calls 'frames of war'. According to Butler, images of war can function normatively, in that within a particular context they create and propagate the discourses that provide justifications for war. However, they can also call these normative modes into question, depending on the context in which they are received. For Butler, the image itself as a technologically reproducible object is not ideologically stable: 'the frame, then, as active, as both jettisoning and presenting, and as doing both at once, in silence, without any visible sign of its operation'.[64] In other words, photographic and filmic documents can be vectors of dominant discourses, but they can also, when framed within a particular context, reveal the power structures behind these ideologies.

Naomi Greene writes that the absence of images in the torture sequence is 'an indictment of the harsh restrictions imposed by French censorship at the time of the Algerian war'.[65] Within the climate of French censorship and silence around the Algerian War, a result of the trauma of the conflict and the Evian Accords, both *Le Petit Soldat* and *La Bataille d'Alger* were censored until 1963 and 1971 respectively, and Panijel's *Octobre à Paris* was denied a *visa d'exploitation* (a permit allowing it to be screened publicly) until 2011. Yet I suggest that the revelation of dominant French attitudes towards the war in 1963 comes about though the juxtaposition of words and images, rather than through the absence of image alone. Without the verbal narration, Bernard's footage of Algeria would have conformed to a fairly standard and benign image of the war: mountains, mosques, and soldiers. However, placed within the context of Muriel's story, it becomes evidence of a broader national unwillingness to confront wartime atrocities, atrocities for which no tangible proof remained. Even when Bernard tries to express his involvement in the violence in

FIG. 2.4. Soldiers at war. *Muriel, ou le temps d'un retour*, dir. Alain Resnais (1963).

fragmented, desultory form through the film and documents, gathering vague proofs that seek some form of retribution for the dead woman, the social context in which he is attempting to articulate this is not prepared to listen. Robert, the only character apart from Bernard to make reference to the political climate in France following the conflict says, 'Toi, tu en es encore à Muriel [...]. C'est aux autres de se cacher, pas nous [...]. Chaque Français se sent seul et crève de peur. Il mettra de lui-même des barbelés autour de sa petite personne. Il ne veut pas d'histoires' [You, you are still dealing with Muriel.... It's up to others to hide, not us. Every Frenchman feels he's on his own and is scared to death. He erects a barbed wire fence around himself. He doesn't want trouble].[66]

Furthermore, an excess of visual representation can be associated with a certain aestheticization or spectacularization of the image. Butler writes that images can become 'a visual spectacle that numbs the senses and [...] puts out of play the very capacity to think'.[67] To have portrayed Muriel's torture visually may have detracted from its intellectual impact; by excluding it, we feel its deficiency more keenly because our awareness is drawn not only to its absence, but also to other potential exclusions within the context of combat.[68] Susan Sontag's often-cited articulation of the distinction between the photograph and the verbal narration — that narratives provoke understanding, while photographs 'haunt' — resonates with Bernard's account. In a film that is riddled with temporal and spatial uncertainties, this stark, chronological and detailed account (which is not to say complete), gathers around it a clarity that is at odds with the cluttered visual and audible diegetic world of the rest of the film. Resnais ultimately rejects the potential for falsification implied in direct representation, instead offering the account of one woman's death, an account for which no tangible, empirical 'evidence' may be found. By refusing to offer a visual image of Muriel's torture, Resnais captures and reflects the silence and invisibility imposed on victims, both as a consequence of the shadowy legality of the act in general, and particularly on Algerian female victims because of their gender and nationality. Partial and incomplete, Resnais's desynchronized and disjointed formal structure blocks the viewer's access to Muriel's experience at every turn, and comes to represent the occlusion of Algerian women's experiences from official accounts of the war in its immediate aftermath. Bernard's refrain, 'pourquoi moi?' [why me?] as Muriel stares at him, reverberates outward to the spectator, bemused and tormented by the film, challenging him or her to recognize Muriel in Bernard's account, the only trace of her that remains.

Notes to Chapter 2

1. Alain Resnais, 'Conférence de presses au Palais du Cinéma, Venise', 31 August 1963. Quoted in Rachid Boudjedra, *Naissance du cinéma algérien* (Paris: François Maspéro, 1971), p. 27.
2. Jean Cayrol, *Muriel* (Paris: Éditions du Seuil, 1963), p. 89.
3. Robert Farmer, 'Marker, Resnais, Varda: Remembering the Left Bank Group', *Senses of Cinema*, 52 (2009) <http://sensesofcinema.com/2009/feature-articles/marker-resnais-varda-remembering-the-left-bank-group/> [Accessed 3 April 2017].
4. Emma Wilson, *Alain Resnais* (Manchester: Manchester University Press, 2006); Laura McMahon, 'Untimely Resnais: *Muriel*'s Disarticulations of Justice', *Film Philosophy* 20.2–3 (2016), 219–34; Matthew Croombs, 'Algeria Deferred: The Logic of Trauma in *Muriel* and *Caché*', *Scope: An Online Journal of Film and Television Studies* 16 (2010).
5. Aussaresses, speaking in Kate Townsend, *We Have Ways of Making You Talk* (2005).
6. Jacques Massu, *La Vraie Bataille d'Alger* (Paris: Éditions du Rocher-J.-P. Bertrand, 1997), p. 165.
7. Ali-Yahia Abdennour, *Algérie: raisons et déraison d'une guerre* (Paris: Harmattan, 1996), p. 30.
8. Florence Beaugé, *Algérie, une guerre sans gloire: histoire d'une enquête* (Paris: Calmann-Lévy, 2005), p. 180.
9. Tzvetan Todorov, 'Torture in the Algerian War', trans. by Arthur Denner, *South Central Review*, 24 (2007), 18–26, (p. 19).
10. Mohamed Lebjaoui, *Bataille d'Alger ou bataille d'Algérie?* (Paris: Gallimard, 1972), p. 11.
11. Todorov, 'Torture in the Algerian War', p. 20.
12. Raphaëlle Branche, *La Torture et l'armée pendant la guerre d'Algérie (1954–1962)* (Paris: Gallimard, 2001), p. 298.
13. See Simone de Beauvoir and Gisèle Halimi, *Djamila Boupacha* (Paris: Gallimard, 1962) and Ryan Kunkle, ' "We Must Shout the Truth to the Rooftops": Gisèle Halimi, Djamila Boupacha, and Sexual Politics in the Algerian War of Independence', *Iowa Historical Review*, 4:1 (2013), 5–24.
14. Alistair Horne, *A Savage War of Peace: Algeria 1954–1962* (London: Pan, 2002), p. 402.
15. Marnia Lazreg, *Torture and the Twilight of Empire: From Algiers to Baghdad* (Princeton: Princeton University Press, 2008), p. 162.
16. The interviews Rotman and Tavernier conducted for the film are also available in Patrick Rotman and Bertrand Tavernier, *La guerre sans nom: les appelés d'Algérie (1954 — 1962)* (Paris: Seuil, 1992).
17. Raphaëlle Branche, 'Sexual Violence in the Algerian War', in *Brutality and Desire: War and Sexuality in Europe's Twentieth Century*, ed. by Dagmar Herzog (Basingstoke: Palgrave Macmillan, 2009), pp. 247–60, (p. 256).
18. Branche, *La Torture et l'armée*, p. 290.
19. Djamila Amrane-Minne, *Des Femmes Dans La Guerre d'Algérie: Entretiens* [*Women during the Algerian War: Interviews*] (Paris: Karthala, 1994), p. 119.
20. Branche, 'Sexual Violence in the Algerian War', p. 256.
21. Lazreg, *Torture and the Twilight of Empire*, pp. 165–66.
22. Ibid., p. 159.
23. De Beauvoir and Halimi, *Djamila Boupacha*, p. 103.
24. The term *maquisard* or *maquis* was originally used by French partisans fighting Nazi occupation in World War II. The FLN resistance movement adopted it as a term for their own guerilla fighters during the Algerian War.

25. Branche, *La Torture et l'armée*, p. 297.
26. Kunkle, 'We Must Shout the Truth', p. 6.
27. Darcy Grimaldo Grigsby, 'Origins and Colonies: Delacroix's Algerian Harem', in *The Cambridge Companion to Delacroix*, ed. by Beth S. Wright (Cambridge: Cambridge University Press, 2001), p. 79.
28. Malek Alloula, *The Colonial Harem* (London: University of Minesota Press, 1986), p. 118.
29. Boudjedra, *Naissance du cinéma algérien*, p. 27.
30. 'Le viol de la femme algérienne dans un rêve d'Européen est toujours précédé de la déchirure du voile' [In the European man's dream, the rape of the Algerian woman is always preceded by ripping off the veil]. In Frantz Fanon, *L'an V de la révolution Algérienne* (Paris: Découverte, 2001), p. 28.
31. Darius Rejali, *Torture and Democracy* (Princeton: Princeton Univeristy Press, 2007), p. 5.
32. Ibid., p. 447.
33. Tom Milne, '*Muriel ou Le Temps d'un retour*', *Monthly Film Bulletin*, 31:364 (1964), 70–71 (p. 71).
34. Peter Brooker, 'Key Words in Brecht's Theory and Practice of Theatre', in *The Cambridge Companion to Delacroix* ed. by Peter Thomson and Glendyr Sacks (Cambridge: Cambridge University Press, 1994), p. 193.
35. Max Silverman, 'Horror and the Everyday in Post-Holocaust France: *Nuit et brouillard* and Concentrationary Art', *French Cultural Studies*, 17:1 (2006), 5–18 (p. 10).
36. Quoted in René Prédal, *Alain Resnais* (Paris: Minard, 1968), p. 153. This is the society that Kristin Ross maps in *Fast Cars, Clean Bodies: Decolonization and the Reordering of French Culture* (Cambridge, Mass.: MIT Press, 1996).
37. Cayrol, *Muriel*, p. 59.
38. Ibid., p. 41.
39. These objects almost torment the viewer, and Wilson has suggested a tentative parallel might be drawn between the grotesque magnification of these everyday items in *Muriel* and the experience of the victim of torture, an effect not of reflection, but rather 'infection and contamination'. Wilson, *Alain Resnais*, p. 100.
40. Cayrol, *Muriel*, p. 41–42.
41. James Monaco, *Alain Resnais: The Rôle of Imagination* (London: Secker & Warburg, 1978), p. 92.
42. Alyssa J. O'Brien, 'Manipulating Visual Pleasure in *Muriel*', *Quarterly Review of Film & Video*, 17 (2000), 49–61 (p. 51–52).
43. Cayrol, *Muriel*, p. 115.
44. Ibid., p. 44.
45. Ibid., p. 41.
46. Ibid., p. 103 and p. 119.
47. Ibid., p. 7.
48. Suzanne Gauch, 'Muriel, or the Disappearing Text of the Algerian War', *Esprit Créateur*, 41 (2001), 47–57.
49. Email correspondence with François Thomas, 6 April 2017.
50. Elaine Scarry, *The Body in Pain: The Making and Unmaking of the World* (Oxford: Oxford University Press, 1987), p. 35.
51. Cayrol, *Muriel*, p. 89–90.
52. Ibid., p. 57.
53. See de Beauvoir and Halimi, *Djamila Boupacha*, and Louisette Ighilahriz and Anne Nivat, *Algérienne* (Paris: Calmann-Lévy, 2001).
54. De Beauvoir and Halimi, *Djamila Boupacha*, p. 64.
55. Celia Britton, 'Broken Images in Resnais's Muriel', *French Cultural Studies*, 1 (1990), 37–46 (p. 45).
56. Wilson, *Alain Resnais*, p. 97.
57. Ibid., p. 79.
58. Todorov, 'Torture in the Algerian War', p. 21.
59. Quoted in Prédal, *Alain Resnais*, p. 113.
60. Scarry, *The Body in Pain*, p. 49.

61. Rejali, *Torture and Democracy*, p.8.

62. Cayrol, *Muriel*, p. 99.

63. Ibid., p. 89.

64. Judith Butler, *Frames of War* (London: Verso, 2009), p. 73.

65. Naomi Greene, *Landscapes of Loss: The National Past in Postwar French Cinema* (Princeton NJ: Princeton University Press, 1999), p. 48–49.

66. Cayrol, *Muriel*, p. 11.

67. Butler, *Precarious Life* (London: Verso, 2006), p. 148.

68. The notion that a lack of visual images leads to an incomplete form of representation privileges the visual over all other senses. Indeed, as Derek Jarman's *Blue* (1993) or Nicolas Klotz's *La Blessure* (2004) show, an audible narrative with little visual stimulation can have a powerful effect on the viewer, especially when the subject is emotive or traumatic.

❖

PART II

Histories of Violence: Algeria

CHAPTER 3

❖

Deep Wounds: Personal and Collective Histories in Assia Djebar's *La Nouba des femmes du Mont Chenoua*

If Algeria remains a remote, off-screen space in *Muriel*, France is situated beyond the cinematic frames of Assia Djebar's *La Nouba des femmes du Mont Chenoua* (hereafter referred to as *La Nouba*). Although both films deal with marginalized histories, their conditions of production, distribution, and reception differ dramatically. By 1963 when *Muriel* was released, Resnais was an established filmmaker, who had gained renown for his exposition of troubled national memories in *Nuit et Brouillard* and *Hiroshima mon amour*. Djebar, having garnered initial success as an author in the 1960s, had not published anything for almost ten years when *La Nouba* appeared on Algerian screens in 1978, sixteen years after the conflict. Although both films treat the question of gendered violence during the Algerian War, the results of these explorations diverge significantly. Djebar's film exposes precisely what is absent from *Muriel*: the visual presence of Algerian women, and their direct, first-hand testimonies. If Resnais was a male French director with no direct experience of Algeria or the war, *La Nouba* presents a paradoxical set of parameters: a female Algerian filmmaker, talking about and with women, aimed at a television audience comprised of many Algerian women. Set in the predominantly Berber-speaking region of Mount Chenoua to the west of Algiers, the site of Djebar's maternal ancestors, the film combines documentary sequences of interviews with the women of the region with a fictionalized account of the central character Lila (Sawsan Noweir), an architect, as she navigates an uneasy marriage and the loss of her brother during the war. The state-controlled 'Radio-Télévision Algérienne' funded the film and despite the fact that it garnered plaudits abroad, winning the International Critics Prize at the Venice Biennale in 1979, it only aired once on domestic television. *La Nouba* was also omitted from the celebration of Algerian cinema published by ONCIC (Office National pour le Commerce et l'Industrie Cinématographique) in 1984.[1] The film's extremely limited distribution at the time of its release highlights the state's desire to exclude a particular vision of national history that recognizes the political contributions of Algerian women during the Algerian War. Public showings of the film are rare, and currently, the film is procured with difficulty: distributed by the American non-profit media arts organization, 'Women Make Movies', a DVD version of the film with English subtitles can be purchased for US$295.00.[2]

Djebar's early life and education situate her as a figure who straddles French and Algerian cultures and languages. Fatima-Zohra Imalayen, the birth name of Assia Djebar, was born in Cherchell, a small coastal town near Algiers on 30 June 1930. Her father, Tahar Imalayène, was a French teacher and a native Berber speaker, who encouraged Djebar to pursue a Western education: at her high school, the 'Collège de Blida' in Algiers, she was the only Muslim in her class. Djebar assumed the pen name under which her work is known upon completing her first novel, *La Soif* [*The Thirst*, 1957], a semi-autobiographical account in the style of Françoise Sagan of a young Westernized Algerian woman's experiences of love and infidelity in upper-class Algiers society. Following her studies in history at the École normale supérieure de Sèvres, and at Paul-Valéry Montpellier 3, Djebar returned to Algeria after independence in 1962, and taught history, French literature, and film at the University of Algiers. In 1980, she moved back to Paris, because 'il n'y avait plus que les hommes dans les rues d'Alger' [there were only men on the streets of Algiers].[3] She later moved between France and the United States where her work amassed academic followers, and she taught French Literature, first in Louisiana State University and later at New York University. Over the course of her career, Djebar penned more than seventeen works of literature, including novels, poetry and plays and was frequently cited as a potential recipient of the Nobel Prize for Literature. She was elected to the Académie française on 16 June, 2005. On the occasion of her death on 7 February, 2015, French President François Hollande described Djebar as 'une grande intellectuelle algérienne' [a great Algerian intellectual], lauding her as, 'cette femme de conviction, aux identités multiples et fertiles, qui nourrissaient son œuvre, entre l'Algérie et la France, entre le berbère, l'arabe et le français' [this woman of conviction, whose multiple and fertile identities, between Algeria and France, between Berber, Arabic and French, enriched her work].[4]

La Nouba marks Djebar's return to public creativity after a self-imposed thirteen-year silence, and the experience of making the film inspired what is perhaps her best known work, the short story collection *Femmes d'Alger dans leur appartement* [*Women of Algiers in their Apartment*], hereafter referred to as *Femmes d'Alger*.[5] The collection offers a thorough exploration of many themes that occur in *La Nouba*: the self-imposed and state-imposed silences of women, their attempts to speak about the memories of traumas experienced, and their sense of betrayal and disillusionment that the nation they fought for should disavow their contribution. The play of fiction and fact has been central to Djebar's writings, and many works meld autobiographical events, as well as primary and secondary historical sources, women's testimonies and reflections on contemporary political turmoil. Djebar has continued to explore the question of generic fluidity throughout her creative trajectory: reworking Koranic tales in theatrical form in *Loin de Médine* (1991); mixing history, autobiography and fiction in *Vaste est la prison* (1995); intertwining biography and fiction in *Le Blanc de l'Algérie* (1996); and combining oral testimony with fictional invention in *La Femme sans sépulture* (2002). In many of these texts,

Djebar, or a figure that approximates to her, acts as a collector and repository of women's stories: there is an emphasis on person-to-person communication, and no one character is the locus of liberating speech. No single person acts as a confidant for all the others and Djebar calls her short stories 'quelques repères sur un trajet d'écoute' [a few frames of reference on a journey of listening] implying that rather than imposing the structure of a narrative form onto her experiences of the world, she allows the real women's voices she hears to guide her.[6]

The centrality of storytelling and female narratives to Djebar's written work is also evident in *La Nouba*: in the opening credits, the viewer is informed that the word 'nouba', in Djebar's repurposing of the term, comes to mean 'histoire quotidienne des femmes (qui parlent "à leur tour")' [the everyday story of women, who take it 'in turns' to speak]. A *nouba* is also a genre of Arabo-Andalucian music, which originated in Spain in the eighth and ninth centuries, but later spread to North Africa, and is found in the musical traditions of Algeria, Tunisia, Morocco and Libya. The film is constructed around this musical form, which, as Réda Bensmaïa notes, 'is itself made up of heterogeneous fragments', resulting in a filmic narrative (or lack of narrative) which 'seems to take a perverse pleasure in thoroughly disappointing any desire on the viewer's part to tie up loose ends or reach closure'.[7] In this sense, *La Nouba* is a resolutely, and one might say, deliberately difficult film, a structurally abstruse work of experimental cinema whose narrative strategies appear to work against a clear interpretation of the lost female narratives of the war that it aims to reveal. Many of the film's challenges lie at the intersection of the dual meanings of the word *nouba*, as a complex musical form that lends structure to the film and 'the everyday story of women'. The film combines the fictional Lila's real interviews with the women of Chenoua with footage of the Algerian war, wartime photographs, abstract, experimental sequences that feature Lila, her child, and her husband Ali (Mohamed Haymour), and scenes which imaginatively reconstruct some of the narratives that the women describe.

If *Muriel* invited a consideration of how a director might represent a violent history that is precisely not one's own, *La Nouba* opens a debate about how one might represent a violent history that is at once private and public, personal and communitarian. Djebar, an educated and Westernized Algerian woman, discloses her own story alongside that of a group of women who were considerably marginalized in historiographical accounts of the war: rural women (*moussebilate*). *La Nouba* has generated significant academic criticism to date, covering a range of thematic and formal issues in the film: grief (Bensmaïa); the film's 'palimpsestic' structure (Donadey); *La Nouba* as 'fourth cinema' (Khanna); narrative transvergance (Martin); the film's wider relation to Algerian cinema (Austen); gender and community (Flood); space (Sharpe); and linguistics and voice (Bentahar).[8] My intervention here considers how Djebar uses both documentary and fictional elements, the play of space, and female storytelling to counter women's return to the private sphere and to disrupt post-Independence Algerian narratives about the war. I examine the intersecting personal and historical narratives in the film, the role that Djebar as filmmaker plays in the transmission of these accounts, and how

Djebar the individual situates herself within the female Algerian community she represents. Djebar's self-representation in the film through the character of Lila, and the ways in which Lila is visually and behaviourally distinguished from the other women, may trouble a conception of what Mildred Mortimer describes as Djebar's 'polyphonic', non-hierarchical female communities.[9] My analysis here proceeds upon the assumption, also made by Bensmaïa and Donadey, that Lila represents Djebar's fictional double: on camera, she undertakes the interviews that Djebar herself conducted, and her dress, manner, profession, and character allow the figure of Lila to be clearly transposed onto the filmmaker herself.

After the War: Gendered Spaces and Nationalist Myths

While FLN propaganda and works like Fanon's *L'An V de la révolution algérienne* [*A Dying Colonialism*] and *La Bataille d'Alger* helped to contribute to the image of the female bomb carrier as a self-emancipating figure, the alluring implications of such depictions were quite far from the realities experienced by most women.[10] The conservative element of the FLN, aligned with the military and led by Ahmed Ben Bella and Houari Boumédiène, defeated the weaker socialist and liberal factions of the revolution in 1962. In the years following independence, women's liberation, their public prominence, and the recognition of their political achievements, became associated with French values and a return to colonial rule. As Zahia Smail Salhi outlines:

> The roles of women were seen at the top of the list of things that should be restored to their original places and, in a society where cultural values have been dislocated for so many decades by the forces of occupation, women were quickly identified as the repositories of these values and the guardians of traditions and customs, all fundamentally important components of the Algerian national identity.[11]

Within this schema, the notion of the silent, proud, and suffering Algerian woman emerged: to voice pain, trauma, or discontent was unpatriotic. Women found themselves in the paradoxical position of wanting to speak about experiences that had contributed to the gaining of independence, experiences that they undertook because of their patriotism, but finding that to voice such memories went against the dominant national narrative. Historians have further questioned the legitimacy of the FLN's posited gender progressiveness during the war, highlighting a consistent tendency to view women's participation and their future in the movement as tied to the domestic sphere. Jean-Charles Jauffret and Charles Ageron suggest that women were generally confined to tasks that were never too far removed from 'l'univers censé leur appartenir en propre, celui du foyer' [the world that was considered to be their domain, that of the home].[12] There was, moreover, a pre-existing religious conservatism that Mohammed Harbi and Gilbert Meynier have recognised in FLN documents from 1957–1958 onwards. A note taken by a senior member of the FLN, Captain Si Allal in Wilaya V, supposed to have been made in 1957, suggests that even during the war, women's emancipation was conceived as a temporary affair:

'dans l'Algérie indépendante, la liberté de la Femme musulmane s'arrête au seuil de sa porte. La femme ne sera jamais l'égale de l'homme' [In independent Algeria, a woman's freedom ends on the threshold of her door. Women will never be equal to men].[13] These citations highlight the significance of women's return to domestic life, a process that was painfully underscored by a series of legislative changes that foreclosed women's rights in the public sphere. Echoing Partha Chatterjee's statement that 'the story of nationalism is necessarily a story of betrayal', the introduction of the Family Code on 9 June, 1984 was the culmination of a series of regressive measures designed to exclude women from public life.[14] The Family Code, which combined Napoleonic resonances with Islamic *sharia* doctrines, effectively reduced women to the status of minors in Algerian society. Its principal dictates legalized polygamy, allowed a man to divorce his wife at will while placing strict barriers against a woman initiating divorce procedures, prohibited adoption, and instituted the system of guardianship (the *wali*) for all women.

La Nouba recognizes the marginalization of women from public life, and foreshadows the social changes that would ultimately lead to the Family Code. In order to highlight women's return to the sphere of the domestic, the documentary and fictional elements of *La Nouba* invert the social hierarchy of masculine and feminine spatial relations through a series of reimaginings of the implied gendered power relations in the gaze. In a montage of documentary-style shots of a town, a few men sit on pavements, ride on horse-drawn carts, or loiter outside cafés, smoking. In the post-independence Algeria of 1978, the street remains a definitively masculine domain, yet the male groupings depicted appear to be fraught and uncertain: these men do not appreciate the invasion of their space by the camera, and in one shot, a man waves a stick angrily at the lens. The whole scene is overlaid with a desynchronised soundtrack of eerie flute music and wartime sounds of shouting and gunfire. The scene shifts to images of men beating animals and gesticulating with hostility towards the camera, imagery which creates a sense of a masculine space founded upon violence and aggression in the face of perceived threat. Although it is unclear whether Djebar herself is holding the camera or not, it appears that the inversion of the scopic hierarchy, that is, the dominance of the male gaze in Algerian public space, threatens the values of this insecure community: men become the objects of a gaze that they cannot control, rather than the dominant spectator. This overturns the classic model of male voyeurism in film spectatorship identified by Laura Mulvey. In Mulvey's often-cited 1975 analysis, she writes that 'in a world ordered by sexual imbalance, pleasure in looking has been split between active/male and passive/female'.[15] By assuming control of the camera, Djebar assumes an active role that distinguishes the viewing subject from the viewed object, a dynamic that the men she films clearly resent.

Mulvey's thesis also posits that while men are active agents within filmic narratives, driving the action forward, women exist as static objects: the woman's 'visual presence tends to work against the development of a story-line, to freeze the flow of action'.[16] Yet Lila is the only character in the film who appears to enjoy an unfettered liberty of movement: her corporeal mobility is frequently contrasted

FIG. 3.1. Lila and Ali. *La Nouba des femmes du Mont Chenoua*, dir. by Assia Djebar (1978).

FIG. 3.2. Through the window — the inverted gaze.
La Nouba des femmes du Mont Chenoua, dir. by Assia Djebar (1978).

with the physical confinement of her husband, and her perambulations drive the story [Figure 3.1]. Djebar has often described the importance of female movement. In an interview with *Le Monde* in 1978, she says, 'En Algérie, une femme non-voilée n'est pas forcement libérée. Une femme libre, c'est une femme libre de circuler' [In Algeria, an unveiled woman is not necessarily a free woman. A free woman is a woman free to circulate].[17] In *La Nouba,* the inversion of the power of the male gaze converges with images of female mobility. In one sequence, Ali, who is in a wheelchair and therefore physically unable to partake in the exterior world of male community, is sitting by a window in his house and he watches women outside from behind bars of a window working, cutting and hoeing the ground in long, muscular strokes. A young girl, perhaps eleven years old and therefore just at the threshold of potential sequestration, comes to the window and stares in unashamedly at him, with a coy half-smile. He is powerless to alter his position of physical stasis, and the spectator is privy to his visible discomfort as the young girl gazes at him for perhaps a minute or more. When she leaves, she closes one of the shutters behind her, thus further inhibiting Ali's view onto the outside world. This sequence inverts the male gaze and the paradigm of female sequestration: the experience of a man who is physically impaired is compared to the situation of confined women [Figure 3.2]. These reversals point to the constructed nature of the visual hierarchy; the male right to gaze is shown to be the manifestation of a power relation that resists threats to its scopic prerogative. Djebar further elaborates upon this theme in a scene where positions of power in relation to public space are imaginatively reversed. Three women in white *haïks* are walking in an enclosed yard in the city, and a crowd of men cling onto the bars that surround this space; whether they want to climb in, or just look at the women, remains unclear. Djebar zooms in and pans across their faces slowly, capturing an unspecified longing in their expressions as the black iron railings frame their faces. It seems as if men are imprisoned, rather than women, gazing outwards at the women who walk freely. These images are an inverse echo of Djebar's description in *Femmes d'Alger* of women trapped in the modern harems of city houses and apartments: 'cette ville étrange, ivre de soleil mais des prisons cernant haut chaque rue' [this strange city, intoxicated with sunshine but shadowed by the high prisons encircling every street].[18] Djebar's disruption of gendered modes of looking, which she explicitly links to the practices of veiling and sequestration, is aptly captured in the words of Lila, who pronounces, 'as an architect, I always wanted to build houses of glass, transparent houses. Then, we wouldn't look that way at veiled women'.[19]

Gender distinctions are inscribed in the mise-en-scène, cinematography, and framing of *La Nouba*. The women (with the exception of Lila) are presented overwhelmingly in outdoor and rural spaces, working, chatting, surrounded harmoniously with animals and children. Their clothes, in bright yellow, green and blue tones, are designed to reflect the natural world around them of sand, cliffs and sea, and to contrast with the darker tones and urban settings associated with depictions of male spaces. Images of male groupings are frequently overexposed, and shot in a colour scheme dominated by black, grey, brown and beige. Sharp lighting contrasts also punctuate the film; in one particular shot, images of male and female groupings are intercut with shots of doves trapped in an enclosed space, flitting between areas of extreme brightness and darkness, suggesting that both men and women are fenced in by gendered separations. In Lila's excursions into the women's homes, her entry into the woman's house is preceded by shots of other women and young girls peeking out over lintels, framed by walls and doors, their bodies visually segregated by branches or wires. The penetration of the outside into this enclosed and private world arguably marks a greater traversing of codified space than the filming of public scenes in the town, yet these women do not resent the intrusion of the camera. Rather, they appear to welcome Lila's visits, which furnish the possibility of sharing their stories of the war with another person. As the *leifmotif* of Djebar's literary work, female storytelling and the image of what Djebar describes as 'une femme qui parle devant une autre qui regarde' [a woman speaking in front of another who's watching][20] structures women's exclusively female encounters in these texts. Djebar appears to move from motifs of failed male communication towards the invocation of a plurality of female voices. These women are 'in the frame' for the duration of the film, at both the discursive and the visual centre of this work, offering alternatives to imposed national myths.

This presentation of male communities as social spaces that need to be aggressively defended from both physical and ideological outside intrusion accords with Jean-Luc Nancy's consideration of dominant forms of community, which he characterizes as domains that function according to a gendered hierarchy: 'c'est la fraternité qui désigne la communauté' [fraternity designates community]. For Nancy, myth is what the dominant polity employs to perpetuate the idea of community as a shared essence, providing a structure and an ideological framework upon which communitarian practices can be based. He notes that 'rien n'est plus *commun* aux membres d'une communauté [...] qu'un mythe, ou un ensemble de mythes' [nothing is more *common* to all members of a community [...] than a myth, or a set of myths].[21] The fraternal community unites around a common narrative, or myth, recounted by central male grouping: 'nous les disons "frères", parce qu'ils sont rassemblés, et parce qu'ils écoutent le même récit' [we call them 'brothers', because they are gathered together and because they listen to the same story].[22] Yet the identity that myth aims to propagate, be it based on nation, race, religion, culture or gender, can never be fully assumed, because it will always be haunted by other emerging and contradictory narratives. These narratives trouble the monolithic conception of community that myth propagates, threatening to undo its unity. The stories that the women tell in *La Nouba*, and the mingling of fictional and documentary accounts, function as interruptions in this sense. They offer counter-narratives to the isolationist discourses of the Algerian state about the role of women within this national community.

Telling Tales: Between Fiction and Documentary

A form of Algerian nationalist filmmaking, the *cinéma moudjahid* [freedom fighter cinema] was popularized in the immediate aftermath of the war. This movement included films like Mohammed Lakhdar-Hamina's *Chronique des années de braise* [*Chronicle of the Years of Fire*, 1974] (winner of the Palme d'Or at Cannes in 1975), and Tewfik Farès's *Les hors-la-loi* [*The Outlaws*, 1969]. These works examined the anti-colonial conflicts of the war years, the brutality of the French, and the nobility of the Algerian martyrs who gave their lives for the liberation of the country. However, they focused almost exclusively on the patriotic struggles of the male liberation fighters. Female participation in the Algerian War was largely ignored. As Guy Austin notes, 'the labour of the female revolutionary fighters, the *moudjahidat*, [...] was gradually erased from history and from its representation as myth in the *cinéma moudjahid'.*[23] By charting the experiences of women during the war and the marginalization of women's narrative in post-independence Algeria, *La Nouba* runs deliberately counter to the narrative and thematic concerns of the *cinéma moudjahid*. In this sense, it can be said to participate in the *cinéma djidid* [young cinema] of the 1970s, which depicted many of the social and political issues in Algeria at the time, offering a darker and more nuanced conception of the nation.[24] As part of this movement, *La Nouba* offers a deliberate counter-narrative to patriarchal and nationalist accounts of female participation in the conflict, focusing particularly on the role of female resistance fighters and on the experiences of rural women.

The stories told by rural women and recorded by Djebar in *La Nouba* are among the most silenced of post-war histories, and these accounts disrupt many of the nationalist myths that the post-1962 Algerian state promulgated, principally around the role played by Algerian women in the conflict. In the case of urban women and female resistance, the FLN loudly promoted female figureheads like Zohra Drif, Djamila Amrane Minne, Djamila Bouhired and Djamila Boupacha internationally with the aim of politicizing other women. An FLN communiqué from 1958 entitled 'Directives sur la propagande et la contre-propagande au sujet de la femme' [Directives on propaganda and counter-propaganda in the subject of women] highlights the distinction between the FLN's perception and recruitment strategies for urban and rural women. For urban women, the organization sought to appeal to divergent ideas of female liberation and autonomy, linking it not to Western feminism, but to female liberation in other majority Muslim countries: 'Faire miroiter l'émancipation des autres sœurs musulmanes des pays indépendants, exemple ÉGYPTE, SYRIE, TURQUIE...Il ne faut pas être française pour s'émanciper' [Dangle before their eyes the emancipation of other Muslim sisters from independent countries, for example, EGYPT, SYRIA, TURKEY...You do not have to be French to become emancipated]. However, in relation to rural women, the FLN propaganda took on a rather more menacing tone, and it appealed to the affective registers of patriotism and religion, rather than female emancipation. The same directives outlined a much more socially conservative strategy to appeal to rural women against a proposed French initiative to offer women the vote: 'notre sœur bédouine: Par ce vote, tu t'engages, toi Algérienne, à être Française, donc tu renies ta RELIGION, ta PATRIE,...tu t'engageras à faire de l'Algérie une terre française' [our Bedouin sister: by this vote, you, an Algerian women, commit to being French, so you disown your RELIGION, your HOMELAND,...you commit to making Algeria a French land].[25]

The differential treatment of urban and rural women during the war continued in the aftermath: as Marnia Lazreg states, 'the history of women's lives during the war will remain incomplete because it does not include the standpoint of rural women — prime targets of military action'.[26] In 1974, the Ministry for Veteran's Affairs in Algeria reported that 11,000 Algerian women had fought for the liberation of the country, of which 22% were from urban areas, with the remaining 78% from rural parts of the country. However, Djamila Amrane Minne considers this figure to be a serious underestimation of women's participation.[27] The diversity and informality of women's contributions to the liberation effort may also account for the uncertainty of the statistics around female participation, particularly in the case of rural women. In many cases, rural women were not recruited as official members of the FLN, and instead fulfilled functions that can be considered gender-traditional: as the guerrilla fighters passed through villages, women gave them food and shelter or hiding places, they washed clothes and cared for wounds as well as preparing food for the onward journey. They frequently suffered violent reprisals at the hands of the French army for their support of the FLN, including mass rapes and being forced to witness the killing of family members, as well as the destruction of their homes, animals, and food supplies.[28]

In this sense, the interviews Djebar/Lila conducts with the rural women of Chenoua themselves become rare historical documents. The film counters author Rachid Boudjedra's criticism of Algerian cinema in 1970: 'le cinéma algérien crée une Algérie monolithique et se coupe de la réalité vivante' [Algerian cinema creates a monolithic Algeria, that cuts itself off from lived reality] by presenting a range of viewpoints on contemporary Algeria and the War of Independence.[29] During one of Lila's visits, a middle-aged woman tells her of forced collaboration with the FLN partisans, noting that when they came, the attitude was simply 'roll up your sleeves, knead the bread, do the laundry'. In return for this effort, the French bombed her house, she was taken prisoner, and left to die in the slums. She survived, but without any assistance from the FLN 'frères' whom she had helped, a tale reiterated by another woman who sheltered Djebar/Lila's brother during the resistance. Although a 'Christian' gave her land when she needed it, as her father-in-law and husband were both dead, she notes that members of the *mujahideen* took food from her farm for three days continuously, leaving her nothing to feed her own family. Djebar also treats the issue of female collusion with patriarchal policies through the story of a resistance fighter, Cherifa, who as a thirteen year-old followed her brother into the guerrilla army. The French forces tracked them and killed her brother while the girl dangled from the branches of a tree, watching. Djebar dramatizes this scene in the opening shot of the film, where an indistinguishable figure hangs from a tree, hesitating to jump. In the latter stages of the film the viewer connects these opening images with Cherifa's mother recounting her daughter's story to Lila in a documentary section. However, the mother appears to have disassociated herself from Cherifa, saying, 'I won't see her now; I don't need to open new prisons'. Although she has lost three sons, a husband and a brother, Cherifa's mother excommunicates her daughter, due to the pain and shame the association causes her. This scene is intercut with images of women in *haïks* walking in public places, carrying loads or children, and this editing strategy points towards the fundamental opposition that entrenched discourses pose to their own reconfiguration: women can participate in their own oppression, or the oppression of other women.

The theme of communal female oppression is also addressed in a fictional episode, which dramatizes the myth of the creation of the community by Chenoua's saint, St. Abdel Rahnan el Shamir. El Shamir had many wives, and the seventh was a stranger to the Chenoua community. The voiceover tells us that 'the day she arrived she went to every jar, just to see for herself', and released the doves that were the magical source of never-ending food. The scene is visually dramatized for the viewer, and as the girl releases the doves she swirls in the middle of the room, hair flowing, as if in a trance, to the soundtrack of cacophonous violin chords. The supply of food is lost, and the saint tells the villagers 'that woman stripped you of my blessings'. This foundational communitarian tale functions according to two divisive tropes. The girl is an interloper within the community, and her actions, cutting off the village's food source, lend justification to the mistrust of foreigners and outsiders: a position for which Djebar, an exile in France and a French-educated woman, had a keen appreciation. In addition, this myth also propagates a profound mistrust of the curiosity of young girls; by simply wanting to 'see and know', she cuts off the community's food supply that allowed them to lead a privileged, work-free existence. Djebar reframes this story by offering a reconfiguration of its central message in a scene where Lila and her daughter are in their bedroom. Lila tells the story not as the tale of a girl who cut off a community's food source, but as that of a release of the doves that was concomitant with the girl's own liberation. The voiceover links this scene to the present in Algeria, 1978: 'Why tell her about the tragedies of the past? The occupation, the war and the hatred. It's better for her to dream of birds'. This implies that a constant retelling of nationalist narratives only serves to propound further hatred and division, while offering a new counter-narrative, one which bolsters ideas of female agency and freedom.

La Nouba further addresses the issue female resistance fighters, women glorified by Fanon's work as 'la chair de la révolution' [the flesh of the revolution] whose role assumed, he argues, 'des dimensions véritablement gigantesques' [truly gigantic dimensions].[30] In one sequence, Lila visits the daughter of Zoulikha, a wartime heroine who carried food and arms to the soldiers in the mountains, where the guerrillas called her 'mother'. This story is also the subject of Djebar's novel, *La Femme sans sépulture* (2002). Through Lila's voiceover, the spectator learns that French soldiers shot Zoulikha and that her body was abandoned in the centre of a village for several days. Eventually, she was buried anonymously in an unmarked grave, reflecting the lack of recognition surrounding her accomplishments during the war. Indeed, for Djebar, the real war heroes and heroines she has encountered are silenced by their experience, and the inability they feel to articulate it beyond the pressure of communal mythologization. She notes that many of the women from the Mont Chenoua area were reluctant to speak and when they did it was often in a cold, detached manner: 'plus les femmes avaient souffert, plus elles en parlaient sous une forme concise, à la limite presque sèchement' [the more the women had suffered, the more sparingly they talked about it, in a manner bordering on terseness].[31] This reluctance to speak, sometimes amounting to silence, is reflected in Djebar's paring down of the visual imagery of the film: interviews with women about their experiences during the war take place in their homes, modest rural farmhouses with animals and children scurrying about in the background. Moreover, on the soundtrack Djebar uses traditional songs sung by female vocalists, which sometimes resound in a solitary haunting cry, and at other times reverberate with a throb of drums. The disconnection between the music and the speakers disorientates the viewer, and serves to further underline the difficult articulation of traumatic memories.

Djebar was an academically trained historian, and in the 1960s she undertook a doctorate on the early medieval Tunisian saint Lalla Manoubia at the University of Rabat. Djebar's interest in Maghrebi history is evident in the film as she intersperses the women's testimonies and Lila's narrative with dramatizations of various events in Algeria's colonial pasts, thus destabilizing received notions of the war, and of the process of historicization itself. For example, in a montage sequence of the town, Djebar refers obliquely to the Roman occupation of territory in 44AD while filming in the area around Cherchell. The camera lingers on Roman ruins, tracking over the rough, weathered stone surfaces, illuminated by blazing sunlight, and the shot cuts to an image of Lila scrambling over the ruins, a peaceful smile on her face, as Ali sits and watches from his wheelchair. By referring back to the various histories of the country, and interweaving these narratives into the testimonies and fictional sequences, Djebar suggests that the present and past overlap and influence one another, refusing a linear and chronological account of history. The film also shows how the French colonial past, and the recent history of the War of Independence, impact upon the lives of present day Algerians. She visually reconstructs the insurrection of Sidi Malek El Sahaoui of the El Berkani tribe against the French in 1871, as well as the massacre of civilians, mostly women and children, by French soldiers in the cave of Dahra in 1845. Djebar also uses archive footage of French soldiers in Algeria, mixing the political and the personal in her presentation of these images; thus, the thud of Ali's fall from the horse, a flashback to the accident that resulted in his confinement to a wheelchair, coincides with a sharp cut to photographs of French soldiers shooting civilians during the war. The intersections of personal and collective trauma are reiterated in a sequence depicting Lila's dreams, where shots of women cut up by doorways and frames are intercut with photos of soldiers laughing and smiling with confiscated guns. This section links the French discourse of war to the situation of women in Algeria in the 1970s, demonstrating how French colonialism, with the subsequent counterbalancing insistence upon a return to traditional values, contributed to the isolation of Algerian women.[32] In another sequence, an image of Ali slumping forward on his crutches and falling through the ground leads to an abrupt cut to jaundiced archive footage of French soldiers shooting Algerian civilians. The soldier shoots a man at point blank range and the man crumbles to the ground, echoing Ali's movement in the previous shot [Figure 3.3]. The archive footage continues, and it depicts more soldiers shooting civilians at close proximity, one woman holding her hands above her head in a gesture of surrender. This footage dissolves into a close up of Lila's face as she sleeps fitfully, suggesting that these images from the war return to her in dreams.[33]

The archive images function like the newsreel sequence in *Muriel*, because by placing the photographs within the specific context of these women's stories, their meaning is altered. The personal accounts of the women frame these images,

FIG. 3.3. Archive footage. *La Nouba des femmes du Mont Chenoua,*
dir. by Assia Djebar (1978).

demonstrating how documents of public discourse cannot be separated from the individuals and private events to which that they refer. This corresponds to what Sontag perceives as the shifting signifier inscribed in the war photograph, because in its very reproducible materiality, it can be interpreted differently depending on the audience and the context of reception: 'the photographer's intentions do not determine the meaning of the photograph, which will have its own career, blown by the whims and loyalties of the diverse communities that have use for it'.[34] The photographs and footage shown in the film were initially conceived as documents of the success of the war effort in Algeria and were designed to foster a sense of colonial community, but through Djebar's reconfiguration they become forms of evidence, linked to the women's narratives for which no such 'evidence' can be found. Images from times of war haunt us not only with a vision of human vulnerability in the face of possible death, but also with those lives or experiences that lie beyond the frame of the image. As Ranjana Khanna points out, Djebar uses the women's testimonies in conjunction with the archive image to find 'through the voice-over, a memory that fits these images — a counter-hegemonic memory that has no images but those produced by the French'.[35] The rural women that Djebar presents to the viewer were among the most marginalized by the hegemonic narratives of Algerian national unity at that time and, by placing the women on a collective platform, Djebar challenges the attempts of governing socio-cultural norms to position their stories beyond the bounds of depiction. Political implications arise from these women's stories because they can be placed within the framework of other structures (male communities, dominant Algerian national narratives, French wartime images) and they provide a template for the recognition of lives lost and forgotten.

Self-Representation: Personal Histories

The documentary sequences of *La Nouba* present undeniably real people to the spectator, and these images form one half of the film's narrative structure, the other being Lila's personal trajectory. This raises the issue of whether Djebar is creating a fictionalized community of real individuals, or representing an existing social and political collectivity. Jane Hiddleston argues in relation to Djebar's literary works that the author is emphatically not attempting to found a 'real' community of Algerian women: '[the] constructed nature of the voices in her texts [...] warns against collating these with a real collectivity'.[36] Nevertheless, *La Nouba* offers Djebar an advantageous means of cultural and affective engagement with the Algerian women who form the subject matter of most of her texts. Because many of these women may be Arab or Berber speakers, Djebar's novels, written exclusively in French, remain inaccessible to the vast majority.[37] Indeed, Djebar states that *La Nouba* was conceived as a means to speak directly to Algerian women through the medium of television:

> 'Fin des années 70 dans les villes d'Algérie, dans les salles obscures, c'était un public presque exclusivement masculin. Or, les femmes de tous les âges, de tous niveaux regardaient en majorité la télévision. Ainsi *La Nouba des femmes du Mont Chenoua* fut une production de la télévision algérienne, originellement'.

> [In Algerian cities at the end of the 1970s, cinema audiences were almost exclusively male. However, the majority of women of all ages and all backgrounds watched television. That is the reason why *La Nouba des femmes du Mont Chenoua* was originally produced for Algerian television].[38]

Although Djebar uses the interviews she records with the rural women of Chenoua in another text, *L'Amour, la fantasia*,[39] in the latter, these interviews have been translated into French and are interwoven with a narrative that is fictionalized, autobiographical, and quasi-historical, while within the context of *La Nouba*, these voices are unmediated by translation or the textually marked interpretative interventions of the author.

While Djebar represents herself in many of her written texts, the techniques she uses are a direct consequence of the medium employed and have a clear impact on the relations posited between Djebar (or her fictionalized counterparts) and the Algerian women whose testimonies she conveys. The role that Djebar plays as recorder and transmitter of testimonies in *La Nouba* thus merits consideration within the context of the medium of documentary itself, and the ethics of documentary (re)presentation. The potentially hierarchical relation between the viewing film-maker and the viewed subjects of a documentary is addressed by Calvin Pryluck in one of the earliest interventions into the debate on ethics in documentary film-making. He notes that 'there is typically an unequal power relationship between investigators and subjects'.[40] This power can be ethnically, economically, socially, or linguistically marked, and in Djebar's case, her international education, her *francophonie*, and her status as a writer and an academic certainly distinguish her from the rural, agricultural women who she films. Further attention should be paid to the role that the documentary maker plays in their own film: whether they are present on screen, either in the background or front and centre, as in *cinéma vérité*, or whether the documentary operates either as a 'fly on the wall' piece, designed to offer the illusion of complete objectivity. For Bill Nichols, the relation of the filmmaker to the subjects of a documentary is not merely an aesthetic issue; rather, ethical and political concerns arise from the documentary maker's presence or absence from the diegetic space. Nichols argues that the most common formulation of the relation between the subjects of a documentary, the audience, and the filmmaker is 'I speak about them to you', whereby 'the filmmaker represents others' and 'the third person pronoun implies a separation between speaker and subject'.[41]

However, Djebar's position regarding the women she films, and her imagined audience, is particularly complicated in *La Nouba*, because while Djebar herself is not featured in the film, Lila operates as her doppelganger, straddling the boundary between fiction and documentary in the narrative. Djebar's role in this process of testimonial recording and her self-representation, trouble often unspoken critical assumptions that Djebar's status as a woman and an Algerian allows her to assume a position of figurative privilege. In many respects, Djebar, '*de l'Académie française*', came to embody Algerian letters and a particular representation of the Maghrebi (female) intellectual in France. Academic studies of her work abound, some with which Djebar herself was certainly familiar, as the personal photographs contained therein attest.[42] Although the effect of her own interaction with academic criticism of her work is beyond the scope of this study, her role as a representative (willing or otherwise) of Algerian women is rarely problematized and the image of Djebar as a transmitter, translator, and representative of 'Algerian women' has been central to academic studies of her work. Djebar's literary reputation has been founded on speaking for or about Algerian women: her desire to find a collective 'langue des femmes' has been documented in her literary texts and by academic critics. Many readings favour a thematic examination, thus selecting a recurrent problematic in Djebar's work and exploring it across a range of texts in relation to gender: space (Best); silence (Budig-Markin); resistance (Calle-Gruber, Clerc); violence (Gracki); identity and history (Hiddleston); the gaze (Huugue); victimization (O'Riley); French feminism (Ringrose); and writing (Zimra 1992).[43] Critics have also seized upon the vocal multiplicity of Djebar's work, and the abundance of rarely heard, marginalized voices therein, with Mildred Mortimer defining Djebar's literary outputs as 'polyphonic texts that combine personal and collective memory'.[44]

Yet even if personal and group memory combine in storytelling, the extent to which Djebar's self-implication in the film troubles a non-hierarchical conception of this community should be questioned within the film. While her literary works gesture towards the difficulties and gaps created around the representation of another's pain (through use of silences, italicisation, and clear delineations between Djebar and her characters), within the visual context, the blunt divisions between Lila and the other women raise doubts about equality of this group. The uncertain frontiers between the character of Lila and Djebar (including physical and biographical resonances) seem to furnish Djebar with a concealing cloak of fiction, while the other women remain steadfastly real. From the outset of the film it is difficult not to notice the marked visual and thematic separation between Lila and the other women: Lila herself says, 'I'm a stranger in my own country'. While Lila's clothes are distinctly westernized (she wears slim-fitting skirts and trousers), other women dress in more traditional and loose-fitting garments, and generally wear *hijabs* or *haïks*. Lila is frequently depicted walking or driving in wide, open spaces, while other women are shown working the land, walking with heavy loads, or carrying children. In one scene, a horse-drawn cart passes in the opposite direction, and she recalls going to that market in a cart with her father and brother, at a time when 'I welcomed the world of men coming toward me'. This suggests that from a young age, Lila, like Djebar, enjoyed comparatively greater liberty than other female children. Lila's freedom is further underlined in the many scenes where she visits the women whose stories she will gather, and they watch her arrival from behind barred windows and doorways. There is even a separation on the level of filmic texture and technique: while the shots of other women carry a documentary-like colour scheme, using natural lighting and medium straight-angle shots to create a sense of objective distance, the scenes depicting Lila's perambulations are shot in a more stylised, fictionalised texture, through the use of softer lighting, sharper colour contrasts, close-ups, and both low-angle and high-angle shots.

In another scene, the face of Cherifa, cradling the corpse of her brother, merges into the face of Lila as a child sitting on her grandmother's bed, listening to stories. The voiceover states, 'that was her...and that was me', a linking of identities that serves to emphasize the difference between the fortunes of the thirteen year-old resistance fighter and the young Lila. This association is complicated by the fact that at no point in the story is Cherifa present to represent herself and this coupling threatens the posited goal of female stories that emerge quasi-independently of Djebar's mediation. As Lila listens to her grandmother recounting tales of past wars, they are raised on an ornate golden bed, but as the camera zooms out, it reveals rows of grandmothers and children telling and listening to stories, with these groups all seated on the ground [Figures 3.4]. Given the position of importance that Djebar accords to the female storyteller, and to female narration in general throughout the film, this mise-en-scène seems to imply that some storytellers are more equal than others. The image of the grandmother telling stories to the female grandchild is a consistent feature of Djebar's texts and may certainly be linked to the autobiographical elements contained therein. If Djebar's project in relation to the women she depicts is to speak near these women, rather than for them, this conception appears problematized by the position of privilege that Lila and her grandmother enjoy. At the end of the film, the women of Chenoua gather in a sea-cave to dance, dancing and clapping to rhythmic music. Intercut with this scene are shots of Lila in another part of the cave alone, accompanied by the sound of an eerie solitary flute. Dressed in a white cloak that recalls the *haïk* but is closer to the garb of a pagan priestess, Lila lights individual candles as the voiceover tells us that 'she has kindled the spark of the past'. For Donadey, this phrase summarizes Djebar's œuvre, her texts hinging upon a 'palimpsestic structure' that layers official history, oral testimonies, and personal narratives, ultimately revealing new meanings in accepted histories.[45]

Combined with the visual images it accompanies, the phrase, 'she has kindled the spark of the past' suggests a privileging of Lila, and by extension, Djebar. The candles, each singular yet together providing the light that allows the women to dance, can be read as symbols of the disparate threads and fragments of narrative that can combine to illuminate a past, but only Lila lights them. The voiceover states plainly that she alone has illuminated the past and the fact that Lila is separated from all the other members of the group seems to suggest that kindling the spark of the past constitutes a solitary effort. A later text, *La Femme sans sépulture*, hints that a plurality of voices can collapse into a privileging of authorial influence, as one of the characters, 'l'étrangère' [the female stranger], appears to be Djebar describing herself in the third person. Her very presence liberates the blocked speech of Mina, the youngest daughter of the heroine, Zoulikha: 'cette inconnue, au visage aigu et non fardé, seuls les yeux couleur noisette, noircis de khôl, et qui a une façon lente de vous fixer — déclenche, par son arrivée, des tornades de souvenirs' [This unknown woman — whose sharp face is unmade-up except for the black kohl applied to her hazel eyes, and who slowly fixes her gaze on you — triggers a whirlwind of memories with her arrival].[46] Djebar's listening presence releases these 'tornades', implying transcendental benevolence, rather than a bilateral sharing or exchange.

Djebar's self-representation raises important issues about the extent to which she and her critics place her in the position of a singular liberator of Algerian female speech. Emer O'Beirne has pinpointed a blind spot in Djebar's reading of Delacroix's *Femmes d'Alger dans leur appartment* and Picasso's *Femmes d'Alger*. Despite Djebar's clear appreciation of the liberty of physical movement accorded to the women of the harem in Picasso's reworking of Delacroix's canvas, she fails to recognize that the black slave has embodied this freedom of circulation all along: 'cultural and political factors [...] thus combine to facilitate the elision of a figure in whose very cultural otherness are exhibited, alongside her servitude, the physical freedoms that Djebar seeks for her own oppressed kind'.[47] It seems that Djebar's desire for identification with the Algerian women whose voices and bodies she so desires to free, has blinded her to an individual whose social marginalization, gender, and race might offer a potent and fruitful point of comparison.

Djebar's position in relation to the other women in *La Nouba* can be clarified by considering the particular concerns of the postcolonial writer, situated at the intersection of cultures, languages, and gendered roles: in Djebar's case, the French, Arabic and Berber languages, Western/French and Islamic/Maghrebi cultures, and male and female communities. Nicholas Harrison questions the frameworks that influence the Western critic's conception of the postcolonial writer and their project. Many Maghrebi writers choose to write in French, which may mean that their audience will live mainly in metropolitan France. For Harrison, these writers are bracketed as 'postcolonial', even if this is a label they never sought, and in some cases, they are promoted by critics and publishers as examples of their country, gender, or of the postcolonial 'genre' itself: 'being (seen as) representative (where representativity = typicality) and *acting* as a representative are very different matters, even if, as I have already noted, it is often expected of the minority representative in particular that s/he "be" "typical"'.[48] A key issue in this sense is language. Djebar initially experimented with filmmaking in an attempt to resolve her struggles with the political implications of using French as a language of literary expression, an interior conflict that the film helped to resolve.[49] Moreover, Djebar's concern with her use of French as a language of literary expression amounts to an apprehension regarding her community, and her place within it as a writer or intellectual. Lila speaks only in French and frequently Arabic voices are played simultaneously with French overlay. Although Lila's words are louder, neither voice, neither language, succeeds in drowning out the other; they co-exist in an uncertain and ill-defined relation. On the one hand, Djebar seems to suggest that languages and cultures can co-exist, if not side by side at least in layers, but nevertheless, the film allows French to dominate over these women's Arabic dialect, reinstating a questionable trope of colonial domination.

While publishing and critical pressures may influence the postcolonial writer or artist in terms of didacticism and typicality, it cannot be said that Djebar rejects the accolades accorded through her role, and the examples outlined above indicate that she actively pursued the role of cultural intermediary. However, this is a position that troubled her deeply. In her speech to the *Académie française* in 2006, she refers on several occasions to the 'immense plaie' [deep wound], and the 'blessures' [wounds] that French colonialism inflicted on the people of Algeria and other ex-colonies, including the imposition of the French language. She evokes the many Algerian men and women who died in the Algerian Civil War in the 1990s for writing and speaking in French:

> Mes confrères — écrivains, journalistes, intellectuels, femmes et hommes d'Algérie qui, dans la décennie quatre-vingt-dix ont payé de leur vie le fait d'écrire, d'exposer leurs idées ou tout simplement d'enseigner...en langue française. Depuis, grâce à Dieu, mon pays cautérise peu à peu ses blessures.

> [My colleagues — writers, journalists, intellectuals, women and men of Algeria who, in the 1990s lost their lives because they wrote, expounded their ideas or simply taught...in the French language. Since then, thank God, my country is gradually healing its wounds].

The image of the wound immediately evokes a sense of separation and pain. Yet just as the skin breaks apart, the wound of language points the immense cleavage Djebar feels between her use of French as a language of literary expression, her deep connection to it, and her emotional and affective ties to Algeria and its people, with all the deep hurts that this history entails. She also describes French as the 'espace de ma méditation ou de ma rêverie, cible de mon utopie, [...] tempo de ma respiration' [space of my meditation or of my musing, target of my utopia, [...] rhythm of my breath].[50] Algerian author Amara Lakhous recalls that in his final encounter with Djebar in 2006, she expressed concern about how her election to the *Académie française* would be perceived in Algeria. Lakhous reports that she repeated on several occasions, 'je ne suis pas une écrivaine française, je suis écrivaine francophone' [I'm not a French writer, I'm a francophone writer], and she expressed great sorrow that she never mastered Algerian Arabic or Berber because French colonialism had deprived her of her native tongue. Lakhous finds this excuse somewhat unconvincing: 'our fathers used to blame French colonialism for everything that went wrong. Assia Djebar was 26 years old when Algeria became independent, so she had enough time to learn Arabic if she wanted, though she didn't. Why?'.[51]

Djebar's insistence on her *francophonie* may move in some way towards answering this question. To be a 'francophone' writer is explicitly not to be French: it marks an individual as an exile, either in body or in language, and situates them at the intersection of at least two different cultures. Tzvetan Todorov describes this interstitial individual as what he terms an *exote*: someone who is neither wholly integrated into one culture nor another, but resides somewhere on the boundary. While no direct translation exists for this neologism, the root *exo-* ties it to Greek, meaning 'outside', and to the French terms 'exotique' [exotic] and 'exode' [exodus]. The *exote* differs from the exile, who Todorov says emigrates to a foreign country but remains immersed within the community, traditions, and language of their birthplace, without ever running the risk of being changed or challenged by the host culture. The *exote*, by contrast, sees both the home and host culture afresh: he or she is not blinded by everyday habits, and so continually notices differences in customs, behaviours, and language. It is for this reason that the *exote* is frequently an artist, who consciously cultivates a feeling of alienation, of being surprised by difference. However, residing in this liminal space presents a particular set of challenges:

> 'Il [...] s'agit [...] d'une équilibre instable entre surprise et familiarité, entre distanciation et identification. Le bonheur de l'exote est fragile: s'il ne connaît pas assez les autres, il ne les comprend pas encore; s'il les connaît trop, il ne les voit plus. L'exote ne peut s'installer dans la tranquillité.[52]

> [It is [...] an unstable equilibrium between surprise and familiarity, between distance and identification. The *exote*'s happiness is fragile: if he doesn't know others well enough, he doesn't understand them yet; if he knows them too well, he is no longer able to see them. The *exote* cannot settle peacefully].

Although the *exote* is exiled from both of their native and host culture, they retain a perspective that sees both contexts as exotic, because they continually view them with fresh eyes.

Therefore, rather than situating Djebar as a cultural representative or mediator of Algerian women's experiences, we might instead consider that it is the difference between Djebar's cultural norms and those of the women she portrays that furnish the possibility of a productive, creative, and testimonial exposition. The unique and rare personal narratives in this film and the character of Lila allow Djebar to uncover her own position in this community. Looking with a renewed perspective on a country she has been absent from, Djebar brings to light the wartime narratives that, in 1978, had been absent from official histories, while at the same time, positioning herself as both within and outside the community of women she represents. At one point in *La Nouba*, Lila cries out, 'I feel like an exile in my own country'. This line is repeated verbatim in Yamina Bachir-Chouikh's 2002 film *Rachida*, which exposes the devastating effects of the Civil War of the 1990s on Algerian civilians.

The eponymous heroine in *Rachida* utters these words when she is confronted with television images of the on-going terrorist atrocities, and unlike others around her, she insists on recognizing and voicing her fear, but without reacting with anger or hatred. This suggests that the feeling of exile is not only a question of geographical or even linguistic difference: it is seeing what others refuse to acknowledge, having the courage to stand outside the norm and to confront truths that others are willing to ignore. As Djebar writes in a story entitled 'Il n'y a pas d'exil' [There is no exile] from the *Femmes d'Alger* collection, 'il y a ceux qui oublient, ou simplement qui dorment. Et ceux qui se heurtent contre les murs du passé, [...] ce sont les véritables exilés.' [There are those who forget, or simply sleep. And those who hurl themselves against the walls of the past,...they are the real exiles].[53] Djebar's vision is forged against forgetting, oblivion, or the endless repetition of the past through the lens of nostalgia, national glorification, or bitterness: she examines the past in order to pose questions of the present, questions about herself, and questions about the women and men she encounters.

Notes to Chapter 3

1. Guy Austin, *Algerian National Cinema* (Manchester: Manchester University Press, 2012), p. 76.

2. This figure is accurate as of 11 June 2017. The Franco-Algerian collective 'Le Cercle des amis d'Assia Djebar' runs occasional screenings to small audience in Paris. To this date, the film is owned by only a small number of university libraries in France, the UK and the US and the vast majority of these versions are in the 'Women Make Movies' version, in the original Arabic with English subtitles. Currently, the only versions in Europe in French are held in Merseburg, Germany, and Bremen, Germany. I have therefore chosen to use the 'Women Make Movies' version which is more widely accessible.

3. Raphaëlle Leyris, 'Mort de l'académicienne Assia Djebar', *Le Monde* (7 February 2015) <http://www.lemonde.fr/culture/article/2015/02/07/mort-de-l-academicienne-assia-djebar_4572120_3246.html> [Accessed 26 October 2016].

4. Fabien Morin, 'Disparition de l'académicienne Assia Djebar: les hommages se multiplient', *Le Figaro* (7 February 2015) <http://www.lefigaro.fr/livres/2015/02/07/03005-20150207ARTFIG00077-disparition-de-l-academicienne-assia-djebar-les-hommages-se-multiplient.php> [Accessed 26 October 2016].

5. Marguerite Le Clézio, 'Assia Djebar: écrire dans la langue adverse', *Contemporary French Civilization*, 9 (1985), 230–31, (p. 242).

6. Assia Djebar, *Femmes d'Alger dans leur appartement: nouvelles* (Paris: Albin Michel, 2002), p. 7.

7. Réda Bensmaïa, trans. by Jennifer Curtiss Gage, 'La Nouba Des Femmes Du Mont Chenoua: Introduction to the Cinematic Fragment', *World Literature Today*, 70 (1996), 877–84, (p. 877).

8. Bensmaïa, 'Introduction to the Cinematic Fragment'; Anne Donadey, 'Rekindling the Vividness of the Past: Assia Djebar's Films and Fiction', *World Literature Today*, 70 (1996), 885–92; Ranjana Khanna, *Algeria Cuts: Women and Representation, 1830 to the Present* (Redwood City: Stanford University Press, 2008); Florence Martin, *Screens and Veils: Maghrebi Women's Cinema* (Bloomington: Indiana University Press, 2011); Austin, *Algerian National Cinema*; Maria Flood, 'Common Vulnerability: Considering Community and its Presentation in Assia Djebar's *La Nouba des femmes du Mont Chenoua* (1978)', *Modern and Contemporary France*, 21:1 (2013), 73–88; Mani Sharpe, 'Representations of Space in Assia Djebar's *La Nouba des femmes du Mont Chenoua*', *Studies in French Cinema*, 13:3 (2013), 215–25; Ziad Bentahar, 'A voice with an elusive sound: aphasia, diglossia, and arabophone Algeria in Assia Djebar's *The Nouba of the Women of Mount Chenoua*', *The Journal of North African Studies*, 21:3 (2016), 411–32.

9. Mildred Mortimer, 'Assia Djebar's "Algerian Quartet": A Study in Fragmented Autobiography', *Research in African Literatures*, 28 (1997), 102–17, (p. 102).

10. Catherine Lloyd, 'From Taboo to Transnational Political Issue: Violence against Women in Algeria', *Women's Studies International Forum*, 29:5 (2006), 453–62; Maria Flood, 'Women Resisting Terror: Imaginaries of Violence in Algeria (1966–2002)', *The Journal of North African Studies*, 22:1 (2017), 109–31; Zahia Smail Salhi, 'The Algerian Feminist Movement between Nationalism, Patriarchy and Islamism', *Women's Studies International Forum*, 33:2 (2010), 113–24; Meredeth Turshen, 'Algerian Women in the Liberation Struggle and the Civil War: From Active Participants to Passive Victims?', *Social Research*, 69:3 (2002), 889–911. Natalya Vince's *Our Fighting Sisters: Nation, Memory and Gender in Algeria* (Manchester: Manchester University Press, 2015) intervenes in this debate with a new oral history, examining how women's memories of the War of Independence interact with official state narratives.

11. Smail Salhi, 'The Algerian Feminist Movement', p. 116.

12. Jean-Charles Jauffret and Charles Robert Ageron, *Des hommes et des femmes en guerre d'Algérie* (Paris: Autrement, 2003), p. 309.

13. Cited in Mohammed Harbi and Gilbert Meynier, *Le FLN, documents et histoire: 1954–1962* (Paris: Fayard, 2004), p. 607.

14. Partha Chatterjee, *The Nation and Its Fragments: Colonial and Postcolonial Histories* (Princeton, NJ: Princeton University Press, 1994), p. 154.

15. Laura Mulvey, 'Visual Pleasure and Narrative Cinema', *Screen*, 16:3 (1975), 6–18 (p. 19). Although Mulvey's theory has been much interrogated and reconfigured since 1975, its use here is relevant to Djebar's knowledge of feminism in the 1970s. As Priscilla Ringrose has shown, Djebar engaged with the work of Julia Kristeva, Luce Irigaray, and Hélène Cixous, all of whom, like Mulvey, dialogue with Lacanian psychoanalysis. See Priscilla Ringrose, *Assia Djebar: In Dialogue with Feminisms* (Amsterdam: Rodopi, 2006).

16. Mulvey, 'Visual Pleasure', p. 17.

17. Marie-Françoise Levy, 'Interview: Assia Djebar', *Le Monde* (28–29 May 1978).

18. Djebar, *Femmes d'Alger*, p. 124.

19. Quotations from the Arabic in *La Nouba* are in English, because of the fact that the most readily available version of this little-distributed film is that of 'Women Make Movies'.

20. Djebar, *Femmes d'Alger*, p. 122.

21. Ibid., p. 104.

22. Jean-Luc Nancy, *La Communauté désœuvrée* (Paris: Christian Bourgois Éditeur, 2004), p. 30 and p. 109.

23. Austin, *Algerian National Cinema*, p. 65.

24. See Sharpe, 'Representations of Space', p. 218.

25. 'Directives sur la propagande et la contre-propagande au sujet de la femme' (2ème semestre 1958). Text reproduced in full in Harbi and Meynier, *Le FLN, documents et histoire*, p. 608.

26. Lazreg, *Torture and the Twilight of Empire*, p. 169.

27. Djamila Amrane-Minne, *Femmes au combat: la guerre d'Algérie* (Algiers: Éditions Rahma, 1993), p. 231.

28. See Lazreg, *Torture and the Twilight of Empire,* and Neil MacMaster, *Burning the Veil: The Algerian War and the 'Emancipation' of Muslim Women, 1954–62* (Manchester: Manchester University Press, 2009).

29. Rachid Boudjedra, *Naissance du cinéma algérien* (Paris: François Maspéro, 1971), p. 90.

30. Frantz Fanon, *L'an V de la révolution algérienne* (Paris: Découverte, 2001), p. 36–37.

31. Quoted in Mortimer, 'Assia Djebar's "Algerian Quartet"', p. 202.

32. Fatima Mernissi argues that 'the French protectorate actually helped bring about an astonishing consolidation of traditions and breathed new life into existing hierarchies and inequalities'. Fatima Mernissi, *Beyond the Veil: Male-female Dynamics in Modern Muslim Society* (Cambridge, MA: Saqi Books, 2003), p. 153.

33. Having consulted with Amel Chaouati and the members of 'Le Cercle des amis d'Assia Djebar', many of whom knew Djebar personally, it seems the origin of this archive footage is uncertain.

34. Susan Sontag, *Regarding the Pain of Others* (New York: Farrar, Straus and Giroux, 2004), p. 35.

35. Khanna, *Algeria Cuts*, p. 125.

36. Jane Hiddleston, *Assia Djebar: Out of Algeria* (Liverpool: Liverpool University Press), p. 58.
37. Clarisse Zimra, 'Writing Woman: The Novels of Assia Djebar', *SubStance*, 21 (1992), 68–84 (p. 77).
38. Kamal Salhi, 'Assia Djebar Speaking: An Interview with Assia Djebar', *International Journal of Francophone Studies*, 2:3 (1999), 168–82 (p. 177).
39. Assia Djebar, *L'amour, la fantasia: roman* (Paris: Lattès, 1985).
40. Calvin Pryluck, '"Ultimately We Are All Outsiders": The Ethics of Documentary Filming', *Journal of the University Film Association*, 28:1 (1976), pp. 21–29, (p. 25).
41. Bill Nichols, *Introduction to Documentary*, 2nd edn (Bloomington and Indianapolis: Indiana University Press, 2010) p. 59 and p. 61.
42. Mireille Calle-Gruber, *Assia Djebar, ou, la résistance de l'écriture: regards d'un écrivain d'Algérie* (Paris: Maisonneuve and Larose, 2001) and *Assia Djebar, nomade entre les murs: pour une poétique transfrontalière* (Paris: Maisonneuve & Larose, 2005).
43. Victoria Best, 'Between the Harem and the Battlefield: Domestic Space in the Work of Assia Djebar', *Signs*, 27 (2002), 873–79; Valérie Budig-Markin, 'Writing and Filming the Cries of Silence', *World Literature Today*, 70 (1996), 893–904; Calle-Gruber, *Assia Djebar, ou, la résistance de l'écriture*; Jeanne-Marie Clerc, *Assia Djebar: Écrire, Transgresser, Résister* (Paris: Harmattan, 1997); Katherine Gracki, 'Writing Violence and the Violence of Writing in Assia Djebar's Algerian Quartet', *World Literature Today*, 70 (1996), 835–43; Hiddleston, *Assia Djebar*; Laurence Huughe, *Écrits sous le voile, romancières algériennes francophones, écriture et identité* (Paris: Editions Publisud, 2001); Michael F. O' Riley, *Postcolonial Haunting and Victimization: Assia Djebar's New Novels* (Oxford: Peter Lang, 2007); Ringrose, *In Dialogue with Feminisms*; Zimra, 'Writing Woman'.
44. Mildred Mortimer, 'Assia Djebar's "Algerian Quartet": A Study in Fragmented Autobiography', *Research in African Literatures*, 28 (1997), 102–17 (p. 102).
45. Donadey, 'Rekindling the Vividness of the Past', p. 885.
46. Assia Djebar, *La Femme sans sépulture* (Paris: Albin Michel, 2002), p. 50.
47. Emer O'Beirne, 'Veiled Vision: Assia Djebar on Delacroix, Picasso, and the Femmes d'Alger', in *Romance Studies*, 21:1 (2013), 39–51 (p. 48).
48. Nicholas Harrison, *Postcolonial Criticism: History, Theory and the Work of Fiction* (West Sussex: Wiley, 2003), p. 102.
49. Le Clézio, 'Assia Djebar', p. 242–43.
50. Assia Djebar, 'Discours de Mme Assia Djebar', *Le Figaro* (22 June 2006) <http://www.lefigaro.fr/pdf/AssiaDjebar.pdf > [Accessed 10 April 2017], p. 13 and p. 15.
51. Email correspondence of author with Amara Lakhous, 26 October 2016.
52. Tzvetan Todorov, *Nous et les autres* (Paris: Seuil, 1989), p. 381.
53. Djebar, *Femmes d'Alger*, p. 160.

CHAPTER 4

Algiers as Heterotopia:
Mothers and Whores in *Viva Laldjérie*

Although it was made twenty-six years after Djebar's *La Nouba des femmes du Mont Chenoua*, Nadir Moknèche's second feature film, *Viva Laldjérie* (2004) shares similar concerns, examining politics, violence, and the role of women in Algerian society. Set in Algeria in the early years of the twenty-first century following the decade of the Algeria Civil War in the 1990s, it tells the story of a mother-daughter duo, Papicha and Goucem, who have been displaced by the conflict and have moved from their home in Sidi-Moussa to the *Pension Debussy*, a boarding house in central Algiers. Goucem Sanjak, played by the Moroccan actress Lubna Azabal, is a twenty-seven year old photographer's assistant, who is engaging in an unhappy love affair with an older married man, the upper-middle class doctor, Aniss (Lounès Tazairt). Papicha, incarnated by the popular Algerian actress and performer Biyouna, is a widowed former cabaret dancer with a penchant for emotional theatricality. Emotionally and financially dependant on her daughter, Papicha harbours dreams of reopening the club where she used to work, the *Copacabana*. The film charts both women's very different attempts to fulfil their desires and ambitions: for Goucem, this means marriage, and for Papicha, returning to her work as a stage performer. A host of dynamic and colourful characters populate the film, in an array of genders, guises, and garbs. There is the prostitute Fifi (Nadia Kaci), who occupies the apartment adjacent to Papicha and Goucem and is abducted and killed by government agents, Yacine (Akim Isker), the closeted homosexual son of Aniss, and Samir (Jalil Naciri), a young man who is eager to escape to Europe.

The film situates itself confidently, but at times uneasily, between French and Algerian culture; the dominant language is French, and the film treats themes that seem distinctly Western, such as women's rights, sex, prostitution, and homosexuality. Yet the narrative is also deeply grounded in the specific socio-historical context of early twenty-first century Algeria, in the fragile accord following the Civil War. The dual cultures that inform the narrative and themes of *Viva Laldjérie* reflect the director's artistic influences, and like Djebar, he has biographical and artistic connections to both France and Algeria. Moknèche was born in Paris in 1965 to Algerian parents, and he returned to Algiers with his family when he was one month old. He witnessed the sweeping changes that occurred throughout Algerian society in the latter half of the twentieth century under the governments of Houari

Boumédiène and Chadli Bendjedid, including the Arabization of national curricula, rising Islamic fundamentalism, and the democratic movements around the Berber Spring of 1981. Moknèche has called himself 'un produit de l'Algérie indépendante' [a product of independent Algeria]: bilingual in French and Algerian Arabic, he passed through a brief period of religious fervour before leaving Algeria for France when he was sixteen years old.[1] This rich personal history informs Moknèche's work, and the title of *Viva Laldjérie* reflects his connections to both France and Algeria. *Laldgérie* is a mix of French and Arabic: the inserted 'd' references the Arabic name of the country, *El Djezaïr*, and 'one, two, three, *Viva Laldjérie*' is one of the slogans chanted by Algerian football fans in the 'July 5, 1962' stadium in Algiers. As Moknèche notes, these supporters are often called *hittistes*, a word that also combines French and Algerian lexicons: it is a combination of the Algerian 'hit' [wall] and the French suffix 'iste'. Represented in *Viva Laldjérie* in the figure of Samir, *hittiste* can be translated as 'those who hold up the walls', referencing the generation of jobless young men who loiter on city streets in the capital.

With its allusions to present-day youth culture, and its joyful, rhythmic inflection, the title of *Viva Laldjérie* suggests that the film will be an all-encompassing and celebratory examination of contemporary Algerian society. Yet *Viva Laldjérie* is set in the fragile peace of the post-war years, and while the looming threat of terrorism and state terror punctuate the story, Moknèche eschews a detailed consideration of the Civil War in favour of a character-driven narrative, that could be considered largely ahistorical. Moreover, although a cast of humorous and vibrant characters populates the film, they are socially marginalized individuals: single or widowed women, prostitutes, homosexuals, and the economically disenfranchised. The city spaces the characters frequent and the people they encounter seem to accommodate some fundamental contradictions: they are secure and dangerous, free and constrained, sexually fluid and rigidly heteronormative. This reflects a contradiction that Moknèche perceives in the city of Algiers itself: 'pour moi, Alger, c'est la maman et la putain, cette dualité permanente' [Algiers, for me, is the mother and the whore, this permanent duality].[2] The gendered characterization of the city also mirrors Moknèche's focus on women, as both maternal figures and social outsiders — characteristics that are embodied in the three central female characters, Goucem, Fifi, and Papicha. In foregrounding excluded social groups, Stora suggests that Moknèche 'attaque la société par ses marges et en touche le cœur. Le cœur de "Laldjérie"' [attacks society from its fringes and reaches its heart, the heart of 'Laldjérie'].[3] Yet where exactly might this Al(dj)erian 'heart' be located, in France or in Algeria? Moknèche has been charged with catering to Western values and tastes, and his narrative and aesthetic choices in *Viva Laldjérie* have been roundly criticized in online forums, particularly for his use of the French language and the depiction of women, sex, and sexuality.

In this chapter, I begin by considering *Viva Laldjérie*'s engagement (or lack of engagement) with the recent past of national violence in the 'black decade' of the 1990s. I ask how and why Moknèche marginalizes terrorism and fundamentalist threats, insisting instead on the continuation of everyday life in the face of historical trauma and present-day insecurity. I then examine Moknèche's depiction of his female characters, demonstrating the ways in which this representation can be aligned with historical accounts of women's roles both during and after the conflict. I discuss the critiques of Moknèche's depiction of women, and the supposed dearth of realism, which opens a debate on genre and typicality in the postcolonial text. I then consider whether *Viva Laldjérie* simply offers the Western viewer a comfortable, ideologically familiar, and ultimately false picture of Algerian life. Finally, I bring together these concerns in a discussion of heterotopic spaces within the film, as spaces that accommodate marginalized individuals and that contain fantasy and realism in the present, in the face of past atrocity and future insecurity.

Terrorism Marginalized: Humour and the Persistence of the Everyday

The Civil War began in Algeria in 1991 following the victory of the Islamist party, the FIS (Front islamique du salut), at the first round of general elections in the first democratic electoral process ever permitted in the country. The FLN-led government, with the backing of the army, effectively cancelled the second round of elections, ironically citing the threat that Islamic radicalism posed to 'democratic' values. This decision led to brutal reprisals from the Islamists and the concomitant state response, resulting in a decade-long civil war between the government and the army, and the various terrorist groups: the FIS, the MIA (Mouvement islamique armé), the AIS (Armée islamique du salut), and the GIA (Groupe islamique armé). According to Lahouari Addi, the army generals saw the elections as a way to give the impression of democracy, both within and outside Algeria, and never intended to allow the FLN to lose.[4] The Algerian government wanted to contain and manage terrorist violence within its own borders, and it regulated the dissemination of images of the conflict to the international community. The control the state exerted over representations of the conflict resulted in what Stora calls 'la persistence d'absence, la sensation de "vide" d'images' [the persistent absence, the feeling of an image vacuum]. He asks, 'une guerre non montrée peut-elle exister?' [Can a war that is not shown really exist?].[5] The questionable role of the army and the state in responding to the Islamist threat, as well as potentially contributing to the on-going cycles of violence, may explain their reluctance to allow widespread media coverage of the conflict. Lahouari Addi and John Entelis suggest that the government responded to the Islamists with excessive force; more than 7000 people disappeared in police custody during the conflict, a phenomenon referenced in *Viva Laldjérie* through the disappearance of the prostitute, Fifi.[6] In the years following the worst of the violence, the government attempted to restore peace and a sense of community in a fractured nation. Inaugurated on 15 August 2005 by President Bouteflika, the 'Charter for Peace and National Reconciliation' was designed to bring a ceasefire to Algeria, and to legally mark an end to the violence of the past. Put to a vote in a referendum on 29 September 2005, the proposition won 98% of popular support.[7] However, this charter granted blanket amnesty to both state and terrorist militias who surrendered their arms, and it was criticized as another instance of pervasive national silencing by organizations like Djazairouna, an association of victims of terrorism. Nacera Dutour, speaking on behalf of Djazairouna, believes that in implementing this charter, Bouteflika had 'ended the dreams of truth and justice for thousands of families of the disappeared'.[8]

In the face of this blanket amnesty, the task of rendering the trauma, losses and interpersonal fractures experienced by Algerians during the war is not insignificant. Stora outlines the complexity of the representational, historical, and political entanglements faced by Algerian writers and artists in the following terms: 'Comment parler des blessures personnelles, enfouies, au travers desquelles se profilent la complexité des nœuds de l'histoire coloniale et post-coloniale, l'impossibilité de les dénouer sereinement, tant ils sont constitués de violences, de non-dit?' [How should we speak of the hidden personal wounds, intertwined as they are with the complex knots of colonial and post-colonial history, the impossibility of gently undoing them, made up as they are of violence and all that is left unsaid?].[9] In response to this 'non-dit' of representational and political omissions and imposed silences, Algerian filmmakers in the 1990s and the 2000s produced a series of works that examined terrorism and the state's response during the 'black decade' of civil strife. Participating in the *cinéma de l'urgence* [cinema of crisis] movement, films like Merzak Allouache's *Bab El-Oued City* (1993), Yamina Bachir-Chouikh's *Rachida* (2002), Djamila Sahraoui's *Barakat!* (2006) and *Yema* (2012) tackle the problematic intersections of fundamentalist and state terror, and unlike *Des hommes et des dieux* discussed in the following chapter, these films explicitly address the trauma and losses of Algerian civilians during the conflict. Set during the peak years of hostility between the state and the Islamists, from 1991 to 1999, the films of the *cinéma d'urgence* movement foreground individual protagonists who resist the dictates of the terrorists using both violent and non-violent means. These films focus on the lives of ordinary individuals facing extraordinary circumstances, and the central protagonists in these films are depicted as particularly exposed to terrorist violence through age, gender, or socio-economic circumstance.

The films of the *cinéma de l'urgence* movement demonstrate the close proximity between Algerian civilians and terrorists who are, in many cases, members of their families and communities. Intimate social groups were divided by the conflict, a situation that is achingly rendered in Sahraoui's *Yema*, which depicts a mother (an allegorical representation of the Algerian nation) who is caught between two sons, one a terrorist and the other a member of the armed forces. Wendy Kristianasen summarizes the conflicting position that many Algerians hold: 'for most Algerians, including moderate Islamists, the conflict was not a civil war, which is an idea too painful to articulate, but *le terrorisme*: armed insurgents against the state and those that the state had armed for self-defence'.[10] Marking the insurgents as 'terrorists' allows an affective distancing to occur, whereby the agents of violence are viewed as renegades and deviants, pushed outside of the national community, psychologically if not spatially. This emotional disassociation occurs on a formal level in Bachir-Chouikh's *Rachida*: although the terrorists are shown to move freely amongst the villagers, this movement is always one of violence, and the spectator never gains any knowledge of their personalities, motivations, or backgrounds.

In contrast to the films of the *cinéma de l'urgence* movement, *Viva Laldjérie* appears to reiterate some of the silence and invisibility that surrounded the conflict by pushing terrorism and the ongoing fundamentalist threat to the margins of the narrative. The action takes place a mere four years after the official cessation of hostilities between the government and the majority of the Islamist groups through the 'Civil Harmony Act' in 1999. Yet, instead of positioning terrorism and the memory of the Civil War at the centre of the story, the on-going terrorist threat in the country hovers in the background. Moreover, in contrast to *Des hommes et des dieux*, which depicts the group of French monks as politically and spatially positioned between the Algerian state and the Islamic fundamentalists, in *Viva Laldjérie* the dominant actors in the conflict are largely absent. Rather, small, individual actions propel the narrative forward, and Algerian civilians, mostly depicted as apolitical, take centre stage: the historical backdrop seems to function almost incidentally compared to the sustained focus on the everyday lives of the central characters. Moknèche's decision to sideline terrorism and the Civil War relates to the conditions of civil discord that increased the need for reunification in the wake of the violence.

A consideration of the temporal proximity of the film's creation to the conflict can also help clarify Moknèche's position. The closer one is to a perturbing past, the more complex its relation is to the present: Moknèche notes that Algeria, 'comme toute société qui traverse ce genre d'épreuves, dans un premier temps, elle veut oublier, elle veut vivre' [is like every society that has gone through this sort of ordeal, initially, it wants to forget, it wants to live].[11] Rather than bringing to mind the horror of the 'black decade', Moknèche wanted to depict the resilience of the Algerian people, and the persistence of everyday life in the face of an on-going terrorist threat. Stora, in his interview with Moknèche, appears to endorse the director's choice of deliberate forgetting, as an action that can benefit a society in the wake of a conflict. He writes: 'une société qui vivait tout le temps dans le ressassement de la guerre serait une société morte. [...] Le bilan du fondamentalisme politique et religieux est tiré: le fait que les gens vivent' [a society that constantly dwelled on the war would be a dead society...the outcome of political and religious fundamentalism can be assessed: the fact that people live].[12] Moknèche foregrounds these intersecting desires, the desire to forget and the desire to live, through an insistence on the everyday lives of his characters and the use of humour. *Viva Laldjérie* is, in broad terms, a drama, but humour is a recurring means through which characters lampoon their oppressors, make light of their circumstances, and mock their own fears of terrorist violence. Many studies have pointed to the deployment of humour as a political strategy and a rhetorical tactic that counters extremist narratives. For Hannah Arendt, humour fundamentally undermines the authority of those in power, by demonstrating a lack of respect: 'the greatest enemy of authority, therefore, is contempt, and the surest way to undermine it is laughter'.[13] Goodall et al reiterate Arendt's statement, specifically in relation to terrorism: 'the appeals of humour as "rhetorical charms" or stylistic seductions [are] based on surprising uses of languages and/or images designed to provoke laughter, disrupt ordinary arguments, and counter taken-for-granted truths'.[14] By mocking the once omnipotent oppressor, as the protestors in Tahrir Square did in 2011 through satirical depictions of Hosni Mubarak, the sensations of fear that these figures induce are redirected into laughter. Power, in short, changes hands.

In *Viva Laldjérie*, the all-powerful persona of Osama Bin Laden is ridiculed, in a joke that also subtly highlights the inadequacies of the forces of order that are supposed to protect citizens and punish terrorist criminals. In one sequence, Papicha, a little drunk, comments on Bin Laden's picture in the paper: 'Bin Laden reste introuvable. Il est trop fort. Ils peuvent jamais le capturer' [Bin Laden still hasn't been found. He's too strong. They'll never be able to capture him]. In lofty tones of false admiration, she lays stress on the 'fort', jokingly suggesting that she perceives Bin Laden's apparent inviolability to be a positive attribute. In doing this, she is mocking American and Algerian state narratives of Bin Laden as an almost preternatural figure, the human embodiment of superhuman evil, and thus mitigating some of the fear that he inspires. Humour can also serve as a panacea to those suffering psychological trauma following terrorist attacks, and the ability to laugh at one's own vulnerability triggers not only mental and emotional, but also, physiological release. As Elaine Pasquali notes, 'terrorism may threaten the physical, psychosocial, and spiritual aspects of one's personhood, the effects of humor strengthen these dimensions of self [...] humour thus has the potential for healing the wounds inflicted by terrorism'.[15] Humour has the ability to strengthen social bonds, and when Papicha expresses anxiety that there is bearded man outside, a terrorist who may be watching them, Goucem goads her, saying 'je vois un homme...il achète des fleurs...c'est pour me demander en mariage' [I see a man... he's buying flowers...it's to ask for my hand in marriage], doubly mocking both her mother's fear of terrorists and their shared concern that she is unmarried. In other instances, terrorism is conceived as a normal occurrence, an easy lie to tell your boss, like a traffic jam: when Goucem is late for work because she has been visiting a 'voyante' [psychic], she excuses herself calmly, saying that there was a terrorist attack. Similarly, a cross-cut scene shows Aniss lying to Goucem about why he cannot meet her: he says he is in Oran hospital, caring for the victims of a terrorist attack, while in the background of the shot, a blonde woman waits for him at the entrance to an apartment building.

This focus on humour in the face of possible violence demonstrates the ways in which terrorism comes to be integrated into the structures of everyday life. The targeting of innocent civilians gives terrorism its shocking impact, and the random, unqualified nature of terrorist attacks means that even individuals who support or are sympathetic to the cause may be victims. This lack of predictability, and the break from a logic of means and ends, alters the discursive and physical space in which victims live. Charles Townshend writes that, 'war is in essence physical, terrorism is mental'.[16] The core of terrorism lies not in the destruction it causes or the lives lost (for these are correlative with war) but in the mental fear it induces: if anyone can be a target, anywhere, at any time, the delineated mental and physical space of the war-zone no longer exists, and dread and danger become ever-present realities. All time becomes the time of war; all spaces are potentially and unpredictably lethal. Adriana Cavarero summarizes the spatio-temporal specificity of life amid a terrorist threat: 'disengaged from the intensive continuity of war, the time of violence thus dilates and finishes by coinciding, through unfathomable intermittence, with the banal dimensions of daily life'.[17] Moknèche creates this sense of lingering fear and routinized caution throughout the film by introducing murky, isolated statements that hint at the personal and collective violence of the past. The absence of Goucem's father, Papicha's husband, remains unexplained, but when they visit his grave the tombstone informs the spectator that he died in 1991 at the age of 51, at the beginning of the Civil War in Algeria. When Papicha is asked for the cause of his death, she spits out that 'il est mort du dégout' [he died of disgust]. This ambiguous answer suggests that her husband may have been a political adversary of the state, or an opponent of the Islamists: at whom his disgust was directed remains unclear. Sidi-Moussa, Goucem and Papicha's village of origin, was at the centre of the 'triangle of death', a non-urban area of intense violence, where the monk's monastery at Tibhirine was also located. The viewer is informed that the two women have not been living in the *Pension Debussy* for long, and they form part of a group of displaced individuals who had to move home because of the Civil War. Papicha still owns a house in Sidi-Moussa, which she wants sell in order to use the money to buy the *Copacabana*. Goucem disparages this idea, asking, 'tu veux te faire égorger?' [Do you want to have your throat cut?], highlighting the on-going dangers in the area.

Yet aside from these brief moments that hint at dark past events, Moknèche insists upon his character's will to continue in the wake of violence. The opening sequence highlights the centrality of the everyday in this depiction of Algiers and the return to the quotidian after conflict in *Viva Laldjérie*. As the credits roll, the camera captures in medium shot a city street in Algiers, and a multitude of people bustle past, talking, laughing, and shopping. Men and women, young and old, dressed in torn tracksuits or heavy fur coats, the women veiled and unveiled, file past the camera. Filmed in a quasi-documentary style in muted tones of brown and grey, the sequence is accompanied by Pierre Bastaroli's plaintive piano score, a muted melancholic refrain that recurs throughout the film. By opening with these images, snapshots of daily life in the city recorded live in the streets of Algiers without actors or extras, Moknèche underscores his vision of a vibrant and dynamic Algeria.

Characterization, Gender, and the Question of Realism

Viva Laldjérie dramatizes the ways in which individuals strive to carve out spaces of meaning and fulfilment in the wake of conflict and women occupy a position of tremendous importance in this endeavour. Moknèche's childhood also goes some way towards explaining his focus on women: his father died from a work-related accident in 1968, and his mother, a switchboard operator at the central Post Office in Algiers, began working as a seamstress in their home. Every day, groups of women would gather in the house, and Moknèche recalls the diversity of his encounters, as he would listen to their stories: 'j'ai vu défiler toutes sortes de clientes qui racontaient leur vie' [I saw all sorts of clients passing through, who would talk about their lives].[18] Moknèche's focus on women also reflects historically the socio-political targeting of women during Algerian Civil War by both the FLN-led government and by terrorist organizations. Although the 200,000 people who died in the conflict and the 7000 or more who disappeared were almost all men, some of the most horrific acts were perpetrated against women.[19] Moreover, violence against women was not confined to the space and time of war, nor was it solely the preserve of the Islamic fundamentalists. Violence against women can be situated within a decades-long framework, where symbolic and discursive violence restricted women's rights (for example, the Family Code), where incidents of domestic violence were rising, and where extreme physical aggression against women was tacitly ignored or even sanctioned by government institutions who refused to adequately punish perpetrators under law.[20]

In terms of radical Islamism, the control of women's bodies became a point of emblematic contestation, and women found themselves increasingly the targets of brutal and horrific attacks. Catherine Lloyd summarizes the extent of the violence:

> Women teachers were beheaded in front of their pupils, women related to government officers or security workers were also targeted. In remote areas whole villages were massacred, young girls were kidnapped, gang raped and turned into sex slaves, divorced women or widows who lived alone were also targeted.[21]

Unsurprisingly, given their increased exposure to threat, Algerian female activists were among the first to recognize the growing menace that Islamic fundamentalism represented to their freedoms and those of Algerian society as a whole. They organized huge demonstrations in all the major cities of Algeria on 2 January 1992 against the FIS, to protest their victory in the elections displaying photographs of the victims of terrorism and distributing documents that outlined FIS leaders statements against democracy.[22] These protests carried a weighty symbolic dimension, as they were an attempt to occupy communal forums that the Islamists were controlling through violence, particularly in relation to female participation in the public sphere. Smail Sahli suggests that women's resistance during the Civil War was often constituted by small, everyday acts of normality, by striving to preserve the structures of daily life in a climate of generalized fear: sending their children to school, going to hairdressers and beauty salons, showing up to work. For Sahli, 'these women stood for life and for the continuance of life in Algeria despite the roaming danger of death in an extremely dangerous and hostile environment. This in itself is an extraordinary act of resistance and societal cohesion'.[23]

Resistance — figured as the simple will to exist in everyday life, to work, to live — is the cornerstone of Moknèche's depiction of the three central characters in *Viva Laldjérie*: Papicha, Goucem, and Fifi. The name 'Papicha' itself underscores the notion of everyday resistance. Originally a slang term for the madam of a brothel, the word was re-appropriated in the 1990s by the *papichettes*, working-class girls of eighteen to twenty-five years of age. During the years of the conflict, these young women would walk out in public in the suburbs of Algiers wearing tight clothes, heels, and make-up in order to flout the conventions of the Islamists. The actions of these young women contravened the dictates of the terrorists and state-controlled terror: by asserting their right to dress and circulate as they pleased, they countered the fear that sought to control behaviour, through an unabashed assertion of individuality. In a 1999 study undertaken by Chams Benghribil of the *papichettes* in the Algiers suburb of Belcours, one of the young women describes the reasons she and her friends took dangerous risks in defying the Islamists:

> Nowadays all the girls dress like this. It is normal, they want to live. If you take that away from us, there is nothing left. That is all there is to raise our spirits. If they kill me, I may as well die beautiful, I will at least have lived.[24]

For these women, and for the characters in the film, the threat of punishment does not outweigh the need to live with agency. Papicha's actions echo this resistance: although fearful of the 'barbus' [literally 'bearded men', but in this case it signifies the terrorists], she launches whole-heartedly into the project of reviving the *Copacabana*, before it was shut down in 1991 because of terrorist threats. She resurrects her old dancing costumes, parading about their living quarters in a dazzling ensemble of crimson red satin and chiffon, draped in gold tassels and jewellery. Goucem is critical of this project, suggesting that it is dangerous, and that she is too old: she scorns her mother, saying 'à ton age on ne refait pas sa vie' [you can't rebuild your life at your age]. But Papicha remains unbowed, and goes to the local council in order to procure a licence to reopen the *Copacabana*. She is confronted with what is a clear reference to the remnants of French bureaucracy: the attendant at the Ministry, who has blue eyes and blond hair, invents a series of nonsensical reasons to avoid helping her. Instead, Papicha uses overt sexual charm to lure an older man at the ministry into providing her with information, and in the end, the former owners, a gay couple returned from exile in Paris, reopen the club. The final sequences of the film depict Papicha singing a song about the betrayals of love and loss, 'Mouaoud Lik', written by Biyouna herself [Figure 4.1].

FIG. 4.1. Papicha/Biyouna. *Viva Laldjérie*, dir. by Nadir Moknèche (2004).

This final sequence, which overlays the character of Papicha with Biyouna, exists as a kind of homage to and celebration of the resistance of the iconic performer, who in the face of real-world terrorist threats, remained, in Moknèche's terms, 'violente, provocatrice, irrévérencieuse' [violent, provocative, irreverential].[25]

Yet the fact that Papicha is the only character who succeeds in fulfilling her goals, while the younger characters, embodied in Goucem and Fifi, are thwarted, captures the particular concerns faced by younger generations in Algeria. Goucem is caught between conflicting desires: for marriage, stability, and conformity on the one hand, and a quest for personal autonomy and independence on the other. For Moknèche, 'Goucem est le fruit de l'Algérie socialo-islamiste. [...] Elle a grandi en réaction aux contraintes, aux principes, aux fausses espérances. Elle oscille entre désir de normalité et désir de transgression' [Goucem is the product of a socialist and Islamist Algeria. [...] She grew up responding to its constraints, principals, false hopes. She oscillates between the desire for normality and the desire for transgression].[26] Goucem's frequent costume switches between modest brown *abayas* and skimpy mini-dresses encapsulate these dual desires, and her behaviours also alternate between provocation and reserve. While she expresses a gloomy awareness of her nonconformity, and her potential difficulty in finding a husband — 'vingt-sept ans, deux avortements, une mère danseuse' [twenty-seven years old, two abortions, and a mother who's a cabaret dancer] — her gestures in the opening sequences of the film point to an almost excessive sexuality. Pouting, thrusting her hips, and flicking her hair, she plays the role of coquette with her lover Aniss and with men at a nightclub. Yet Moknèche subtly hints at the fragility of such outward displays of sexual power: Goucem's monthly salary is stolen, leaving her without the means to pay the rent, and Aniss abandons her for another mistress. One sequence in particular illuminates Goucem's conflicting motivations: sitting on her bed with Fifi, Goucem's grabs her friend's breasts lightly and playfully, and when Fifi gently rebuffs her, Goucem says quietly, 'j'ai besoin de tendresse' [I need affection]. Acting as an emotional and financial carer to her mother, and rebuffed by her lover after a three-year affair, Goucem's apparent independence is gradually revealed as an imposed state, rather than chosen liberation. Goucem's naïve assertions of control are in part responsible for her friend's eventual death: entering Fifi's room clandestinely, Goucem steals a gun from the coat pocket of one of Fifi's clients, a government official. Mocking the figures in action movies, she points the gun at her reflection in the mirror, making explosive noises, mimicking an aggression and control that is denied to her in real life.

Fifi is the only character that offers emotional support to Goucem, stating that they are like 'sœurs' [sisters], and for the most part, they are sketched in the drama as close and caring friends [Figure 4.2]. The audience is first introduced to Fifi through the sound of her tinkling laughter and this light-hearted joviality is consistent with Fifi's approach to her profession throughout the film. She appears to delight in her work, never expresses any moral qualms, instead celebrating in the financial freedom it offers. Even more than Goucem, Fifi's appearance changes constantly throughout the film: adorned in a variety of wigs, she moves from a slick, razor

FIG. 4.2. Fifi and Goucem. *Viva Laldjérie*, dir. by Nadir Moknèche (2004).

straight blond bob to the thick brown corkscrew curls of her natural hair. She wears delicate, transparent silk negligées in peach, blue and white silk, and fur and feather collared nightgowns for her clients, but when she walks out on the street, she dons the traditional white *haïk* with a face covering, completed with a pair of high heels. These changes of appearance highlight the fluidity of Fifi's character, the white *haïk* implying a traditionalism and modesty that is at odds with Fifi's profession and persona. Fifi's phone message — 'je suis occupée ou dans les bras de Morphée' [I'm busy or in the arms of Morpheus] — points to these shifting personas, as well as foreshadowing her tragic end. Morpheus, the god of dreams depicted in Ovid's *Metamorphosis*, could mimic any human form, just as Fifi's physical incarnations change almost every time she appears on the screen. Moreover, as a god of dreams, Morpheus can be linked to the fine line between consciousness and unconsciousness, and between life and death. The murder of Fifi at the hands of government officials, and the reaction of her friends and acquaintances to her disappearance, highlights her liminal status. Apart from Goucem who reports her disappearance and tries to find her, no one else in the *Pension Debussy* seems overly concerned. The family who act as caretakers in the hotel take some of her clothes, and Papicha even says to Goucem, 'tu vas quand même pas faire la bile pour une putain?' [Come on, you're not going to upset yourself over a whore?] When Goucem goes to file the missing person's report, the policeman remarks dismissively that thousands of people are disappearing everyday: Fifi is not only a prostitute without close relatives, but also a single missing person among a multitude of lost bodies.

Although Fifi's murder in the film's closing sequences could be inscribed in the pan-cultural paradigm of the sacrificial death of the uncontrollable and sexually liberated women, Fifi is not killed because she is a prostitute, but due to Goucem's betrayal. The focus on excluded individuals throughout the film and alternative logics of honour contrasts sharply with the state-controlled Algerian cinema of the 1960s to the 1980s, which concentrated on narratives of male sacrifice, honour, and political intrigue.[27] Following the French-Algerian War, filmmaking in Algeria was run by the state, which produced works like Mohamed Lakhdar-Hamina's *Le Vent des Aurès* [*The Wind of the Aurès*], Lakhdar-Hamina's *Chronique des années de braise* [*Chronicle of the Years of Fire*] and Pontecorvo's *La Bataille d'Algers* (1966). Characterized as the *cinéma moudjahid* [freedom fighter cinema], these films sought to glorify the FLN's role in the War of Independence through the figure of the male political martyr, dying nobly in the name of the liberation cause. Roy Armes points out that the post-independence Algerian cinema of the 1960s and 1970s served an 'ideological function' in terms of nation building, but 'Algerian audiences could not recognize themselves in their cinema's deformed image of the struggle'.[28]

For Ratiba Hadj-Moussa, the monolithic cinema of the 1960s and 1970s has given way to 'portraits of new identities', where the themes include 'first, the absence of strong male characters and the political and social marginality of female characters, and second, the contemporary expression of the logic of honour'.[29] *Viva Laldjérie* certainly foregrounds its female protagonists, but the extent to which these 'portraits of new identities' invite recognition from Algerian audiences, recognition that was absent from the state controlled cinema of the post-independence years, remains open to question. For Moknèche, the concern is not only that national cinema has failed to provide Algerians with identifiable images of their lives, but also that the history of French colonialism means that for many Algerians, representation in any form carries uncomfortable associations:

> Les Algériens ont un rapport épineux avec l'image, leur image. Ils ont commencé par se voir à travers le regard colonial, en une masse de gens indifférenciés, et à l'indépendance, en archétypes réalistes socialistes: le Combattant, le Paysan, l'Ouvrier. Rarement en individus ayant une personnalité propre.[30]

> [Algerians have a thorny relationship with the image, their image. Initially they saw themselves through the colonial gaze, as an undifferentiated mass, and then, following independence, through the archetypes of socialist realism: the Soldier, the Peasant, the Worker. Rarely as individuals having their own personality].

The tension created by the colonial gaze, as well as the characters and lifestyles depicted in the film, is evident in online responses: *Viva Laldjérie* did not conform to many viewers' conceptions of a 'real' Algeria. The YouTube streaming version of the film is followed by a series of comments that vary from a muted appreciation for the film and its evocation of a seldom seen vision of daily life in Algeria, to extreme outrage, anger, and disgust.[31] Overwhelmingly, the derisive comments appear to be from men, and the appreciative reactions appear to be from women. Judging by the nature of some of the more violent reactions, the most contentious issues evoked are the representation of women and prostitutes, the depiction of male homosexuality, and the lack of overtly political content. The film is also criticized for catering to Western and French tastes, and for demeaning Algeria for the pleasure and gratification of Western audiences.

Viva Laldjérie explicitly treads a delicate line between an undeniable 'Algerianness' and generic attributes that lend it a much larger appeal. While the many long takes in the streets and alleyways of Algiers ground the film in a concrete geographical setting, the treatment of space and time is conventional, the action is chronological, and the characters are sympathetic and recognizable. The film often stresses the pan-national aspects of the characters' lives, and of Algeria itself, enlarging its scope beyond the paradigm of the strictly national concerns that populated the *cinéma moudjahid* [freedom fighter cinema]. Moknèche notes that during his time in France, 'je suis devenu profondément méditerranéen' [I became profoundly Mediterranean].[32] Indeed, Stora likens Moknèche to the Italian director Pier Paolo Pasolini, as well as to Spanish director Pedro Almodóvar, and the comparison with Almodóvar merits further scrutiny. Both directors began their careers in fractured national forums, post-Franco Spain and post-Civil War Algeria. Thematically, they share a focus on flamboyant and socially transgressive female characters, the overt depiction of homosexuality, and critiques of religion and repressive social values. Both directors employ a camp, tragi-comic aesthetic with strong female leads, which reappear in multiple films. Just as Carmen Maura, Penelope Cruz, and Rossy de Palma star in diverse roles in multiple Almodóvar works, Biyouna and Nadia Kaci have also starred in Moknèche's *Le Harem de Mme Osmane* (2000) and *Délice Paloma* (2007), while Louba Azabal features in *Goodbye Morocco* (2013).

For Patrick Crowley, 'Moknèche is a *bricoleur* of images and motifs. He draws on a repository of Algerian, North African, and European images in ways that visually signal Algeria's connections to ideas and images that have circulated across the Mediterranean sea'.[33] Crowley cites the painting of Saint George slaying the dragon, which Fifi buys for Goucem moments before she is kidnapped, as a decisive transnational reference [Figure 4.3]. This iconography was originally Egyptian in origin, and was brought back to Europe and adopted by Christianity during the Crusades. The colours of red and green feature heavily in this painting, and as Crowley suggests, it can also be read as a symbol of contemporary Algeria: green representing the colour in the Algerian flag, red signifying a decade of violence and bloodshed, and both colours combining in the figure of the dragon's scales and scarlet tongue, perhaps representing the 'dragon' of terrorism that could be slain.[34] This emphasis on a trans-Mediterranean cultural history neither ignores nor privileges exclusively the colonial past. Instead, Moknèche points to a much broader history of trans-Mediterranean interaction and exchange and also exploitation and appropriation: the Crusades were an attempt to eradicate the Muslim infidel, although elements of the Islamic cultural imaginary were also integrated. Yet the history of exploitation does not feature in any direct way in *Viva Laldjérie*, even if the traces of the French past in Algeria are ever-present through the language the characters speak, through the subtle references like the painting, or the complicated bureaucracy that Papicha must navigate in attempting to purchase the *Copacabana*. Like the treatment of terrorism and state-control, these historical fragments are tributaries, feeding into the main plot, which remains focused on the lives of the central characters. Moreover, sex scenes, the adoption of French as the principal language, the personalities of the characters, and the themes of the film further hint at an implicit or explicit catering to European and American tastes and values,

FIG. 4.3. Saint George and the Dragon. *Viva Laldjérie*, dir. by Nadir Moknèche (2004).

appearing to offer Western and French audiences confirmation of their ideological assumptions, particularly regarding Muslim-majority states and the oppression of women and minority groups.

Thomas Elsaesser addresses these concerns around realism and audience expectation in relation to the broad category of 'world cinema', which comes to encompass all filmmaking outside of a Euro-American context. Elsaesser argues against dividing films along colonial, postcolonial, or national lines. He instead notes that cinema nowadays is principally distinguished by a 'Hollywood and all the rest' division, and the notion of 'world cinema' risks becoming the catchall term for this non-Hollywood remainder. For Elsaesser, worldwide film markets dictate themes, and 'what matters is how well local/national provenance can communicate with global/transnational audiences'.[35] Films are no longer (if they were ever) being made within a national context for distribution in that context; more and more, what has come to be called 'world' cinema addresses a transnational audience, particularly on festival circuits and in art house cinemas, rather than the local or national group they represent. This is what Elsaesser designates 'art house cinema light', a form of cinema that may portray 'exotic' (i.e., non-Western) locations, but with the comfortable characterization and formal techniques that will ensure wider circulation. According to Elsaesser, this is a cinema that 'others' the other, with the collusion of the other, and, by portraying what the 'native' thinks the 'non-native' (read Western) observer wants to see, becomes engaged in a kind of 'auto-ethnography' and 'self-exoticization'. Elsaesser formulates a list of common preoccupations of world cinema and the majority of these themes feature in *Viva Laldjérie*: identity politics, women's rights, nationalism, terrorism, contested spaces, everyday lives in harsh national conditions, difficult political circumstances, human rights, conflicts between history and tradition, and social exclusion.[36]

Viva Laldjérie was funded primarily by French sources, including government subsides from Centre National de la Cinématographie (CNC), Région Ile-de-France, Ministère des Affaires étrangères et du Développement International, and

Arte France Cinéma, as well as several small, private production companies from Belgium, France, and Algeria. No Algerian government funding was obtained. For Walid Benkhaled, funding issues are part of a 'double distortion' of verisimilitude in Algerian cinema: firstly, through the influence of European, and principally French, funding bodies, and secondly, through Anglo-American academic criticism, which takes these works as a form of factual 'proof' of Algerians' lived experiences — what he calls 'unfiltered documentary evidence of the desires and frustrations of Algerian youth'.[37] For Benkhaled, the linguistic and cultural limitations of European funding mechanisms fundamentally constrain the characters and themes represented, and this has an impact upon 'what "types" of Algerians (in terms of socio-economic profile and geographic location) can be represented cinematographically'.[38] Certainly, having Algerian characters of varying social classes speaking in French for the duration of the film is not a realistic reflection of contemporary Algeria, and Moknèche's choice of French as a dominant language may be a result of the language clauses in French funding conditions. However, Moknèche justifies his choice of language in different terms, citing the massive Arabization of Algeria in the decades following Independence, which makes the Classical Arabic spoken on television as distanced from ordinary Algerians as French. He also notes that Lubna Azabal is a native Moroccan speaker, and having her speak in Algerian Arabic would have been 'ridicule' [ridiculous]. He further cites Algeria as the country with the second highest number of French speakers in the world.[39] Benkhaled finds these explanations to be tenuous, and it is possible that the director is being disingenuous about the conditions of production and the influence that Western funding bodies had over his directorial choices. For Benkhaled, Algerian filmmakers like Moknèche are 'alienated from the realities which they claim to represent' and the assumptions of Western critics, who interpret these works as ethnographic testaments to a 'real-life' Algeria, compound the misrepresentation of the country.[40]

Yet on the level of characterization, Moknèche is eager to stress that the people he presents in his films are grounded in actual encounters: 'une chose est sûre, mes personnages sont des gens que j'ai croisés au moins une fois' [one thing is certain, my characters are people who I've met at least once].[41] Yet behind these assertions or critiques of realism in *Viva Laldjérie* lies the implicit assumption that film must represent reality and that it should reflect and recreate a concrete socio-political context. This desire for film to perform a didactic function, to tell 'us' the viewer about a particular country or people, is, as Elsaesser outlines, an issue that is particularly pertinent to non-Western filmmakers. Moreover, in the case of *Viva Laldjérie*, I suggest that it be treated as a cultural document, one that can be analysed not for its proximity to or illumination of a given reality, an endeavour that is inevitably partial and incomplete, but rather for its depiction of a world that exists between reality and fantasy. Indeed, as Moknèche notes, the film moves between the real and the imaginary throughout: 'le film commence dans un "réel fantasmé": veille de week-end dans une ville "normale"; pour découvrir petit à petit un "réel quotidien"' [the film begins in a 'fantasized reality': the beginning of the weekend in a 'normal' city; and bit by bit, it uncovers a 'daily reality'].[42] Rather than depicting the past, or attempting to create a realistic image of contemporary Algiers in 2001, Moknèche has instead created a fantasized present, one that may point towards possible futures. He does this through emphasizing spaces of fantasy that exist between the realms of the public and the private, spaces where socially unacceptable behaviours are practised: what Michel Foucault calls 'heterotopias'.

Heterotopias: Private Deviation and Public Conformity

In 1994, Hadj-Moussa wrote that the dominant characteristic of Algerian cinema 'est de mettre en relief la sexualité toute en la biffant: plus il la couvre, plus il la dé-couvre et plus il montre qu'il la recouvre' [is that it foregrounds sexuality, while also erasing it: the more it covers it, the more it dis-covers it, and it then shows the process of re-covering].[43] This is certainly not the case in *Viva Laldjérie*. Sixteen minutes into the film, the spectator has already seen frontal female nudity and extra-marital sex, sources of veritable outrage for certain YouTube commentators. The question of the 'reality' of the depiction again becomes pertinent: apart from the most virulent, the majority of online commentators acknowledge that Algerian women certainly have casual sex, sometimes have affairs, and that prostitution and homosexuality exist, 'comme partout' [like everywhere], as they are eager to point out. Yet, as Hadj-Moussa highlights, there is a fundamental difference between a tacit acceptance of such practices and their representation to an international audience through film. What appears to emerge, therefore, is not the question of whether such practices occur, but the space in which they occur: public and visible (in literal public space or the public space of a broadcast film) or private and largely unseen.

From the outset, *Viva Laldjérie* emphasizes the character's lack of privacy: Goucem lives in a cramped room with her mother, where they change clothes and use the toilet in front of one other, and share a double bed on which they eat their meals. Likewise, Goucem frequently interrupts Fifi's sexual activities in her bedroom, and her work is common knowledge to the landlords and lodgers at the *Pension Debussy*: cries of pleasure circulate through the corridors, just as Fifi's clients are often found wandering the halls looking for her room. Indeed, the central narrative thread of Fifi's abduction and death is a result of a lack of privacy: Goucem steals into her room, unbidden, because the doors are always open. If private spaces are never completely sealed, neither is public space secure. Acts or potential acts of state or Islamist terror take place on the streets, and public space is depicted as fraught with potential dangers, particularly for socially marginalized characters. Yacine is beaten up by his former lover in a motorway underpass, and when Goucem's pay is stolen in a public bar, her friend tells her that she should consider herself lucky: recently, two women walking home at night had their throats cut. The scene of Fifi's attempted escape from the government officials takes place in the heart of the city and it is intercut, firstly, with a wedding cortège, and secondly, with Goucem gazing wistfully at this same spectacle from the door of the photography shop where she works. The proud display of the legitimate, socially condoned, practice of marriage in the centre of Algiers contrasts sharply with the semi-private spaces that Fifi and Goucem inhabit. All of the sexual acts that are depicted or referenced in *Viva Laldjérie* take place in semi-public spaces: Yacine's homosexual tryst, interrupted by the police, is outdoors, and Goucem's liaisons with Aniss are conducted in a room in the hospital, with the staff's tacit acknowledgement of what is taking place.

Much of the film's narrative centres on the characters' quests to find physical spaces, and private spaces, in which they can live out their dreams and fantasies. Papicha wants to resurrect the *Copacabana* under her own stewardship, while Goucem dreams of marriage and her own home. Fifi wants to make enough money to afford an Ottoman house in the Kasbah with a courtyard, and Yacine notes that he will leave Algeria for Europe, in order to find a space in which he can live as a homosexual without fear of violence and police reprisals. Yet although no character succeeds in fully realizing their ambitions, throughout the film, these socially ostracized individuals find spaces within their environment hidden away from visible, conventional, and sanctioned modes of existence on the streets. These semi-private spaces, containing small groups or communities of marginalized people, can be aligned with Foucault's concept of heterotopias, as spaces of otherness ('les espaces absolument autres' [spaces that are absolutely other]) that function under non-hegemonic conditions.[44] If utopias are fantasized spaces of essential perfection and dystopias evoke the nightmarish inversion of social codes, heterotopias exist alongside, rather than in between these concepts as real spaces that contain individuals or acts that are deemed unacceptable by the rest of society. Heterotopias are intended to purge these unacceptable elements from public spaces: they are 'des lieux qui s'opposent à tous les autres, qui sont destinés en quelque sorte à les effacer, à les neutraliser ou à les purifier. Ce sont en quelque sorte des *contre*-espaces' [Spaces that are opposed to all other spaces, that are in some way designed to erase them, to neutralize them or purify them. They are, in a way, *counter*-spaces].[45] Heterotopias are spaces in which marginalised outsiders exist and engage in behaviours that deviate from a national and hegemonic norm, spaces 'plutôt réservés aux individus dont le comportement est déviant par rapport à la moyenne ou à la norme exigée' [reserved rather for individuals whose behaviour is considered deviant, compared to average or required norms].[46] These are what Foucault calls heterotopias of deviation: real spaces created for 'undesirable' bodies, which allow the rest of society to exist and remain 'pure', or functional in some sense; examples include brothels, asylums, hospitals, and cemeteries, all of which appear or are referred to in *Viva Laldjérie*.

The nightclub scene of *Viva Laldjérie* drew particular opprobrium from online viewers for its depiction of active female sexuality and promiscuity. The sequence occurs approximately sixteen minutes into the film. Goucem prepares to go out for the night wearing heavy make-up and a skimpy dress which she covers in an *abaya* in the streets on her way to the club. There is an emphasis on the international influences in their domestic arrangement. Papicha sprawls on the shared bed, eating 'Pizza Rapido — Quatre Saisons', smoking cigarettes, and watching a French reality television programme about Miami, featuring bronzed Western bodies, blond hair, tight-fitting skimpy swimwear, and the dialogue 'tu veux qu'on baise?' [Do you want us to fuck?]. This question foreshadows her daughter's plans for the night. There is an abrupt visual and auditory transition to the nightclub scene, as *raï* music saturates the acoustic space. Native to Oran on the coast of the Mediterranean, known even in colonial times as the most liberal city in Algeria, *raï* music was traditionally renowned for its sexually and politically provocative lyrics. Performed in cafes, bars, and brothels, heterotopic spaces *par excellence*, its counter-cultural resonances ensured that *raï* was banned from Algerian broadcast media until the 1980s. As Hana Noor Al-Deen outlines, '[Raï] has also been regarded as music of rebellion and the symbol of cynicism [...] rai [sic] performers, especially the newest and younger artists among them, have adeptly set the dissatisfaction of an upcoming generation to music'.[47] Cheb Abdou, one of *raï*'s most famous artists and a publicly proud gay man, has two songs featured on the soundtrack of *Viva Laldjérie*, and his work fits into the themes of the film, thus confirming Moknèche's assertion that *raï* is 'la musique des marginaux' [the music of the marginalized].[48] *Raï* also captures the trans-Mediterranean interconnections that characterize Algerian culture. Thought to originate in a combination of *andalusi* and *melhun* music, of Spanish and Baghdadi origin respectively, *raï* is principally sung in conversational Algerian Arabic, although contemporary forms also mix Arabic with French, Spanish, Italian, Berber, and even English vocabulary. *Raï* thus integrates broader European and Islamic influences in an intermingling that is in itself profoundly Algerian: author Boualem Sansal describes Algerians as 'des êtres multicolores et polyglottes, et nos racines plongent partout dans le monde. Toute la Méditerranée coule dans nos veines et, partout, sur ses rivages ensoleillés, nous avons semé nos graines' [Multi-coloured and multi-lingual beings, our roots reach throughout the world. The whole Mediterranean courses through our veins, and we have sown our seeds all over its sunny shores].[49]

The linguistic and cultural diversity of *raï*'s origins, as well as its socially unconventional stance, find an echo in the space of the nightclub. Aptly named 'Paradoxe', the old colonial façade of the club's exterior contrasts with the brash and shiny interior. Although there is a predominance of men over women in the club, it seems nevertheless to be a shared space (male, female, queer, straight). Women and gay men control sexual availability, as is shown through the belly dancer presiding over the scene, and Goucem's lip pouting and hip thrusting at the man she chooses to seduce. In this space, gay men are 'out'; the straight man who seemed comfortable and in control in the streets earlier in the day is teased, taunted, and flirted with by two gay friends who appear at home and at ease in this space [Figure 4.4]. In the heterotopic world of the club, the socially undesirable can be contained and hierarchies of sexual orientation and gender are reversed: sex is chosen or controlled by the publicly less powerful. This mixing of sexes and sexualities continues into the following sequence, a sex scene in a disused reservoir. In this dirty, abandoned space, at once both interior and exterior, public and private, the figuratively marginalized literally move outside to engage in 'illicit' sexual activities: an unmarried man

FIG. 4.4. The club as heterotopia. *Viva Laldjérie*, dir. by Nadir Moknèche (2004).

and woman, and a homosexual encounter between two men. The space seems to encompass a cross section of class, sexuality, and gender: Goucem, in her late twenties and mistress to a married man; her sexual partner, carrying a gun and therefore most likely a government official; Yacine, the upper-class son of a doctor, hiding his sexuality; and finally, Samir, the apparently straight, unemployed man who desperately wants to get to France, whom we have seen pursuing Goucem, yet who is now with a man, perhaps for money. One couple arrives as the other is leaving, and these overlapping spatial utilities again accord with the functionality of the heterotopia: 'l'hétérotopie a pour règle de juxtaposer en un lieu réel plusieurs espaces qui, normalement, seraient, devraient être incompatibles' [one of the rules of the heterotopia is to juxtapose in a real place several spaces which usually would be, and should be, incompatible].[50]

For Foucault, the heterotopia is a heterogeneous site that challenges and subverts the culture that surrounds it 'en créant une illusion qui dénonce tout le reste de la réalité comme illusion' [by creating an illusion which denounces the rest of reality as an illusion].[51] The overlapping identities and narrative threads that structure *Viva Laldjérie*, as well as its shifts between the sites of daily life and real places where fantasies are enacted, point towards the space and time of the film itself as a kind of heterotopia. Adrian Avakiv argues that cinema is always fundamentally heterotopic: 'like a mirror, cinema is heterotopic in that it presents the world to us, but differently, in a reconstituted manner, with its presentation affecting the world in heterogeneous ways'.[52] The deliberate and sustained attempt in *Viva Laldjérie* to portray an atypical aspect of Algerian life, beyond the customary depictions of violence, terrorism, religious conservatism, female oppression, and monolithic tragedy, points to a desire to envision alternate futures for Algeria, through a representation of a heterotopic present which is part real, part fantasy. Fifi, Goucem and Papicha are sustained throughout by fantasies of alternative futures, futures that they can glimpse, but never quite attain. Concerns regarding the authenticity of the characters' actions, as well as the language of the film, might be assuaged if we consider that according to Foucault, the heterotopic space exists somewhere in between fantasy and reality. Therefore, Moknèche is not trying to represent Algiers and its inhabitants, or the brutal history of the Civil War according to an ethnographic logic of truth, but instead, as Hadj-Moussa eloquently argues, he instead offers a vision of 'a present that is coming into existence'.[53]

By presenting alternative worlds, film, like heterotopic space, exerts a counterbalancing pressure, and may have the power to alter social attitudes towards socially marginalized bodies in the real world. Moknèche describes the enthusiasm in an apartment building in Bâb El-Oued provoked by a screening in 2000 of *Le Harem de Mme Osmane* on French satellite television: '[ma parente] a entendu ses voisines faire des youyous en criant que madame Osmane [sic] était à la télévision' [my relative heard her neighbours crying out excitedly that madame Osmane was on television].[54] *Le Harem de Mme Osmane* is not a realist film, and it contains the same colourful characters, provocative themes, and moments of fantastical excess that are found in *Viva Laldjérie*. This suggests that not all audiences want robust, true-to-life representations, and that occasionally, the greatest merit of a film can be its capacity to represent an alternative social world, perhaps even one which distances the spectator from immediate reality, a heterotopic space which is 'assez subtile ou habile pour vouloir dissiper la réalité avec la seule force des illusions' [subtle or deft enough to want to dissipate reality with only the force of illusion].[55] Ultimately, *Viva Laldjérie* reminds us that when conflicts of the past shadow and haunt the present, an overt exposition of the already all-too-present realities of violence may lend further weight to the fears that terrorism inspires. By pushing historical violence to the margins of the narrative, Moknèche retains a focus on individuals, foregrounding minor, everyday acts of resistance, acts that define and sustain everyday life. In this way, filmic fantasies of escape and freedom, however unrealistic, atypical or illusory, may open roads towards possible futures.

Notes to Chapter 4

1. Benjamin Stora, 'Entretien avec Nadir Moknèche, réalisateur de "Viva Laldjérie"', *Dossier de presse: Les Films de Losange* (2005) <http://www.filmsdulosange.fr/uploads/presskits/4ae93e0a97 07b0b588761335dcbd5d0ffb756da2.pdf> [Accessed 2 May 2017], p. 12.
2. Nadir Moknèche, 'Nadir Moknèche à Alger', *Le Monde* (1 August 2003) <http://www.liberation. fr/cahier-special/2003/08/01/cette-ville-c-est-la-maman-et-la-putain-nadir-mokneche-a-alger_441196> [Accessed 2 May 2017].
3. Stora, 'Entretien', p. 5.
4. Lahouari Addi, 'Algeria's Army, Algeria's Agony', *Foreign Affairs*, 77.4 (1998), 44–53 (p. 49).
5. Benjamin Stora, *La Guerre invisible: Algérie, années 90* (Paris: Presses de Sciences Po, 2001), p. 7–8.
6. Addi, 'Algeria's Army'; John P. Entelis, 'Algeria: Democracy denied, and revived?' *The Journal of North African Studies*, 16:4 (2011), 653–78.
7. Wendy Kristianasen 'Truth & Justice after a Brutal Civil War: Algeria: The Women Speak', *Review of African Political Economy*, 33:108 (2006), 346–51, (p. 347).
8. Quoted in Kristianasen 'Truth & Justice', p. 346.
9. Stora, *La Guerre invisible*, p. 113.
10. Kristianasen, p. 347

11. Stora, 'Entretien', p. 15.
12. Ibid., p. 15.
13. Hannah Arendt, *On Violence* (Orlando FL: Harcourt Books, 1969), p. 45.
14. H.L. Goodall, Jr, Pauline Hope Cheong, Kristen Fleischer and Steven R. Corman, 'Rhetorical Charms: The Promise and Pitfalls of Humor and Ridicule as Strategies to Counter Extremist Narratives', *Perspectives on Terrorism*, 6:1 (2012), 70–79, (p. 70).
15. Elaine Anne Pasquali, 'Humor: An Antidote for Terrorism', *Journal of Holistic Nursing*, 21:4 (2003), 398–414 (p. 401).
16. Charles Townshend, *Terrorism: A Very Short Introduction* (Oxford: Oxford University Press, 2002), p. 14.
17. Cavarero, Adriana, *Horrorism: Naming Contemporary Violence* (New York: Columbia University Press, 2009), p. 73.
18. Stora, 'Entretien', p. 13.
19. Entelis, 'Algeria: Democracy revived', p. 659.
20. See Catherine Lloyd, 'From Taboo to Transnational Political Issue: Violence against Women in Algeria', *Women's Studies International Forum*, 29:5 (2006), 53–62 and Kristianasen, 2006.
21. Lloyd, 'Violence Against Women', p. 120.
22. Ibid., p. 121.
23. Zahia Smail Salhi, 'The Algerian Feminist Movement between Nationalism, Patriarchy and Islamism', *Women's Studies International Forum* 33:2 (2010), 113–24, (p. 121).
24. Chams Benghrebil, 'La Décomposition sociale du djihad dans un quartier populaire d'Alger', *Annuaire de l'Afrique du Nord*, XXXVIII (1999), pp. 137–41, (p. 145). Also quoted in Ratiba Hadj-Moussa, 'Marginality and Ordinary Memory: Body Centrality and the Plea for Recognition in Recent Algerian Films', *The Journal of North African Studies*, 13 (2008), 187–99, (p. 195).
25. Stora, 'Entretien', p. 10.
26. Ibid., p. 9.
27. *Omar Gatlato*, dir, Merzak Allouache, 1977, constitutes a notable exception to the themes of the *cinéma moudjahid*, recounting the tale of a young man who likes to dance, party and play soccer. For more on the *cinéma moudjahid*, see Guy Austin, 'Representing the Algerian War in Algerian Cinema: *Le Vent des Aurès*', *French Studies*, 61:2 (2007), 182–95.
28. Roy Armes, 'From State Production to *Cinéma d'Auteur* in Algeria' in *Film in the Middle East and North Africa: Creative Dissidence*, ed. by Josef Gugler (Austin: University of Texas Press, 2011), pp. 294–306, (p. 295).
29. Hadj-Moussa, 'Marginality and Ordinary Memory', p. 187.
30. Stora, 'Entretien', p. 8.
31. The comments that follow the streaming version of *Viva Laldjérie* offer an interesting insight into the division of opinion regarding the film and for the violence with which it is both vilified and defended: <http://www.youtube.com/watch?v=iwohr3NI2vY> [Accessed January 8 2013].
32. Stora, 'Entretien', p. 12.
33. Patrick Crowley, 'Images of Algeria: Turning and Turning in the Widening Gyre', *Expressions maghrébines*, 6 (2007), 79–92 (p. 87).
34. Ibid., pp. 86–87. Goucem and Samir also don the colours of red and green throughout the film, linking them as young people to the future of the Algerian nation.
35. Thomas Elsaesser, *European Cinema: Face to Face with Hollywood* (Amsterdam: Amsterdam University Press, 2005), p. 491.
36. Ibid., p. 509.
37. Walid Benkhaled, 'Algerian Cinema between Commercial and Political Pressures: The Double Distortion', *Journal of African Cinemas*, 8:1 (2016), 87–100, (p. 96).
38. Ibid., p. 93
39. Stora, 'Entretien', p. 5.
40. Benkhaled, 'Algerian Cinema', p. 94.
41. Stora, 'Entretien', p. 13.
42. Ibid., p. 9.
43. Hadj-Moussa quoted in Crowley, 'Images of Algeria', p. 86.

44. Michel Foucault, *Le Corps utopique, les hétérotopies* (Paris: Nouvelles Editions Lignes, 2009), p. 25.

45. Ibid., p. 24.

46. Ibid., p. 27.

47. Hana Noor Al-Deen, 'The Evolution of Rai Music', *Journal of Black Studies*, 35:3 (2005), 597–611 (p. 609).

48. Stora, 'Entretien', p. 13.

49. Boualem Sansal, *Poste restante: Alger. Lettre de colère et d'espoir à mes compatriotes* (Paris: Gallimard, 2006), p. 48.

50. Foucault, *Le Corps utopique*, p. 29.

51. Ibid., p. 24.

52. Adrian Ivakhiv, 'Cinema of the Not-Yet: The Utopian Promise of Film as Heterotopia', *Journal for the Study of Religion, Nature and Culture*, 5:2 (2011), 186–209, (p. 192).

53. Hadj-Moussa, 'Marginality and Ordinary Memory', p. 189.

54. Stora, 'Entretien', p. 6.

55. Foucault, *Le Corps utopique*, p. 35.

PART III

❖

French Histories, Algerian Violence

❖

CHAPTER 5

Of Gods and Terrorists: *Des hommes et des dieux*

Although *Des hommes et des dieux* and *Viva Laldjérie* are both set in Algeria and treat the Algerian Civil War, the former has not been labelled 'postcolonial' in any sense. Indeed, *Des hommes et des dieux* might best be considered as an example of French heritage cinema, as a form that appeals to national discourses of community, nostalgia, and national values. Moreover, while *Viva Laldjérie* stressed the aftermath of the Civil War and the efforts of marginalized individuals to overcome the fear and devastation wrought by terrorism, Xavier Beauvois's *Des hommes et des dieux* is set in the peak years of the conflict, and offers a detailed character study of historic personages who were well-known in France and beyond. *Des hommes et des dieux* is based on the 1996 kidnapping of seven French Trappist monks by the GIA (Groupe Islamique Armée), a terrorist faction in Algeria, at the height of the Algerian Civil War. It offers a slow-moving meditation on monastic life and the values of community, brotherhood, and faith, charting the months and weeks leading up to the monks' abduction. The film begins in a blissful rural world, where the monks worship God, tend the land, grow crops, chop firewood, and make their own honey. They are shown to have a harmonious relationship with the local villagers, as they attend weddings, prayer ceremonies, and have tea with the imam. This idyllic existence is shattered by the arrival of a group of Islamic fundamentalist terrorists, who target foreigners and kill a group of Croatian labourers. The terrorists come to the monastery, seeking medical assistance, and are gently rebuffed by the monks. The Algerian state army also visits the holy sanctuary, and advises the monks in the strongest possible terms to return to their native land, France. Instead, the monks reach the communal decision to stay, and seven of their number are eventually kidnapped: Dom Christian (Lambert Wilson), Frère Luc (Michael Lonsdale), Père Christophe (Olivier Rabourdin), Frère Michel (Xavier Maly), Père Bruno (Olivier Perrier), Père Célestin (Philippe Laudenbach), and Frère Paul (Jean-Marie Frin).

The monk's moral choice, bound up in whether they should stay or leave Algeria when confronted with the threats of the terrorists, forms the focus of much of the narrative. Indeed, if a unifying thread emerges from Beauvois's diverse and extensive body of work, it is a sentimental focus on the fortitude and moral imperatives of an individual or individuals who confront a system or situation that challenges their autonomy. Beauvois's career spans four decades, and he began acting and directing short films in the 1980s. His 1991 debut feature film, *Nord*, is a stark coming-of-age tale starring the director and set in his hometown of Calais. His next work, *N'oublie pas que tu vas mourir* (1995), examines the life of a HIV-positive French art historian who embarks on a frenetic quest of sexual and bodily pleasure, before dying in Croatia in the midst of the Yugoslavian War. *Selon Matthieu* (2000) evokes the dramas of suicide and filial revenge in a working-class community in Normandy, while *Le Petit Lieutenant* (2005) is a detective thriller that charts a young policeman's encounters with murder, corruption, and alcoholism within the Parisian police force. Each of these works depicts characters that are embedded in concrete socio-political contexts, and Beauvois strives for an authentic, unflinching gaze on the individuals and issues in question. To this end, for the making of both *Le Petit Lieutenant* and *Des hommes et des dieux*, he conducted a form of observational research before filming, spending time in a police station for the former, and in a French monastery for the latter.

Des hommes et des dieux is Beauvois's most commercially successful film and it was an unprecedented hit at home and abroad, garnering France's official selection for the Foreign Language Oscar in 2010.[1] The film also won the 'Grand Prix' at Cannes, where it received a ten-minute standing ovation at the end of the official screening. The film was exclusively financed by French production companies, including Canal Plus, the CNC (Centre national du cinéma et de l'image animée), France Télévision, and France 3 Cinéma. Made with a comparatively modest budget of four million euros, *Des hommes et des dieux* nevertheless attracted over three million viewers, the kind of audience figures that are usually reserved for Hollywood blockbusters.[2] Critical reception of the film in France and the United Kingdom was overwhelmingly positive, and centred on its explicitly religious themes. Vanessa Thorpe, writing in *The Guardian*, praised the way the film had 'sparked public debate about faith and self-sacrifice and about how religions might work together'.[3] Both the Bishops' Conference of France and the French Council of Muslim Faith lauded the film for demonstrating the ways in which Christians and Muslims can coexist, something that scriptwriter Étienne Comar cites as particularly relevant in contemporary societies: 'the theme of the relationship between the Christians and the Muslims is absolutely contemporary and will find an echo in many countries'.[4] At Cannes, the film also garnered 'Le Prix de l'Éducation nationale' [The National Education Prize], an award given by the Ministère de l'Éducation nationale [The National Education Ministry] to films that are judged to have future pedagogical merit, with the selection criteria being 'l'intérêt cinématographique et pédagogique et les qualités artistiques et culturelles du film' [cinematographic and pedagogical interest and the artistic and cultural qualities of the film].[5] This prize often awards films with historical settings, and previous prize-winners in this category included Haneke's *The White Ribbon* (2009), a dark tale of social decay set in pre-World War One Germany, and Sofia Coppola's *Marie Antoinette* (2006), a kitsch, youthful rendition of the life of the eponymous French queen.

Des hommes et des dieux's recognition by the Ministère de l'Éducation nationale suggests that the film falls easily into the category of what Robert Rosenstone terms 'mainstream historical drama' — films that 'engage the larger *discourse of history*'.[6] Yet it is difficult to discern whose national and political history is being screened in *Des hommes et des dieux*: the film presents the spectator with a sumptuous North African backdrop for what is depicted as an essentially French tragedy. For Benjamin Stora, the representation of the experiences of Algerian civilians in the film constitutes a notable omission, one which points instead towards an implicit hierarchy: 'cette absence [...] me semble problématique et elle est de nature à accroître l'impression de "deux poids deux mesures" [...] entre les deux rives de la Méditerranée' [This absence [...] seems problematic to me, and it is likely to increase the impression that there is a double standard [...] between the two sides of the Mediterranean].[7] Moreover, unlike the millions of Algerians who could not flee, and the 44,000 to 200,000 who lost their lives, the monks did have the option to leave. In this chapter, I consider the historical circumstances surrounding the position of foreigners in the Algerian conflict, the monk's presence in Algeria and their eventual kidnapping, as well as the controversy around their cause of death. I argue that the film might best be characterized as 'heritage' fiction, rather than historical drama, in line with Andrew Higson's definition of this mode of historical representation with reference to British cinema.[8] Heritage films speak more to the present in which they are made than to the time and places they depict. I outline how the film's neo-colonial resonances evoke a nostalgic vision of French presence in Algeria today, and interact with the ideology of universalism and religious and republican values.

Between the Army and the Terrorists: The Monks of Tibhirine

The monastery where the monks lived at Tibhirine, meaning 'gardens' in Kabyle, was originally established by Cistercian monks in 1934 in an abandoned building that had once been a nineteenth century colonial farmhouse.[9] Léon Duval, Archbishop of Algiers from 1954 to 1988, writes that 'Tibhirine was the symbol of a multi-faith post-colonial Algeria where Christians and Muslims, along with Jews, could live together in mutual respect and dialogue'.[10] However, in the tense atmosphere of 1990s Algeria, the presence of the French monks, however harmonious in relation to the local population, came to be resented by terrorist militants and army officials alike. The monks were trapped between opposing factions; the army, who wished to expel them for fear of outside interference, and the terrorists using them as pawns to gain international attention. For the terrorists, the presence of the French monks on Algerian soil was a blatant mark of the continuing control and infiltration of Western culture into the 'pure' Islamic state they wished to create.[11] Moreover, the assassination campaign against foreigners in Algeria had been one of the most effective means of gaining international coverage of the war. The monks, by deliberate choice unarmed and unprotected by the army, provided easy and high-profile targets. The army, on the other hand, was overtly hostile to the presence of foreign witnesses to the war; as Lahouari Addi explains, 'violence is erupting in Algeria in an almost total information blackout. This is hardly by chance; the regime has always preferred the clandestine to the transparent'.[12] The government forcefully censored media information disseminated to Algerians and the outside world. This heavy-handedness also applied to soliciting or accepting help from outside sources. A panel of United Nations visitors was allowed into the country, but almost no aid was received; the subsequent report noted, 'terrorism in Algeria is to be dealt with by Algerians alone'.[13]

In 1996 Algeria was statistically the most dangerous place in the world for foreigners, most of whom were killed by the GIA, who claimed responsibility for the kidnapping of the monks at Tibhirine. Tibhirine is located in an area of the Atlas Mountains to the south of Algiers that came to be known as the 'triangle of death', whose vertices were Algiers, Larbaa, and Blida. On the night of 26 March 1996, seven of the nine monks, Dom Christian de Chergé, Frère Luc Dochier, Père Christophe Lebreton, Frère Michel Fleury, Père Bruno Lemarchand, Père Célestin Ringeard, and Frère Paul Favre-Miville, were kidnapped; Père Jean-Pierre Schumacher and Frère Amédée Noto evaded capture. On 21 May, two months later, they were proclaimed dead. Their heads were discovered on 31 May 1996 and their bodies have never been found. One aspect of the tragedy is still clouded in doubt: the actual cause of death, and at whose hands. This uncertainty is not surprising, given the environment of disorder and fear that prevailed in Algeria at the time. Officially, the GIA claimed responsibility for the attack that had apparently been orchestrated as an attempt to bargain for the release of terrorist Abdelhak Layada in exchange for the monks. However, John Kiser's 2002 history of the kidnapping, *The Monks of Tibhirine: Faith, Love, and Terror in Algeria* illuminated several factors that point towards the involvement of the Algerian army-controlled government.[14] One issue raised was the fact that the heads of the men were flecked with earth, which meant that they had been buried and then dug up, an action that is not concurrent with the throat slitting without burial that was the GIA's usual method of execution. Following the deaths, no information was forthcoming from the Algerian authorities regarding the discovery of the bodies and questions were raised about how the monks could have remained undetected for so long. The Catholic Church wanted to launch an investigation, but found, to their chagrin, that no Algerian lawyers would accept their civil case. Finally, in 2008, *La Stampa* reported that an anonymous Western government official based in Algeria in the 1990s had revealed that Algerian Intelligence Services infiltrated the GIA and orchestrated the kidnapping. According to this official, later named as François Buchwalter, an Algerian military helicopter had killed the monks accidentally.[15]

Funding for *Des hommes et des dieux* was obtained after Kiser's book was translated into French in 2006 by Franco-American historian Henri Quinson (named as 'conseiller monastique' [monastic advisor] on *Des hommes et des dieux*).[16] Therefore, like *Caché*, *Des Hommes et des dieux* came about as a direct result of historical disclosures in the public sphere. However, while many of the names of the victims of the 17 October 1961 massacre remain unknown and they were denied a form of public mourning, no such occlusion occurred with the monks who died at Tibhirine, whose remembrance was an international affair that united the country. As Martin Evans and John Phillips summarize:

President Chirac called the monks the embodiment of tolerance and on television millions shed tears as they watched Cardinal Lustiger, the archbishop of Paris, snuff out the seven candles that had been brought from Tibhirine to Notre Dame cathedral as a sign of hope. Bells were tolled in every church in France on Pentecost Sunday whilst political organizations from across the spectrum marched in memory of the dead brothers.[17]

Moreover, while the memorialization of the victims of the 17 October 1961 massacre divided the political right and left in France (encapsulated in the historical disputes between Jean-Paul Brunet and Jean-Luc Einaudi), the huge outpouring of national grief about the death of the monks cut across both sides of the political spectrum. In a similar sense, the film garnered plaudits from media commentators on the left and right: *Le Figaro*'s Marie-Noëlle Tranchant describes the film as 'le cinéma en état de grâce' [cinema in a state of grace], while Arnaud and Péron, writing for *Libération*, describe a wide public for the film, composed of 'laïcs, athées, croyants, cinéphiles, adeptes de la méditation, militants de la décroissance, [...] passionnés de la question algérienne, nostalgiques d'une nature virgilienne, fans de Michael Lonsdale' [secularists, atheists, believers, film buffs, disciples of meditation, anti-capitalist activists ... people fascinated by the Algerian question, those nostalgic for a Virgilian existence, fans of Michael Lonsdale].[18]

In contrast to *Caché* and *Muriel*, which bring awareness to the historical and social exclusion of Algerians in the past and the present, Beauvois does not attempt to engage marginalized histories at the level of form or content. There is little evidence to suggest that creating awareness of the plight of the monks of Tibhirine has generated discussion about the Algerian victims of a war that Stora has called 'la guerre invisible' [the invisible war].[19] Viewers do not gain a sense of the outcome of the kidnappings, future doubts raised regarding the machinations of the GIA and the Algeria state army, the wider political scene in Algeria or the causes and roots of this struggle. Reaction to the film in Algeria also focused on these historical omissions, as well as the privileging of the deaths of a small group of French men over the elimination of tens of thousands of Algerians. As Stora summarizes, 'En Algérie [...] les commentateurs ne manquent jamais de rappeler que face à ces sept victimes, il ne faudrait pas oublier les dizaines de milliers morts algériens de l'immense tragédie des années 90' [In Algeria, commentators invariably mention that when confronted with these seven victims, it should never be forgotten that tens of thousands of Algerians died in the immense tragedy of the 1990s].[20]

The ambiguity and the historical imbroglio surrounding the exact cause of the monks' deaths and the identity of the perpetrators are not featured in *Des hommes et des dieux*. A title card at the end of the film evokes the mystery surrounding their deaths, but refuses to implicate the Algerian army, in spite of the fact that significant evidence had accumulated by 2010 that pointed to its culpability. Moreover, this lack of historical accuracy, or what perhaps might be best described as a certain historical nebulousness, also applies to the biographical reasons behind the monk's presence in Algeria. Quinson even expresses regret that the film ignores 'la raison profonde de la présence des moines sur cette terre: L'Algérie, mot quasiment jamais prononcé dans le film' [the basic reason for the monks' presence in this land:

Algeria, a word that is almost never uttered in the film]. Many of the monks had deep colonial ties to the country as veterans of the Algerian War or *pied-noirs*, and Quinson describes the monks' roles during and in the aftermath of the conflict in the following terms:

> Christian de Chergé, l'intellectuel de la communauté, féru de dialogue islamo-chrétien, avait été sous-lieutenant pendant la guerre d'Algérie. Son ami Mohammed, un garde-champêtre, s'était interposé et l'avait sauvé de la mort face au FLN. Quelques jours plus tard, Mohammed avait été retrouvé égorgé. Christian en avait été marqué à jamais. Frère Paul, comme parachutiste, avait fait — ou au moins vu — des choses horribles. Quant à frère Luc, "le toubib", il avait déjà été enlevé, en 1959, par des membres du FLN. Amédée était pied-noir et frère Christophe était venu faire la coopération après 1962.
>
> [Christian de Chergé, the intellectual of the community and passionate about Islamo-Christian relations, had been a sub-lieutenant during the French-Algerian War. His friend Mohammed, a rural police officer, had intervened to save his life from the FLN. A few days later, Mohammed was found with his throat slit. Christian had been permanently scarred by the experience. Brother Paul, as a paratrooper, had done — or at least seen — horrible things. As for Brother Luc, the "doc", he had been abducted in 1959 by members of the FLN. Amédée was a *pied-noir*, born in Algeria of French descent, and Brother Christophe had come to do 'coopération' (a government-led foreign aid service) after 1962].[21]

By ignoring the monks' colonial ties to Algeria, the film leaves their presence in the country unquestioned, and removes any culpability from the French viewer: the monks, and by extension France, bear no responsibility for violence in Algeria. The film's historical omissions can also be linked to what Andrew Higson describes as the heritage film's 'fascination with style which displaces the material dimensions of historical context'.[22] Indeed, *Des hommes et des dieux*'s recognizable stars, its broad appeal to a range of ideological, political, and religious beliefs, and to nostalgia, nature, and anti-consumerism, are characteristics that mark it as a 'heritage film'.

Colonial Nostalgia: *Des Hommes et des dieux* as Heritage Fiction

Closely aligned with nationalism and conservative values, the heritage film was first theorized with reference to the English period dramas of the 1980s. Heritage films have broad appeal to wide swathes of the public, and are financially successful in both domestic and foreign markets, straddling the line between arthouse and commercial film (as was the case with *Des hommes et des dieux*). As Higson notes, 'these are the sort of films that are invited to festivals and that win prizes'.[23] One of the charms of heritage film lies in its evocation of national cannons of artistic high culture: literature, classical music, painting, and sculpture, as well as the simplification of complex historical narratives.[24] Higson reads these films as a response to the sweeping changes occurring in British society in the 1980s: multicultural cities, economic reforms that created instability for the working class, and a post-imperialist nation that was unsure of its place in the world, existing uneasily between the European Union and the post-imperial Commonwealth. In response, heritage films like David Lean's *A Passage to India* (1984) and James Ivory's *A Room with a View* (1986) offered a reassuring vision of a whole and wholesome society in a not too distant twentieth century past, in which moral lines were clearly drawn and class and race structures remained happily intact. Moral and political uncertainties are abandoned in favour of what Bélen Vidal, writing about the European heritage film, describes as 'narratives that minimise ambiguity and seek instead to elicit an emotional response to character-driven storytelling structured around satisfying dynamics of conflict and resolution'.[25] Heritage films are not a politically neutral recreation of the past in the present; rather, as Higson writes, they are 'conservative responses to a collective, post-imperialist anxiety'. By 'retreating from the social, political and economic crises of the present', Higson continues, '[heritage films] strive to recapture an image of national identity as pure, untainted, complete and in place'.[26] Although set in recognisable and highly historicized eras of the national past, with World Wars I and II being popular time periods for the French and European heritage film, these works speak deeply to the discontents of the present.

Nostalgia is a key component of the heritage film, evoked through cinematography, characterization, settings, and props. Nostalgia summons a bygone era of national and personal harmony, and etymologically, the term refers to the longing to return home or the recovery of a lost homeland. However, Higson argues that modern nostalgia, referring to the period after the industrial revolution, evokes a temporal rather than a spatial return, a recovery of the past that is profoundly interwoven with 'the things, people, conditions or values associated with that time'.[27] With post-industrial nostalgia, the past is imagined as a space of communitarian, shared values, what he describes as 'a time of innocent pleasures and the community of family and friends, a particular version of home and homeliness'.[28] Within the French context, Sébastien Fevry has described what he calls a nostalgic 'sepia' turn in French cinema in the 2000s. In this category he includes works like *La Guerre des Boutons* (Yann Samuell, 2001), *Les Choristes* (Christophe Barratier, 2004), *Un long dimanche de fiançailles* (Jean-Pierre Jeunet, 2004), and *Le Petit Nicolas* (Laurent Tirard, 2009). Sepia films refer to a twentieth-century past, and while they foreground the lives of 'ordinary' individuals against the backdrop of extraordinary political circumstances, politics never complicates the person-centred narrative; they remain, in Fevry's terms, 'profoundly ahistorical'. Set in rural idylls and small towns and villages rather than major metropolitan areas, these films whitewash French society, 'with not a foreigner or immigrant who might remind the viewers of the debates surrounding immigration or integration in the suburbs'.[29] These films also feature child protagonists, used to convey an image of lost innocence, as these youthful characters can never be held fully morally responsible for their actions. Although clearly the monks are not children, their innocence, chastity, and purity arguably present them as similarly apolitical figures. Indeed, such a return to the innocence of childhood is advocated by Christian teachings: Matthew 18:3 notes that 'truly, I say to you, unless you turn and become like little children, you will never enter the kingdom of heaven'.[30]

In *Des hommes et des dieux*, Camille Champetier's adroit cinematography captures the mountains, and most specifically the monastery, as a nostalgic space of
prelapsarian communion with nature where the monks live a harmonious and
peaceful existence. The opening shot of the film encapsulates the interconnections
between nature, nostalgia, and religious values. The image is a long shot of a
sparsely populated valley filling with a late summer sunset, as threads of gold streak
through high cirrus clouds that touch undulating layers of mountains receding into
the dark background. This image evokes a strongly Christian iconography of God
in heaven, with the golden rays of hope and light offered by the divine breaking
through the dark clouds of earthly existence. Overlaid onto this natural spectacle is
a quote from Psalm 82 in the Bible: 'Je l'ai dit: Vous êtes des dieux, des fils du Très-
Haut, vous tous! Pourtant, vous mourrez comme des hommes, comme les Princes,
tous vous tomberez [I say: You are Gods, the sons of the most high, all of you! But
you shall die like men and fall like any prince] [Figure 5.1]. This quotation evokes
the importance of the individual, as well as their powerlessness in the face of forces
beyond their control. It also foreshadows the eventual death of the monks, who are
both the Gods and men of the film's title, while highlighting their proximity to the
divine. The superimposition of these words onto the image suggests that though
in this rural idyll, humans can be closer to God, they still retain their human
mortality. This long take cedes in silence to a short scene representing the monks
gathering in the chapel for prayer. The muted greys, blues, and whites of their robes
and of the chapel walls are complemented by a single shaft of yellow light from a
candle above the altar, and this colour and spatial composition directly echoes the
aesthetics of the previous shot. The credits continue to roll, and the title of the film
in an archaic serif typeface appears in the centre of the screen at the precise second
that the monks begin to chant in a low, melancholy refrain.

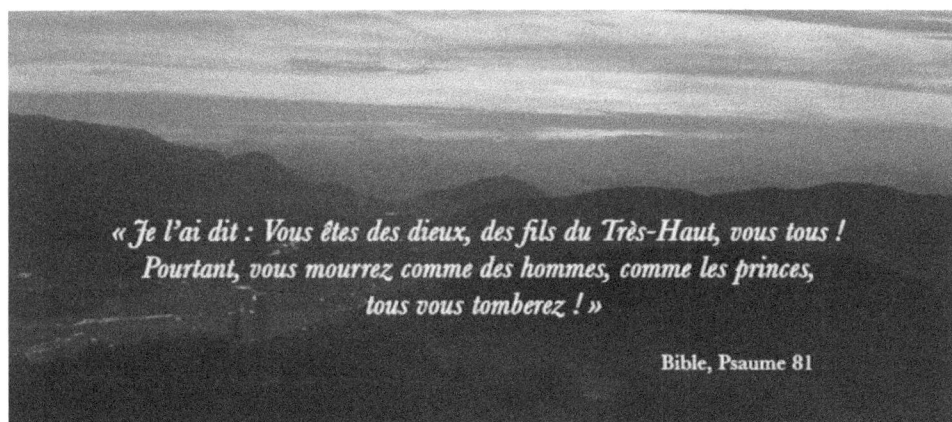

FIG. 5.1. Human and divine landscapes.
Des hommes et des dieux, dir.by Xavier Beauvois (2010).

FIG. 5.2. Harmony and symmetry.
Des hommes et des dieux, dir.by Xavier Beauvois (2010).

There are no jagged edges in this film: the sound and image symmetry of these opening shots mark the spectator's entry into the monastery as an entry into another world, one of seamless harmony and cohesion. The monastery is a religious sanctuary, coded as a space that is separated from the chaos of the outside world. The mise-en-scène also evokes equilibrium and peace: the monks are positioned in a symmetrical V-shape in the chapel, or in lines on opposite sides [Figure 5.2]. As they sit at communal tables in the refectory or the library, they are evenly spaced and positioned at the same height, as are the rustic desks at which they read and write, communally, in silence. The film privileges long, slow takes, and long shots of the monks' prayers and daily duties; this camerawork creates a sense of the timelessness of the monk's simple existences, while creating distance and objectivity in the spectator: we are observers in this world, a world that moves serenely and continually, in spite of our intrusion. Sound and image disjunctions are used to contrast the silence and stillness of the monastery and the scenes in the village. In one of the opening sequences, the perfectly symmetrical image of the monks chanting in the chapel cuts abruptly to the scene of a wedding in the village, where the multi-layering of men, women, and children on walls and steps interrupts this calm cohesion, with the *youyous* (traditional North African incantations) of the women disrupting the steady, melodic chanting of the monks. The cinematography throughout uses colour tonalities to highlight narrative causality: varying shades of cerulean, azure, and navy are associated with times of trouble, for example, the arrival of the terrorists, while yellow tones capture moments of rural harmony as the monks work the land or move through the landscape.

Another aspect of the film's evocation of nostalgia for a lost time of personal and spiritual harmony is its depiction of human communion with the natural world. As Vidal notes, the heritage film creates 'a strong sense place, which arises from evocative landscapes, geographical landmarks, local customs'.[31] The film returns the spectator to an apparently simpler time, and although the film is set in the 1990s, the depiction of a rural setting in a non-Western country creates the sense of a much more distant pastoral past. The monks are shown digging the earth, pausing to smell the air, watering, hoeing, beekeeping, and painstakingly washing the floors on their knees with a cloth and bucket, in slow, meditative circular movements. This is depicted as a world of bucolic, sensory pleasures: eating the food one has grown with one's own hands, and carefully potting honey and attaching handwritten labels that evoke a grounded geographical site: 'Miel d'Atlas' [Honey from the Atlas Mountains]. The monk's intellectual lives are marked by an absence of technology: reading, writing, and contemplation of the dusky, sepia-framed artworks that adorn the monastery occupy their rest periods. Communication with the outside world is limited, and mostly takes place through letters and personal visits, and although there is a telephone, it is a large contraption that would appear more *in situ* in the 1960s, rather than the 1990s, and is rarely used. Technology is presented as both unreliable and unnecessary: even the old tractor malfunctions, and the monks and their Algerian farm labourers return to ploughing by hand. Time moves more slowly in this dewy world: the monks delicately water verdant green plots at sunset, with birds tweeting and a donkey braying in the background. They enjoy late evening strolls on the grounds in companionable silence, and have time to pause in their farming labour to contemplate the landscape. In one such sequence, Frère Christophe is digging the earth with an Algerian worker, who gently castigates the monk: 'tu dors, mon Frère' [Brother, you're half-asleep!], suggesting that perhaps life for the Algerian villagers is more bound up in material concerns than it is for the monks.

By constructing the monastery as a nostalgic haven from the vicissitudes of the modern world, temporal and spatial nostalgia intertwine, and the desire to return to the harmonious, gentle pace of life in the past comingles with the desire to return to a lost homeland, a geographical terrain that is problematically figured as the ex-colonial site of contemporary Algeria. The rose-tinted vision of rural life in an ex-colony points towards a broader refiguring of the colonial past in France, and a reticence in acknowledging colonial violence and exploitation. Nicolas Bancel and Pascal Blanchard remark upon the reluctance of certain French scholars to consider the representational ambiguities of colonial and postcolonial cultural production. They link this hesitancy to the unwillingness of certain factions in French society to admit wrongdoing in their former colonies. As they point out, this has even resulted in a troubling political volte-face: 'over the last decade there has [...] been a desire to "rehabilitate" the colonial project, to deny the link between colonialism and racial hierarchies by proposing a humanist vision of France's colonial activity'.[32] In 2005, this positive reappraisal of France's colonial project assumed a legal visage: the controversial 'Loi 2005–158 du 23 février 2005 portant reconnaissance de la Nation et contribution nationale en faveur des Français rapatriés' [Law 2005–158 of 23 February 2005 acknowledging the Nation and the national contribution in support of repatriated French people] suggests that school curricula should recognize in particular 'le rôle positif de la présence française outre-mer, notamment en Afrique du Nord' [the positive role of the French presence abroad, not least in North Africa].[33]

Nostalgia is not a politically neutral aesthetic; rather, Kimberly Smith argues, it is 'an ideologically charged construct. And its configuration [...] reflects long-standing debates about whose memories count, what kind of attachments and modes of life are valuable, and what harms are politically relevant'.[34] The desire to rewrite the colonial past in nostalgic terms is not only a twenty-first century endeavour, nor is it confined to France. Paul Gilroy coins the term colonial nostalgia to refer to British recreations of the Indian Raj in popular film and television, in examples like David Lean's *A Passage to India*, John Madden's *The Best Exotic Marigold Hotel* (2011) and Danny Boyle's *Slumdog Millionaire* (2008). Gilroy describes colonial nostalgia in the following terms:

> The idea of the empire gets (re)visited obsessively because its loss remains painful but cannot be worked through. Britain might learn too many uncomfortable truths about its history if it was known and considered. In the absence of that encounter, phenomena such as the Raj get recycled as fantasy. The lost greatness of the imperial period can thereby be fleetingly restored.[35]

Gilroy's statement highlights the seductive nature of colonial nostalgia and how it negates historical realities in order to recreate and revisit periods of former national glory. Moreover, the works he cites are set in the period of the Raj, but also in the present day, and they draw on the same stereotypical imagery of India: bright colours, rich foods, populous cities, and white protagonists who seek personal fulfilment in non-Western spaces. *Des hommes et des dieux* draws on a variety of colonial stereotypes in its depiction of a contemporary French presence in Algeria. Indeed, colonial residues are firstly inflected in the setting of the film: filming actually took place at the Benedectine monastery of Tioumliline in Meknès, Morocco, an issue which points towards a perception of exchangeability between one North African former colony and the next. This choice of location also reflects the dangers of filming in Algeria, an issue that is significant in and of itself, because it points towards the continuing violence, a violence that is not gestured towards in *Des hommes et des dieux*.

Indeed, in its depiction of the monks and their relation to the terrorists and the villagers, the film reiterates the colonial stereotypes of the benevolent and Christian colonizer, and the naïve or evil native.[36] Thus, the terrorists in the film are wicked outsiders who transgress the boundaries of the monastery with violent force. The spectator's first introduction to them is when they arrive at a building site where there are Croatian labourers, and brutally cut their throats. Apart from Ali Attiya (Farid Larbi), the terrorists remain an undifferentiated group, in drab garb, with their faces partially concealed [Figure 5.3]. In order to distance them further from the spectator, they are always referred to in the third person plural. The terrorists, like the villagers, are depicted as an undifferentiated grouping, in contrast to the careful humanization of the monks. Terrorism in the film is an act that happens beyond the boundaries of the monks' carefully modulated existences: beyond the monastery and in the distant mountains. At several moments in the film, the villagers disclaim any knowledge of the terrorists' identities. While possibly aiming to depict unity between the peaceful villagers and the monks, such distancing is

FIG. 5.3. The terrorists. *Des hommes et des dieux*, dir.by Xavier Beauvois (2010).

historically inaccurate.[37] As films by Algerians like Bachir-Chouikh's *Rachida*, Sahraoui's *Baracat* and *Yema* demonstrate, terrorists in Algeria were not shadowy, external agents, with little or no ties to the population, but rather brothers, fathers, cousins, sons, and husbands. Indeed, Stora notes, part of the invisibility of the Algerian Civil War arose out of the ordinary civilian's inability to side with either the terrorists or the army: 'l'invisibilité de cette guerre vient aussi de son impossible identification à l'un ou à l'autre des acteurs qui s'affrontent férocement. Et comment trouver la "majorité silencieuse" qui résiste au monde truqué qui l'entoure?' [The invisibility of this war also comes from the fact that the Algerian people cannot identify with either of the principal parties who confront each other so ferociously. How, then, do we uncover the "silent majority" who resist the false world that surrounds them?].[38]

This silent majority remains, for the most part, silent in *Des hommes et des dieux*. If the terrorists conform to the depiction of the sly and malign native, the villagers in the film are the naïve, childlike colonial subjects who live in poverty and are uneducated, and therefore require humanitarian assistance. Villagers, apart from an imam and a woman who works at the monastery, are mostly depicted in groups, huddled fearfully outside its walls when the army arrives, or wandering en masse along the roads and streets surrounding the village. Moreover, the spatial distinctions between the village and the monastery recall the division of the colonial city depicted in *La Bataille d'Alger*, and described by Fanon in the following terms:

> Le monde colonisé est un monde coupé en deux. [...] La ville du colon est une ville en dur, toute de pierre et de fer. C'est une ville illuminée, asphaltée, où les poubelles regorgent toujours de restes inconnus, jamais vus. [...] La ville du colonisé est une ville affamée, affamée de pain, de viande, de chaussures, de charbon, de lumière.

> [The colonial world is a world cut in two. [...] The settlers' town is strongly built, with everything in stone and steel.. It's well-lit; the streets are tarmaced, and the refuse bins are crammed with leftovers that are never seen. [...] The native town is a famished town, starved of bread, meat, shoes, coal and light].[39]

Thus, while the village is consistently filmed in blue or grey light, the monastery glows with golden and sepia tones. The monks' residence is located at the top of a steep slope, and in order to get to the monastery, one must literally ascend, mimicking the language of spiritual ascension predominant in Christianity. While the village is strewn with rubble, rubbish, exposed wires, cracked steps, and fissured gable ends, the stonework of the monastery, although an older building, seems meticulously maintained, retaining only the elegance of age, and not its decay. Although the lands around the monastery are a rich and verdant green, no fertile pastures are visible in the village and its environs.

The fact that villagers are hired by the monks to help cultivate the land, while they have no crops of their own, raises questions about the 'relations de non-puissance' [relationships without power] and 'pauvreté radicale' [radical poverty] to which the monks claim to adhere. The expansive and lush grounds they occupy, the products of land and earth that they cultivate, and the power they wield as doctors and administrative assistants solidifies their position of dominance within this community. This hierarchy is also figured spatially: while the monks pass easily among the locals, highlighting their place of privilege, the locals' access to the monastery is predicated on labour and charity: they may only enter as workers, or recipients of aid. These relations are further underscored by the dependency on the monks the villagers exhibit for protection from the terrorists, in spite of the historical reality that the presence of the monks themselves would have drawn the terrorists to the area. One villager states, 'les oiseaux c'est nous, la branche c'est vous, si vous partez nous ne saurons pas où se poser' [We are the birds, and you are the branches. If you leave, we won't know where to perch]. Frère Christian further evokes his role as a good shepherd leading his flock out of danger: 'un bon Berger n'abandonne pas son troupeau quand le loup arrive' [A good shepherd does not abandon his flock when the wolf appears]. It appears that only French subjects can protect Algerian natives from their compatriots.

Such statements cannot help but carry evident and uncomfortable overtones of the *mission civilisatrice* [civilizing mission], the belief that the French presence in Algeria was a Christian and generous action undertaken for the benefit of a deprived people. A speech in Laurent Herbiet's *Mon colonel*, set during the Algerian War, sums up the core tenets of the civilizing mission, when a party of French *pieds-noirs* organize a politicised picnic on some Roman ruins. The colonel of the title makes a speech, noting that 'ce pays a toujours eu besoin d'une autre civilisation pour le féconder. Il y a plus que 2000 ans c'était les Romains, [...] nous avons aujourd'hui la responsabilité de cette mission civilisatrice' [this country has always needed another civilization to enrich it. 2000 years ago it was the Romans...today, we have the responsibility of that civilizing mission]. Similarly, a scarcely disguised neo-colonialism marks the monks' paternalistic attitude towards the villagers, and the monastery itself seems to serve as a kind of colonial administration centre. The brothers offer employment to locals, acting as doctors, providing clothes and shoes, and assisting in dealing with the French administration. Such actions again have an uncomfortable resonance with the actions of the French authorities preceding and during the Algerian War, when medical assistance and clothing were distributed in villages as a means to gain support among the population for the French cause.[40] These sequences all occur at the beginning of the film, before the terrorists are introduced in the narrative, and they seem designed to stress the benevolence of the monks, their innocent charity. In one such sequence, a woman who visits with a child who has a head wound is treated like a child herself. Luc dresses the wound, but the woman does not leave, and without speaking, she coyly looks down at her feet encased in worn plastic sandals. Luc remarks in a tone of mock seriousness, as one might to a child who has asked for a lollipop, 'oh je vois! Oh là là! C'est grave!' [Oh I see! Dear oh dear! This is serious!]. The woman bites her lip, looking at him from underneath her eyebrows, and silently accepts the shoes, smiling.

In another sequence, Luc prescribes medication to a middle-aged man, and he painstakingly notates the times and quantity of medicine to be taken with pictures of a sun and moon, and single lines on a piece of paper. Adult literacy rates in Algeria in 1997 were 60%, so it is not entirely improbable that the man could not read or write.[41] Yet the fact that the monks have not learned spoken Arabic in their many decades in the country, and the emphasis on the childishness of the drawings as a mode of communication with the villagers again underscores their dependency on the French Christians. Another instance of the infantilizing attitude of the monks towards the villagers occurs when Jean-Pierre is helping an elderly woman to send a letter to her son. Jean-Pierre speaks to her in fragmented sentences in French, and the woman does not reply for the duration of the sequence, except to describe her son's current domicile in France, saying, 'il habite loin maintenant' [he lives far away now]. The woman must know that her child lives in France, but by giving her this vague, simplistic speech, the film distances France from any colonial responsibility (why has he chosen to live there?), while simultaneously underlining the naïve, apolitical, ahistorical mindset of the villagers.

The phenomenon of nostalgia for the French presence in Algeria is common enough to warrant its own neologism: *nostalgérie* [nostalgeria]. Although the term rose to prominence in the 1990s with the publication of Derrida's *Circonfession* (1991) and *Le Monolinguisme de l'autre* [The Monolingualism of the Other] (1996), Philip Dine notes that *nostalgérie* is a constant theme of an entire body of French artistic productions that date back to Louis Bertrand's *Le Sang des races* [*The Blood of Races*] in 1899.[42] Works in the *nostalgérie* mode express a longing for an untainted and peaceful past in the country, and like the films of the sepia wave, many are set in childhood. Derrida's *Circonfession* and *Le Monolinguisme de l'autre* both chart a boyhood lived in the bright streets of Algiers, and the dislocation he felt upon independence in 1962 when he moved to France. Derrida describes himself as neither French nor Algerian, and notes that because of his Jewish heritage, he was an outsider in colonial Algeria under the Vichy regime, and an interloper as a Jew upon independence. Hélène Cixous's texts also focus on her childhood. The short story 'Pieds nus' and *Les Rêveries de la femme sauvage: Scènes primitives* [Dreams of a Wild Woman: Primal Scenes] (2000) take up the theme of the *pied-noir* exile from Algeria, with the title of the later work evoking the stereotype of the wild and primitive colony.[43]

FIG. 5.4. The army invades the monastery.
Des hommes et des dieux, dir.by Xavier Beauvois (2010).

Lynne Huffer argues that this return to childhood innocence allows the protagonists of these works to be removed from the political complexities of their
presence as colonizers in the country, just as the monks' purity and godliness distances
them from any political responsibilities. Huffer discusses the nostalgic discourse
about Algeria in French society and among French intellectuals in the present day,
focusing particularly on Derrida's Algerian works. She argues that the image of a
harmonious past presented in works of *nostalgérie* 'allows France to express horror
at Algeria's current violence without attending to the difficult moral and political
question of France's historical relationship to the present state of affairs'.[44] The only
overt reference to French colonialism in *Des hommes et des dieux* is made by an army
general who implores the monks to leave, and evokes the French imperial mission
as 'ce cambriolage organisé qui nous a retardé' [that organized plundering which
held us back]. The general's statement does underscore the 'retarded' development
of the country, which echoes the monks' neocolonial and paternalistic attitudes
towards the villagers, their handouts and patronizing ministrations. Yet while this
notion of 'organized plundering' alludes to the pillaging of resources enacted by
French authorities during the colonial period, it is implicitly contrasted with the
benignity of the monk's presence in the village as doctors, therapists, peacemakers,
and farmers. The statement is also uttered by a highly suspect and unsympathetic
character, who in the subsequent scene invades the monastery by military force,
enacting another form of state-organized incursion. During this invasion, the army
aggressively coerces the women and children who are waiting outside the medical
centre to check their documentation, lining them up alongside the monks [Figure
5.5]. The composition of this scene almost directly echoes a scene from *Mon colonel*,
where the French army disembark in a rural village and round up its inhabitants
to check their papers. Thus, the memory of French military violence in Algeria is
screened from the spectator by the more immediate association of brutality with
the Algerian army.

When Christian disagrees with the Algerian general regarding their decision to stay in Algeria, stating that 'nous sommes aussi tristes que vous' [we are just as sad as you are], the general responds gruffly, 'qu'est ce que vous en savez? C'est mon pays' [what do you know about it? This is my country]. This again raises the question of why, exactly, the monks have decided to stay in Algeria and what they hope their role in the conflict might be. As the monks struggle to decide whether to stay or go back to France, many of them arrive at the conclusion that there is nothing left for them in their country of origin. Michel says quietly, 'personne ne m'attend nul part. Je reste' [I have no one waiting for me anywhere. I'm staying], while Luc adds, 'partir, c'est mourir' [to leave is to die]. They feel that there is no longer, if there ever was, a space for them in the outside world beyond the monastery and certainly beyond Algeria. In this sense, their predicament echoes many second and third generation Muslims in France, who feel caught between two cultures and two civilisations, and at home concretely in neither.[45] In an essay discussing Derrida's critique of hospitality (based on his own experiences of exile), Kevin O'Gorman notes that 'France had enjoyed one side of the reciprocal arrangement but hospitality was not reciprocated to those who wished to come as "guests" to France; the former hosts were not welcomed as guests'.[46] Hospitality, in *Des hommes et des dieux*, is displaced to the former colony, whose natives extend a heartfelt welcome that has not always been returned to Algerians coming to France. Ultimately, while the inter-religious harmony depicted in the film is certainly admirable, it is worth emphasising that this harmony comes about on Algerian, rather than French soil, and it is a harmony that relies on the hospitality of the locals, founded on unequal economic and social relations.

Postcolonial Malaise: Universalism and Republican Values

Fevry links the sepia wave of film to the politics and memorial practices of the Sarkozy era, which he broadly categorizes as 2002–2012, when Sarkozy served twice as Minister for the Interior and then as President, from 2007–2012.[47] *Des hommes et des dieux* falls squarely within this timeline, and the film's depiction of a nostalgic and colonial past, populated by wise Frenchmen and rustic natives existing outside of historical and political time, corresponds closely to a vision of Africa outlined by Sarkozy in a speech at the Cheikh-Anta-Diop University in Dakar on 26 July 2007. Sarkozy stated:

> Le drame de l'Afrique, c'est que l'homme africain n'est pas assez entré dans l'histoire. Le paysan africain, qui depuis des millénaires, vit avec les saisons, dont l'idéal de vie est d'être en harmonie avec la nature, ne connaît que l'éternel recommencement du temps rythmé par la répétition sans fin des mêmes gestes et des mêmes paroles.[48]

> [The drama of Africa is that the African has no place in history. The African peasant, whose life has been governed by the seasons for thousands of years, whose ideal is to be in harmony with nature, experiences only the eternal renewal of time, cadenced by the endless repetition of the same gestures and the same words].

While Sarkozy's speech was roundly critiqued by many, including Doudou Diène, UN Special Rapporteur on contemporary forms of racism, these words point to deeply held conceptions about France's role in its former territories.[49] While Sarkozy does cite the crimes of colonialism in this speech, including violence, the exploitation of human and natural resources, and the destruction of native cultures, languages, and art forms, he is also at pains to stress the positive aspects of Europe's mission in Africa (reminiscent of the 'Loi 2005–158 du 23 février 2005'). In this endeavour, he consistently lays an emphasis on ideas of universalism and humanity, even going so far as to appropriate chattel slavery not as a specifically African or black experience, but rather as a 'crime contre l'homme, ce fut un crime contre l'humanité toute entière' [crime against man, it was a crime against all of humanity].[50] Indeed, in attempting to justify the speech, special advisor to the Élysée Henri Guaino argues that Sarkozy was simply highlighting the aforementioned 'positive aspects' of French colonialism: 'il y a tous les crimes, mais il y a aussi les droits de l'homme, l'égalité hommes-femmes, l'universalisme' [there are all the crimes, but there are also human rights, gender equality, and universalism].[51] This positive appraisal of France's role in its former African colonies is thus explicitly tied to the idea of universalism, a theme which appears and reappears throughout the speech in relation to the French language, gender, and European values. The most notable example is Sarkozy's description of 'Europe', which in contrast to the ahistorical, pastoral, and 'rhythmic' nature of Africa, 'est l'appel à la raison et à la conscience universelles' [is the call to universal reason and consciousness].[52]

The heritage film is not ideologically impartial, but rather espouses a particular set of values. The principal value espoused by *Des hommes et des dieux* is a form of French universalism which is intertwined with the tenets of Catholicism and republicanism. Universalism is the belief in a shared public existence with a common set of values, values that are immutable and non-relativist. Opposed to the expression of difference in the public sphere, be it ethnic, religious, national, or otherwise, universalism was born out of the 'universal revolution' of 1789, and it is closely interwoven with the Enlightenment philosophies of Rousseau and Voltaire. Universalism, writes Naomi Schor, 'was grounded in the belief that human nature — that is, rational human nature — was universal, impervious to cultural and historical differences. Transcultural, transhistorical human nature was posited as identical, beyond particularisms'. Schor explains that universalism was a key component in France's colonial mission, but the attempted application of the concept in the colonies in fact led to some of the term's current discreditation, due to its association with the denigration and destruction of local cultures and peoples.[53] In the present day, universalism is bound up in an assimilationist approach to immigration, the inverse of a cultural relativism that foregrounds differences, as in the discourses of identity politics and multiculturalism in the UK and the US. Universal citizens in France, Susan Terrio writes, 'regardless of their regional, ethnic, or religious origin, are entitled, even required, to come together as equals to enact secular rituals and to reinforce the shared values of the social order'.[54]

One of the major critiques of universalism by feminists and race theorists is that it assumes the position of the white, male, and often property-owning subject as the norm, and espouses this perspective as an impartial and logical.[55] The monks are universal, Enlightenment subjects *par excellence*: white, male, intellectual, Christian, and French. *Des hommes et des dieux* consistently aligns the spectator with the monks' experiences and consequently, with their values, through narrative perspective, sentimental identification, and point of view shots. As scriptwriter Étienne Comar explains, 'le film a adopté à 100% le point de vue des moines, qui ont toujours veillé à rester neutres, à ne pas prendre parti' [The film adopted the point of view of the monks, 100%. They were always careful to stay neutral, not to take sides].[56] Many of the long panning shots of the idyllic landscape culminate in a medium close up of a monk, surveying the land, a small smile on his face, signalling to the audience that the landscape shot viewed was not neutral, but rather from the perspective of a monk [Figure 5.5]. The landscape sequences in which the monks survey the rolling, empty hills at their feet create an image of the French protagonist as colonial adventurer. In one such sequence, Christian holds his hand above his eyes and takes in a vast empty landscape, smiling with satisfaction, alone with only unpopulated and uncultivated fields and mountains before him. Such imagery recalls the notion of *terra nullius* in Africa and other colonies, the idea that colonial lands were essentially unoccupied before Europeans came, because the 'barbaric' nature of the inhabitants nullified their claims to the territory.[57] The pathetic fallacy is used in a sequence when monastery leader Christian, the good shepherd, tormented by indecision, walks outside alone and is suddenly overtaken by a flock of sheep. He is visually and symbolically transfigured into the beneficent Christian shepherd leading his flock, and the viewer is invited to imagine his inner dialogue, his self-visualization in this role, as the Algerian landscape moulds itself around his mood and his thoughts. Geoffrey Nowell-Smith also remarks on these strategies of audience identification, pointing to a sequence in which two of the monks reach a roadblock that has been set up by the army, and they witness the dead body of a single terrorist, surrounded by tanks and armed militia. The scene

FIG. 5.5. Audience identification and landscapes shots.
Des hommes et des dieux, dir.by Xavier Beauvois (2010).

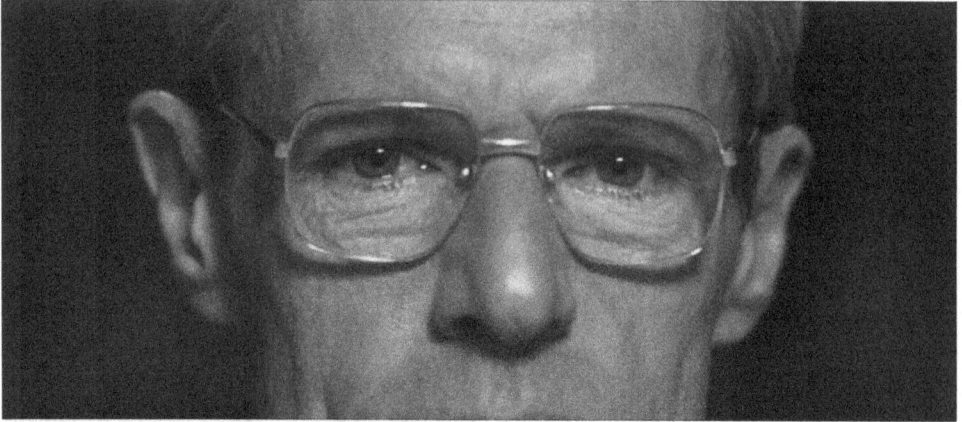

FIG. 5.6. Swan Lake — extreme close ups.
Des hommes et des dieux, dir. by Xavier Beauvois (2010).

is filmed entirely from the monks' point of view, and Nowell-Smith argues that 'the experience of victimhood is transferred from the dead terrorist to the monk witnessing the dead body'.[58]

Such strategies of audience identification are not politically or ideologically neutral; as Susan Hayward notes, 'cinema is an ideological apparatus by nature of its very seamlessness. We do not see how it produces meaning — it renders it invisible, naturalizes it'.[59] It is worth emphasizing the term 'seamlessness', for as I have outlined, *Des hommes et des dieux* is an extremely seductive film because of the smooth, plastic quality of its visual and auditory surface. This flawlessness is combined with a hefty dose of sentimentality and emotion: although the film is generally classified as a drama, it contains many elements of melodrama, the most evident being its narrative trajectory of order and paradise, disorder, and order restored.[60] The film's affective charge is always directed towards eliciting the sympathies of the audience for the monks and sentimentality, melodrama, and audience identification reaches its climax in the final sequences of the film: the monks' Swan Song, their Last Supper which takes place to the famous overture of Tchaikovsky's *Swan Lake*. This musical segment, taken from Act II, No. 10 (Moderato), is first played in the ballet when the owl-like sorcerer Van Rothbart appears on stage to transform the beautiful maiden Odette into a swan. Symbolically coded in black in most productions of the opera, Van Rothbart is the epitome of evil, with Odette, dressed in white feathers, as the representation of fragile goodness. The moral implications of this dance of dark and light in the film are clear: the monks are facing death and abduction, helpless in the face of a great evil that is threatening to engulf them and waiting for the transformation from life into death. The monks are even dressed in white robes, while the terrorists are clad in black. As the music swells, the camera pans across the monks in long shot, and as the sequence progresses, the image moves closer and closer, through medium shots, into close ups of individual faces, and finally resting on extreme close ups [Figure 5.6]. The camera moves in time with the increasing tempo of the music, synching growing proximity with the darkening swells of the score. This progression, combined with the familiar melody that saturates the audible field, draws the spectator into the emotional world of the monks: we know, as they do, that they face imminent death. The faces of the elderly men in close up are extremely emotive: fear, hope, sadness, regret, bravery, acceptance, nostalgia, pensiveness, and love are all made manifest in individual expressions, as the camera captures tearful eyes and wrinkled skin.

This sequence highlights how the monks are individualized and united, separate and together, and this interplay can be tied to Beauvois's conception of the monks' democratic impulses. The opening scenes in the chapel remain resolutely non-hierarchical, as shown in the simple symmetry of the mise-en-scène with four monks on either side, fanning outwards in a V-shape with the camera behind the group. However, after the terrorists first arrive at the monastery and the army moves in to offer protection that Christian refuses, the monks have their first meeting and individual personalities begin to emerge. In the chapel scene following their discussion about whether to leave Algeria, the camera angle shifts: we see the group from the front, and as they each approach the altar with offerings, close-ups of their individual expressions create a sense of singularities within the group that had not been evident up to this point. Beauvois links the monks' decision-making process to a French political and social sense of self: 'ce film montre des hommes libres. Et puis ils décident ensemble, démocratiquement, en se réunissant en chapitres. [...] Je résume cela par: liberté, égalité, fraternité!' [This film shows free men. And then they decide together, democratically, in their assemblies. [...] I sum that up as liberty, equality, fraternity!].[61] The frères insist that Christian's solitary decision to refuse the army's help has endangered the democratic principles upon which the community was founded, and the process is indeed depicted as resolutely democratic. They each form their own opinion individually, come together to discuss it as a group, and happily, they reach the same conclusion, becoming a paragon of the universalist norm outlined by John Bowen: 'citizens must all subscribe to the same values in the public sphere'.[62]

Yet the representation of democratic, universalist, and republican values in the film becomes inseparable from the logic Christian sacrifice. Indeed, although universalism and assimilationist politics in the public sphere in France are, in the present day, closely tied to secularism, Schor argues that universalism as a doctrine actually grew out of France's privileged relationship with the Catholic Church (from the Greek Katholikos, meaning 'universal'). Norman Ravitch even contends that the deepest value in French national identity is religion, rather than universalism: 'it is probably religion which sustains that deeper core of national identity, but certainly not without creating new dilemmas and new controversies'.[63] Des hommes et des dieux both exploits and denies the importance of its religious themes. In terms of the film's promotion and reception, Beauvois stresses the universal values of the film, as a 'drama' that 'describes men', moving beyond religion: '[Le scénario] allait au-delà de la religion. On ne parle pas ici d'un fait divers, mais d'un drame.' [The script] went beyond religion. This isn't just about some minor news item, it's a serious drama].[64] Journalists in France were cautious about overtly praising the religious aspects of the film, yet a muted jubilance peppered with Christian terminology creeps into the writing of many French commentators. For *Libération*, the wide audience that the film managed to reach, which included atheists, Algerian historians, Christians and Muslims, was nothing short of 'un miracle' [a miracle].[65] *Le Parisien*, perhaps unwilling to evoke religious themes that might be at odds with French secularism while also assuaging potential scepticism, asked: 'un film religieux? Non. Un film transcendant? Oui' [A religious film? No. A transcendent film? Yes].[66] This insistence on the film's 'transcendence' rather than its religiosity belies the publicity team's vigorously targeted audience: Catholics in France. Publicist Stéphane Célérier admits to having 'beaucoup ciblé la communauté catholique' [targeted the Catholic community a lot] and Jean-François Petit, who conducted a detailed empirical survey of the promotion of the film in the Catholic Press, goes so far as to call the work 'un phénomène de presse catholique' [a phenomenon created by the Catholic Press] because of the contribution of Catholic networks to the film's success.[67] Moreover, theological journals have published much of the academic criticism of the film, and these articles focus variously on the liturgical and Eucharistic resonances in the film, its depiction of monastic life, and the ideals of Christian hospitality it evokes.[68]

The issue here is not that the film appeals to Catholic and Christian cinemagoers and critics, but that this appeal is couched in a language of universalist, republican values, rather than the language of religion. The intertwining of the monks' fates with religion is coded symbolically throughout the film, beginning with a series of recurring shots of a statue of the Virgin Mary outside the monastery: as the future of the monks looks increasingly uncertain, Mary moves from full, sunlit illumination, through dark, stormy rain showers with water glistening on her upturned hands, to eventually being shrouded in snow. In the final sequence of the film, following the abduction of the monks by the terrorists, the film depicts a series of shots of a snow-covered monastery, the camera lingering on the now whitened, forlorn Virgin Mary statue. As the camera moves through a number of long takes of Christian tombstones, crosses and the silent, abandoned chapel covered in snow, the images are overlaid with the voice of Christian, who says:

> S'il m'arrivait un jour [...] d'être victime du terrorisme qui semble vouloir englober maintenant tous les étrangers vivant ici, j'aimerais que ma communauté, mon église, ma famille, se souviennent que ma vie était donnée à Dieu et à ce pays.

> [If I should one day... become a victim of the terrorism whose target now seems to include all foreigners living here, I would like my community, my church, my family, to remember that my life was devoted to God, and to this country].

These words underscore Christian's and the monks' sense of their duty to the country and the reasons that they decided to stay and be killed, but it is worth noting that he highlights the 'foreigners' who are engulfed by the violence, rather than the country and its civilians as a totality. Moreover, the shots of empty, snow-filled spaces and the Christian crosses overlaid with a melancholy voice strongly echo the final scene in John Huston's adaptation of James Joyce's short story *The Dead* (1987).

Joyce's work and Houston's adaptation explore the existential anxieties of living life in the face of death, and how one might confront mortality in a world where religion and faith no longer provide reassurance. While the final, snowy sequences in both films stress human defencelessness in the face of death, *Des hommes et des dieux* reaffirms the power of religion in the face of deliberate martyrdom, in an Algeria where others are fighting ceaselessly not to die. The monks are marched by the terrorists into a great foggy expanse, still standing in symmetrical lines. The film closes not on their actual death, but rather on a vague departure, as they move out of view into the snowstorm, fading out into a corner of the image like the filmic technique of the iris. There is an odd unity between the monks and their captors at the end, the terrorists moving alongside the brothers, each group having deliberately put itself in this horrific climate out of adherence to a belief system. The final words of the voiceover announce that Christian believes, 'Islam, pour ce pays, c'est un corps et une âme' [Islam, for this country, is a body and a soul].

This leads the audience to ask whether Christianity is to France as the soul is to the body. For Beauvois, the monks' sacrifice is fundamentally tied to forms of Christian courage: 'il y a une phrase de Jean-Paul II qui me plaît: "n'ayez pas peur". Les frères aussi vivent comme ça. [...] Oui, frère Christian ne se laisse pas intimider' [There's a saying of John Paul II's that I like: "do not be afraid". The monks live by this rule too. [...] Yes, Brother Christian does not let himself be intimidated].[69] This association between Christian sacrifice and bravery in the face of terrorism means that the film does not provide the secular, atheist, or non-Christian viewer with any sense of how one resists or confronts terrorism emotionally without the posited reassurances of deep, Christian faith. Nor does it offer any strategy for confronting terror in the political sphere, beyond what appears, removed from the trappings of faith, to be blind acceptance of likely death. At one point in the film, Frère Luc speaks about his lack of fear of the terrorists, citing his time in the French resistance, invoking a shared and glorified moment of the national, republican past. He says to Christian, 'laissez passer l'homme libre' [let the free man pass]. As Fevry points out, references to the Resistance occur frequently in sepia film, because of its perception as a moment of communal national glory. Yet Luc's freedom from fear is twinned to his deep devotion to a Christian God: how those without faith confront terrorism, and why fear is not a rational response to unpredictable violence, is unarticulated, in favour of a glorification of Christian bravery, disguised as republicanism.[70]

The values of French republicanism are notoriously slippery; as Jacques Rancière writes of the national outpouring of patriotic grief in the aftermath of the Charlie Hebdo attacks, 'les défilés ont réuni sans distinction ceux qui défendaient les principes d'une vie en commun et ceux qui exprimaient leurs sentiments xeno-phobes' [The marches brought together, without differentiation, those who def-ended the principles of a shared existence and those who expressed their xeno-phobic sentiments].[71] By eliding the distinction between secular republicanism and religious sentiment, the film implicitly associates French nationalism with a Christian heritage and in so doing, raises questions of cultural belonging and assimilation of second and third generation Algerian and Maghrebi migrants in

France in the present day. In this sense, the film evokes long-standing debates about secularism and the role of the Catholic Church in civic life in France, and there are evident contradictions between the policy of religion as a private practice and the very public role that France's Catholic heritage plays in political and cultural life. Indeed, in an interview with *Le Monde* about the assassination of the monks in May 1996, Cardinal Lustiger argues that Muslims in France must accept that French Catholicism and French republican values are inseparable, by virtue of their shared roots in national history and culture. He further states that immigrants must accept this history in order to claim a French identity: 'chacun de ceux qui se réclament [une identité française] doit se considérer comme un hériter légitime de la totalité de l'histoire de la France, de ses souvenirs glorieux aussi bien que ses obscurités [Everyone who claims [a French identity] must consider themselves a legitimate heir to the totality of French history, to its glorious memories, as well as to its shadows].[72] The extent to which Muslim citizens can also be integrated as French citizens has been the subject of fierce debate in France, and this anxiety resulted in the well-known *affaire du foulard* in 1989, when three girls from the Paris suburb of Creil wore Muslim headscarves within the boundaries of a French republican school. This controversy is referenced in *Des hommes et des dieux* when the village imam, over tea in one of their houses with Christian, cites the example of two schoolgirls in Algeria who were killed by terrorists for not wearing the veil. The imam goes on to note that 'le monde devient fou' [the world is going mad], because Muslim girls in France are making such a fuss in order to be allowed to wear the veil, while girls in Algeria are being killed for not wearing one. Beyond the politicization of women's self-expression through clothing, these issues have little in common. By drawing equivalences between them, the film elides the difference between a non-violent, if potentially polemical, expression of religious autonomy, and the violent elimination of a woman's body. This secularist discourse is conveniently expressed by a Muslim imam, living in Algeria. Given that the film takes place eight years after the headscarf scandal, this anachronistic reference seems to have been deliberately inserted to evoke 'intercultural' shared values, with the value being shared that of French universalism.

The values of universalism are difficult to implement in practice. For example, how does one distinguish between the individual who has only recently been granted the rights of the universal citizen (women, ethnic, racial, and sexual minorities, the differently abled) and those who have enjoyed them all along? Indeed, universalism may be fundamentally predicated on the idea of difference: a community unites around their shared similarities, but also their difference from those who are not part of the group. According to Joan Scott, the universal subject is one 'whose universality was achieved through the implicit processes of differentiation, marginalization, and exclusion'.[73] In *Des hommes et des dieux*, the monks' dress and lifestyle distinguish and separate them from the rest of humanity, and it seems that there is a double standard when it comes to French universalism and linguistic expression and integration. If French universalism emphasizes, according to Veit Bader, a 'universal human liberty, equality, and reason' that is more important than 'specific languages, ethnicity, and particularist culture', in *Des hommes et des dieux*, liberty, equality, and reason are expressed in one language: French.[74] Despite the fact that most of the monks have been in Algeria for several decades, apart from one instance of the words 'Salaam-Alaikum' (hello, or literally 'Peace be upon you'), the monks do not speak in Arabic to the Algerian villagers who come to work on their farm. The villagers and the army speak to the monks exclusively in French, and surprisingly, the terrorists also speak to the monks in the old colonizer's tongue, even quoting passages from the Koran in French. Indeed, the idyll of interfaith understanding in the film is also predicated on the monk's preservation of their values or lifestyle, without conforming to or assimilating into the host culture: the monks do not adopt Muslim religion or dress, obey orders from the Algerian state, or learn the national language. At one point, Christian tells the Algerian army general that 'personne d'autre que nous peut nous décider a quitter ce pays' [no one other than ourselves can make us decide to leave] — a potentially antagonistic stance to assume in front of a state official, and an enviably defiant one for most migrants, be they refugees, asylum seekers, or economic migrants in the present day. This position marks the monks more as colonizers or diplomats, rather than citizens, and underscores their position in this community, as European and Christian, dominant and separate.

Huffer argues that Derrida's *nostalgérie* 'allows him and us to have it both ways': by highlighting his Algerian and Jewish roots, he is the postcolonial excluded subject, and simultaneously a 'postmodern defender [...] humanism's universal man'.[75] In a similar sense, *Des hommes et des dieux* also allows the spectator to have it both ways: we can revel in the exoticism of the location, submerge ourselves in a lush vision of pastoral existence, and marvel at the monk's bravery and humanity, while also profiting from the comfortable distance that a foreign location, Manichean perpetrators, and easy identification with Western protagonists can offer. As a heritage film, *Des hommes et des dieux* presents a glossy and seductive vision of a historical tragedy, set in a world of inter-religious harmony and republican values that is predicated on hierarchical and neo-colonial relations. By disregarding the monks' ambiguous associations with the French colonial past, the film allows violence as well as inter-ethnic harmony to be displaced to another space and another time, beyond French territory in the present. The brothers are depicted as resolutely and nobly apolitical, but just like the French colonizers before them, they refuse to leave. In its evocation of a nostalgic, harmonious, and ultimately colonial past, *Des hommes et des dieux* speaks deeply to present-day anxieties about France and its relation to its former Muslim colonies, and the descendants of these colonies living on French territory today.

Notes to Chapter 5

1. The nomination for the Foreign Language Oscar for Algeria in 2010 was Rachid Bouchareb's *Hors la loi*, a film which inspired considerable controversy. See Ian Merkel, 'Rachid Bouchareb's *Outside the Law*: Aesthetics and Reception in France', *Nka: Journal of Contemporary African Art*, 32 (2013), 62–69.

2. Romain Baro and Michel Guerrin, ' "Des hommes et des dieux", quel succès!', *Le Monde* (28 September 2010) <http://www.lemonde.fr/cinema/article/2010/09/28/des-hommes-et-des-dieux-quel-succes_1417054_3476.html#imcgKLkGXC44FrVX.99> [Accessed 23 May 2017].

3. Vanessa Thorpe, 'The unlikeliest box-office hit: a film about doomed French monks', *The Guardian* (28 November 2010) <http://www.theguardian.com/film/2010/nov/28/film-french-monks-arthouse-hit> [Accessed 31 July 2013].

4. Quoted in Thorpe, 'The unlikeliest box-office hit'.

5. Anon., 'Festival de Cannes: Prix de l'Éducation nationale', *Ministère de l'Éducation nationale* <http://www.education.gouv.fr/cid51423/festival-de-cannes-prix-de-l-education-nationale.html#Le%20prix%20de%20l'Éducation%20nationale%20à%20Cannes> [Accessed 23 May 2017].

6. Robert Rosenstone, *History on Film: Film on History* (London: Routledge, 2006), p. 45 [italics in the original].

7. Didier Péron and Benjamin Stora, 'Interview avec Benjamin Stora: Des victimes françaises de l'histoire algérienne', *Libération* (25 September 2010) <http://next.liberation.fr/cinema/2010/09/25/des-victimes-francaises-de-l-histoire-algerienne_681614> [Accessed 31 May 2017].

8. Andrew Higson, 'Re-Presenting the National Past: Nostalgia and Pastiche in the Heritage Film', in *Fires were Started: British Cinema and Thatcherism*, ed. by Lester D. Friedman (New York: Wallflower Press, 2nd edn 2006), pp. 91–109.

9. Martin Evans and John Phillips, *Algeria: Anger of the Dispossessed* (New Haven: Yale University Press, 2007), p. 225.

10. Ibid., p. 226.

11. See Martin Stone, *The Establishment of Algeria* (London: Hurst & Co., 1997), pp. 1–7, and David J. Whittaker, *The Terrorism Reader*, 3rd edn (London: Routledge, 2003), pp. 151–63.

12. Addi, 'Algeria's Army', p. 45.

13. United Nations General Assembly (July-August 1998), 'Report of the Panel Appointed by the Secretary General to Gather Information on the Situation in Algeria (Report of Emininet Persons Panel)', April 1999. <http://www.un.org/NewLinks/dpi2007/contents.htm> [Accessed 12 January 2012].

14. John W. Kiser, *The Monks of Tibhirine: Faith, Love, and Terror in Algeria* (New York: St. Martin's Griffin, 2002).

15. Anon., 'Extraits de la déposition du général François Buchwalter', *Radio France international* (8 July 2009) <http://www1.rfi.fr/actufr/articles/115/article_82514.asp> [Accessed 28 June 2016].

16. John Kiser, *Passion pour l'Algérie: les moines de Tibhirine*, trans. Henry Quinson, (Paris: Nouvelle Cité, 2006).

17. Evans and Phillips, p. 229.

18. Marie-Noëlle Tranchant, ' "Des hommes et des dieux": le cinéma en état de grâce', *Le Figaro* (7 September 2010) <http://www.lefigaro.fr/cinema/2010/09/06/03002-20100906ARTFIG00802-des-hommes-et-des-dieux-le-cinema-en-etat-de-grace.php> [Accessed 31 July 2013] and Didier Arnaud and Didier Péron, 'La France chauffée aux moines', *Libération* (25 September 2010) <http://next.liberation.fr/societe/01012292294-la-france-chauffee-aux-moines> [Accessed 31 July 2013].

19. Benjamin Stora, *La Guerre invisible: Algérie, années 90* (Paris: Presses de Sciences Po, 2001).

20. Stora and Péron, 2010. On the question of victim visibility and the exclusion of Algerian civilians from the narrative of *Des hommes et des dieux*, see Maria Flood, 'Terrorism and Visibility in Algeria's 'Black Decade': *Des hommes et des dieux* (2010)', *French Cultural Studies*, 27:1 (2016), 62–72.

21. Quinson quoted in Thierry Leclère, 'Derniers mois à Tibhirine', *Télérama* (11 September 2010) <http://www.telerama.fr/cinema/derniers-mois-a-tibhirine,59905.php> [Accessed 16 June 2017].

22. Higson, 'Re-Presenting the National Past', p. 95.

23. Ibid., p. 93.

24. The film uses Classical intertexts to underscore the monk's sacrifice and martyrdom. In one sequence, Frère Luc meditates on a reproduction of Caravaggio's *Christ on the Column* (1607). At the beginning of the shot, the painting is blurred in the background, but as Luc moves in to kiss the body of Christ, the image comes into sharp relief and the painful sacrifice of Jesus

is explicitly contrasted with the knowing sacrifice of the monks. Further classical references in the film include Andrea Mantegna's *Lamentation of Christ* (n.d.) and Rembrandt's self-portraits, evoking loss and grief, and profound, albeit melancholy, self-knowledge.

25. Belén Vidal, *Heritage Film: Nation, Genre and Representation* (New York: Wallflower Press, 2012), p. 53.

26. Higson, 'Re-Presenting the National Past', p. 104.

27. Andrew Higson, 'Nostalgia is not what it used to be: Heritage Films, Nostalgia Websites and Contemporary Consumers', *Consumption Markets & Culture*, 17:2 (2014), 120–42, (p. 123).

28. Ibid., p. 124.

29. Sébastien Fevry, 'Sepia Cinema in Nicolas Sarkozy's France: Nostalgia and National Identity', *Studies in French Cinema*, 17:1 (2017), 60–74 (p. 64).

30. *The Bible: The English Standard Version* (London: Collins Anglicised ESV Bibles, 2012), p. 765.

31. Vidal, *Heritage Film*, p. 53.

32. Nicolas Bancel and Pascal Blanchard, 'From Colonial to Postcolonial: Reflections on the Colonial Debate in France', in *Postcolonial Thought in the French-speaking World*, ed. by Charles Forsdick and David Murphy (Liverpool: Liverpool University Press, 2009), pp. 295–305, (p. 301).

33. 'Loi nº 2005–158 du 23 février 2005 portant reconnaissance de la Nation et contribution nationale en faveur des Français rapatriés', *Légifrance: le service public de la diffusion du droit* <https://www.legifrance.gouv.fr/affichTexte.do?cidTexte=JORFTEXT000000444898&catego rieLien=id> [Accessed 20 June 2017]. For more on this polemical law, see Rosello, *The Reparative in Narratives*, pp. 14–17.

34. Kimberly Smith, 'Mere Nostalgia: Notes on a Progressive Paratheory', *Rhetoric and Public Affairs* 3:4 (2000), 505–27 (p. 515–16).

35. Gilroy quoted in Stuart Jeffries, 'The Best Exotic Nostalgia Boom: Why Colonial Style is Back', *The Guardian* (19 March 2015) <https://www.theguardian.com/culture/2015/mar/19/the-best-exotic-nostalgia-boom-why-colonial-style-is-back> [Accessed 15 December 2016].

36. The polarization of indigenous Algerians into childlike villagers and violent terrorists or army men conforms to Homi K. Bhabha's evocation of the ambivalence of colonial discourses, in which natives are both domesticated and wild, harmless and dangerous. See Bhabha, *The Location of Culture* (London: Routledge, 2009), pp. 145–71.

37. See Wendy Kristianasen, 'Truth & Justice after a Brutal Civil War: Algeria: The Women Speak', *Review of African Political Economy*, 33:108 (2006), pp. 346–51.

38. Stora, *La Guerre invisible*, p. 9.

39. Frantz Fanon, *Les Damnés de la terre* (Paris: Éditions La Découverte Poche [1961] 2002), pp. 42–43; Frantz Fanon, *The Wretched of the Earth*, trans. Constance Farrington (London: Penguin Modern Classics [1967] 2001).

40. On colonial distribution centres during the Algerian War, see Neil Macmaster, *Buring the Veil: The Algerian War and the 'Emancipation' of Muslim Women, 1954–1962* (Manchester: Manchester University Press, 2012).

41. Christof Heyns, *Human Rights Law in Africa: 1999* (The Hague: Kluwer Law International, 2002), p. 410.

42. Philip Dine, *Images of the Algerian War: French Fiction and Film, 1954–1992* (Oxford: Clarendon Press, 1994), p. 148. See also Paul Azoulay, *La nostalgérie française*, (Paris: Eric Baschet, 1980).

43. Jacques Derrida, 'Circonfession', in Geoffrey Bennington and Jacques Derrida, *Jacques Derrida* (Paris: Éditions du Seuil, 1991) and Jacques Derrida, *Le Monolinguisme de l'autre* (Paris: Galilée, 1996). Hélène Cixous, 'Pieds nus', in *Une enfance algérienne*, ed. by Leïla Sebbar (Paris: Gallimard, 1997), pp. 55–66 and Hélène Cixous, *Les rêveries de la femme sauvage: Scènes primitives* (Paris: Gallilée, 2000).

44. Lynne Huffer, 'Derrida's Nostalgeria', in *Algeria & France, 1800–2000: Identity, Memory, Nostalgia*, ed. by Patricia M. E. Lorcin (Syracuse: Syracuse University Press, 2006), pp. 228–46, (p. 230).

45. See Yamina Benguigui, *Mémoire d'immigrées: les enfants* (1997).

46. Kevin O' Gorman, 'Jacques Derrida's Philosophy of Hospitality', *Hospitality Review*, 8:4 (2006), 50–57, (p. 55). See also Jacques Derrida, *De l'hospitalité* (Paris: Calmann-Lévy, 1997).

47. Fevry reads the sepia turn as a response to the 'failures of the memorial politics' of Nicholas Sarkozy, in which he includes the commemoration of communist and Resistance member Guy Môquet and 'Maison de l'Histoire de France' [House of the History of France] to be installed in the National Archives. Fevry, 'Sepia Cinema', p. 68.

48. Nicolas Sarkozy, 'Le Discours de Dakar', *Le Monde* (9 November 2007) <http://www.lemonde.fr/afrique/article/2007/11/09/le-discours-de-dakar_976786_3212.html#IzFdCdfucWIKwEwQ.99> [Accessed 20 October 2016].

49. For critiques of the speech, see Laurent Correau, 'Sarkozy a été "victime de son nègre"', *RFI* (18 September 2008) <http://www1.rfi.fr/actufr/articles/105/article_72481.asp> [23 June 2017], and Anon., 'Ségolène Royal demande "pardon" pour le "discours de Dakar" de Nicolas Sarkozy', *Le Monde* (6 April 2009) <http://www.lemonde.fr/politique/article/2009/04/06/segolene-royal-demande-pardon-pour-le-discours-de-dakar-de-nicolas-sarkozy_1177536_823448.html#THYvofPb2Wyf8Er1.99> [Accessed 23 June 2017].

50. Sarkozy, 'Le Discours de Dakar'.

51. Alain Auffray, 'Le refus de lire la lettre de Guy Môquet est incomprehensible: entretien d'Henri Guaino', *Libération* (20 October 2007) <http://www.liberation.fr/jour/2007/10/20/le-refus-de-lire-la-lettre-de-guy-moquet-est-incomprehensible_104309> [Accessed 14 November 2016].

52. Sarkozy, 'Le Discours de Dakar'.

53. Naomi Schor, 'The Crisis of French Universalism', *Yale French Studies*, 100 (2001), 43–64 (p. 46).

54. Susan Terrio, 'Crucible of the Millenium? The Clovis Affair in Contemporary France', *Comparative Studies in Society and History*, 41:3 (1999), 438–57 (p. 441).

55. For Marxist, feminist and postcolonial critiques of universalism, see respectively Jacques Rancière, 'Who is the Subject of the Rights of Man?', *South Atlantic Quarterly*, 103: 2/3 (2004), 297–310 [original in English]; Joan W. Scott, *Gender and the Politics of History* (New York: Columbia University Press, 1988), and Frantz Fanon, *Peau noire, masques blancs* (Paris: Seuil, 1952), pp. 148–56.

56. Quoted in Christian Georges, 'Résumé — *Des hommes et des dieux*', *Madiana* (2010) <http://www.madiana.ws/pdf/deshommes.pdf> [Accessed 31 July 2013].

57. Edward Saïd evokes this concept in relation to Alphonse de Lamartine's description of his 1833 voyage to Palestine, where the Orient is conceived as 'nations without territory, *patrie*, rights, laws or security...waiting anxiously for the shelter of European occupation'. Saïd, *Orientalism* (London: Penguin Modern Classics [1978] 2003), p. 179. See also Andrew Fitzmaurice, 'The Genealogy of *Terra Nullius*', *Australian Historical Studies*, 38:129 (2007), 1–15.

58. David Nowell-Smith, 'Of Gods and Humanitarians', *Film Quarterly*, 64 (2011), 59–61 (p. 59).

59. Susan Hayward, *Cinema Studies: The Key Concepts,* 2nd edn (London: Routledge, 2000), p. 194.

60. See Linda Williams, 'Melodrama Revised' in *Refiguring American Film Genres: History and Theory*, ed. by Nick Browne (Berkeley: University of California Press, 1998), pp. 42–88 (p. 64).

61. Marie-Noëlle Tranchant, '"Des hommes et des dieux": le cinéma en état de grâce', *Le Figaro* (7 September 2010) <http://www.lefigaro.fr/cinema/2010/09/06/03002-20100906ARTFIG00802-des-hommes-et-des-dieux-le-cinema-en-etat-de-grace.php> [Accessed 31 July 2013].

62. John R. Bowen, *Why the French Don't Like Headscarves: Islam, the State, and Public Space* (Princeton: Princeton University Press, 2007), p. 157.

63. Schor, 'The Crisis of French Universalism', p. 44 and Norman Ravitch, 'Your People, My People; Your God, My God: French and American Troubles Over Citizenship', *The French Review*, 70:4 (1997), 515–27 (p. 526).

64. Beauvois quoted in Christian Georges, 'Résumé — *Des hommes et des dieux*', *Madiana* (2010) <http://www.madiana.ws/pdf/deshommes.pdf> [Accessed 31 July 2013].

65. Arnaud and Péron, 'La France chauffée aux moines'. An analysis of the press and public reception of the film is not out of place in this context; indeed, studies of the heritage film deliberately incorporate reception studies, because these films are designed to appeal to broad swathes of the public and reflect dominant social values. See Paul Cooke and Rob Stone (eds.), *Screening European Heritage: Creating and Consuming History on Film* (London: Palgrave Macmillan, 2016).

66. Anon., '"Des Hommes et Des Dieux" est un chef-d'oeuvre', *Le Parisien* (8 September, 2010)

<http://www.leparisien.fr/loisirs-et-spectacles/des-hommes-et-des-dieux-est-un-chef-d-oeuvre-08–09–2010–1059303.php> [Accessed 31 July 2013].

67. Although the film did attract a wide range of spectators, cinema ushers in the Pantheon in Paris reported a large number of nuns and priests in attendance, and the predominantly practicing Catholic regions of Brittany and Alsace returned the highest audience figures. See Baro and Guerrin, ' "Des hommes et des dieux", quel succès!" ' and Jean-François Petit, 'Des hommes et des dieux: un phénomène de presse catholique?', Transversalités, 2:118 (2011), 123–35 (p. 128).

68. See Giovanna Di Ceglie and Andrea Sabbadini, 'A Camera inside a Monastery: Reflections on Of Gods and Men [Des hommes et des dieux]', The International Journal of Psychoanalysis, 91 (2011), 745–54; Yael Klangwisan, 'Of Gods and Men: Radical Hospitality and the Monks of Tibhirine', Stimulus: The New Zealand Journal of Christian Thought and Practice, 21:1 (2014), 34–35; Anne Thurston, 'The Eucharist: Passion for Life: — a reflection on "Of Gods and Men" ', The Furrow, 62:5 (2011), 259–65; Anne M. Windholz, 'The Terrible and Sublime Liturgy: Sustaining Mission to the Suffering in Beauvois's Of Gods and Men', New Theology Review, 26:1 (2013), 63–74; Wendy M. Wright, 'Of Gods and Men (2010)', Journal of Religion & Film, 15: 2, (2012).

69. Beauvois quoted in Tranchant, 'Le cinéma en état de grâce', 2010.

70. Luc is the only character that remains consistently blasé when confronted with the terrorists, and the casting of Michael Lonsdale in this role is significant. Heritage film uses recognisable actors who are stalwarts of stage and screen, so-called 'national treasures', like Lonsdale and Philippe Laudenbach. Lonsdale has worked in French film and theatre for over six decades, and moreover, he is a devout Catholic who has participated in the Charismatic Renewal in France, and co-founded the prayer group 'Magnificat', aimed specifically at Catholic creative professionals.

71. Jacques Rancière, 'Les idéaux républicains sont devenus des armes de discrimination et de mépris', L'Obs (2 April 2015) <http://campvolant.com/2015/04/04/jacques-ranciere-les-ideaux-republicains-sont-devenus-des-armes-de-discrimination-et-de-mepris/> [Accessed 19 May 2015].

72. Jean-Marie Lustiger, 'Entretien', Le Monde no. 15965, Paris (26–27 May 1996).

73. Scott, Gender and the Politics of History, p. 63.

74. Veit Bader, 'The Cultural Conditions of Transnational Citizenship: On the Interpretation of Political and Ethnic Cultures', Political Theory, 25:6 (1997), 771–813, (p. 779).

75. Huffer, 'Derrida's Nostalgeria', p. 244.

CONCLUSION

❖

In chapters four and five of this book, I argued that film can create fantasy realms, projections of imagined spaces that can impact the real world: that of the heterotopia as a real space created to contain and manage undesirable bodies in *Viva Laldjérie*, and the neo-colonial, nostalgic world of the monastery in *Des hommes et des dieux*. For Foucault, the colony was also a fantastical, heterotopic space. He writes: 'avec la colonie, on a une hétérotopie qui est en quelque sorte assez naïve pour vouloir réaliser une illusion' [In the colony, we have a heterotopia that is, in a way, sufficiently naïve to attempt to make an illusion become a reality].[1] This statement highlights the extent to which the colonial relationship was founded on desire and projection. How the colony represented itself, and was represented by the colonized, generated historical and political reality, even if these representations were naïve or false. Cinema produces worlds, ideas, and fantasies of what was, what is, and what might be, and these images in turn interact and influence the non-cinematic world. Indeed, I have argued here that these French and Algerian histories of violence on screen illuminate the power of representation in the political sphere and the profound interconnectedness of both countries. By avoiding films that are self-evidently historical and by reading one such film against its own aims, this book has demonstrated that attention to the historical context, political resonances, and aesthetic properties of a film can uncover the hidden histories, lives, and ideological motivations that would otherwise remain unarticulated. Moving from metaphors of absence and antagonism in the French texts examined in the first section, through to the reiteration of lost voices in works that straddle the line between reality and fantasy in the Algerian works in the second section, the book closes with a reading of a recent film that is about a history that is both French and Algerian, a film that nostalgically reiterates a lost world of French universalist, republican values.

I have argued that within the French context, paying attention to marginalized histories, and their representation or referencing in film, can bring visibility to otherwise neglected voices and worlds. For example, I showed how Michael Haneke's *Caché* raises questions about the kinds of immediate, inter-personal violence we inflict on others, through exclusion, fear, and prejudice. Drawing on Jacques Rancière's work on aesthetics, politics, and the 17 October 1961 massacre, I contended that the film reflects the delayed recognition of the 17 October 1961 massacre in the public sphere in France, and the invisibility imposed on victims of police violence through state censorship. *Caché* references the unequal dynamics of space and power that played out in the 17 October 1961 massacre through the cultural and social differentiation of Majid and Georges in the mise-en-scène of their living space. Producing spectator discomfort through the identification with Georges and sound image disjunctions, the film enacts a formal questioning of normative frames that posit certain lives, like Majid's, outside the domain of political recognition and empathy through a continuous emphasis on the ambiguity of the image. I argued that Majid's death by suicide shocks the viewer into a new appraisal of the narrative action; if his death occurred off-screen, its emotional and intellectual impact would be significantly reduced. It is the visual and the grotesque physical depiction of this act, and the trauma that it represents, which horrifies. Ultimately, I suggested that Haneke draws on the physical and state violence of the past to highlight that discourses of hatred and inequality continue to impact individuals like Majid in the present.

Made in the immediate aftermath of the Algerian War, *Rive Gauche* director Alain Resnais's *Muriel* references an immediate desire on the part of 1960s French society to forget Algeria, and the atrocities committed there. Like *Caché*, which uses formal techniques to highlight a lack of visibility of Algerian lives following the massacre, *Muriel* references the incredulity that surrounded many women's narratives of torture and violence at the hands of French soldiers. My discussion here emphasized the historicization of torture during and after the Algerian War, with a specific focus on the dehumanization of victims and sexual dimensions of the torture of women. Detailing Resnais's use of visual and verbal disjunctions within the broader aesthetic framework of the film, I connected these aesthetic techniques to the spoken account of Muriel's torture. By offering a detailed close reading of this scene in line with the philosophical work of Elaine Scarry, Judith Butler, and Susan Sontag, I underscored the specifically sexual dimension of Muriel's torture. Connecting Resnais's audio-visual asynchronous techniques and testimonial accounts, I tied the omission of a visual image of the violence of torture in the film to the suppression of the Algeria War in the consciousness of French society in 1963.

In the second section, I examined two works from francophone Algerian directors which considered the role of Algerian women in conflict: in the immediate aftermath of the Algerian War in Assia Djebar's *La Nouba des femmes du Mont Chenoua*, and during the Civil War of the 1990s in the case of Nadir Moknèche's *Viva Laldjérie*. Both directors stress the particular experiences of women in times of conflict in Algerian society, and lay emphasis on narratives of resistance and on female collectivities as sources of strength. Djebar's *La Nouba* is an experimental work that fragments the narrative by combining documentary and abstraction in the form of real interviews with the women of the Chenoua region, and fictional interludes with a character named Lila. I explored how Djebar provides the women of Chenoua with a space within which loss may be articulated, the representational frame of the film itself. Through its creation and production, these real individuals are given recognition within a social and public forum they otherwise would not have received. Yet if *Muriel* elicited debate on how one might depict a violent history that is precisely not one's own, I suggested that *La Nouba* generated questions about the role of the postcolonial writer in relation to their community. Djebar, an educated and Westernized Algerian woman, discloses her own story alongside that of a group of women with whom she explicitly differentiates herself through costumes, lighting, gestures, and characterization. However, in contrast to many studies of Djebar, I demonstrated that it is the author/filmmaker's separation from the women she represents, and not her proximity, that generates productive insights in a vision of history that strikes a stance against nationalism, forgetting, and the exclusion of women's voices from the national narrative.

Unlike the rural spaces and lives depicted in *La Nouba*, *Viva Laldjérie* appears to manifest a bold and sexually fluid Algiers of debauchery, with prostitutes, unmarried women, dancers, and homosexuals taking centre stage. Moknèche's narrative decentres terrorism and the memory of violence, countering these concerns with humour, and offering an exploration of the everyday lives of the central characters. The film highlights the roles played by Algerian women during the Civil War and their specific vulnerabilities to physical and symbolic violence by foregrounding the female characters. I discussed how the film pushes the recent trauma of national civil strife to the margins of the narrative in order to offer a different vision of the city and the country, away from the frequently evoked cycles of terror and counter-terror that populate many representations. The refusal to represent on-going political tensions, the representation of explicit sexual content, and the film's use of the French language and characterization that appeals to Western viewers has drawn criticism for its dearth of realism from popular and academic sources. However, using the concept of the heterotopia I showed that the world conjured in *Viva Laldjérie* is not the representation of the past as it was, or even of a realist present, but rather a heterotopic imagining of what future spaces and imagined existences might be for Algeria and its inhabitants.

If the national past, according to Patrick Wright 'is capable of finding splendour in old styles of political domination and of making an alluring romance out of atrocious colonial domination', it seems that the national present is also capable of conjuring such splendour in old demons.[2] Like *Viva Laldjérie*, *Des hommes et des dieux* creates a fantasy realm, one that acknowledges, and inspires longing for the rustic pleasures that have been forsaken by modernity, while also associating these pleasures with French protagonists and their values of religion and republicanism. This is a moral universe where the lines between good and evil and courage and weakness are clearly drawn, and both goodness and courage are found only in the French, Christian protagonists. I questioned the transplanting of both terrorist violence and inter-community harmony onto Algerian soil, and pointed to many of the colonial stereotypes reproduced and celebrated in this immensely popular film. I demonstrated that the representation of French and Algerian recent histories in *Des hommes et des dieux* can bolster nationalist narratives and mask present day concerns about the memory of colonialism, the posited secularism of the republican state, and the presence of second and third generation Maghrebi French citizens in France.

This study has shown the value of using a tripartite analysis in considering French and Algerian histories of violence, one that engages with the historical context of individual works in order to highlight how artistic techniques can frame and produce political meaning. *Des hommes et des dieux*, with its appropriation of an Algerian tragedy and its faithful staging of proto-colonial behaviours around the *mission civilisatrice* and universalism, points towards the ongoing necessity of examining closely the aesthetic dimensions of works that purport to represent French and Algerian histories. Indeed, the issues that are raised in *Des hommes et des dieux*, namely terrorism, religion and secularism, migration and immigrants, and inter-community harmony, are profoundly pertinent to France and Algeria in the present day. In a recently released anthology, Nicolas Bancel and Pascal Blanchard directly link historical denials of colonial pasts to rising antagonisms between different communities and the terrorist attacks of the twenty first century.[3] There is thus an urgency to the recognition and integration of the colonial past, which films like *Caché* and *Muriel* suggest will continue to return and haunt personal and political relationships in the present. Moreover, the ideological impetus and soaring popularity of *Des hommes et des dieux* demonstrates that there is a continued appetite, conscious or otherwise, for a nostalgic vision of the French colonial presence abroad. However, the works of Algerian francophone directors like Djebar and Moknèche do point to the possibility that fruitful individual, collective and creative identities can emerge from historical violence. In the case of Djebar, her complex negotiation of her position of representational privilege in the community of Algerian women she represents and her *francophonie* offers a productive vision of the exile and the immigrant who negotiates the boundary between two cultures with warmth and insight. Finally, Moknèche's vision of a dynamic and diverse Algeria in *Viva Laldjérie*, however at odds with certain aspects of historical or social reality, demonstrates the power of film as a cultural document in a given space and time, and its capacity to generate spaces that exist between reality and fantasy, resonating in the non-cinematic world.

Notes to the Conclusion

1. Michel Foucault, *Le Corps utopique, les hétérotopies* (Paris: Nouvelles Editions Lignes, 2009), p. 24.
2. Patrick Wright, *On Living in an Old Country* (London: Verso, 1985), p. 254.
3. Nicolas Bancel, Pascal Blanchard, and Dominic Thomas, *The Colonial Legacy in France: Fracture, Rupture, and Apartheid* (Indiana: Indiana University Press, 2017).

BIBLIOGRAPHY

❖

ADDI, LAHOUARI, 'Algeria's Army, Algeria's Agony', *Foreign Affairs*, 77:4 (1998), 44–53

ABDENNOUR, ALI-YAHIA, *Algérie: raisons et déraison d'une guerre* (Paris: Harmattan, 1996)

ALLEG, HENRI, *La Question* (Paris: Les Éditions de Minuit, 1958)

ALLOULA, MALEK, *The Colonial Harem* (London: University of Minesota Press, 1986)

AMRANE-MINNE, DJAMILA, *Des femmes dans la guerre d'Algérie: Entretiens* (Paris: Karthala, 1994)

——*Femmes au combat: la guerre d'Algérie* (Algiers: Éditions Rahma, 1993)

ANON., ' "Des hommes et des dieux" est un chef-d'oeuvre', *Le Parisien* (8 September 2010) <http://www.leparisien.fr/loisirs-et-spectacles/des-hommes-et-des-dieux-est-un-chef-d-oeuvre-08–09–2010–1059303.php> [Accessed 31 July 2013]

ANON., 'Extraits de la déposition du général François Buchwalter', *Radio France international* (8 July 2009) <http://www1.rfi.fr/actufr/articles/115/article_82514.asp> [Accessed 28 June 2016]

ANON., 'Légifrance: le service public de la diffusion du droit', <https://www.legifrance.gouv.fr/affichTexte.do?cidTexte=JORFTEXT000000444898&categorieLien=id> [Accessed 20 June 2017]

ANON., 'Festival de Cannes: Prix de l'Éducation nationale', *Ministère de l'Éducation nationale* <http://www.education.gouv.fr/cid51423/festival-de-cannes-prix-de-l-education-nationale.html#Le%20prix%20de%20ol'Éducation%20nationale%20à%20Cannes> [Accessed 23 May 2017]

ANON., 'Ségolène Royal demande "pardon" pour le "discours de Dakar" de Nicolas Sarkozy', *Le Monde* (6 April 2009) <http://www.lemonde.fr/politique/article/2009/04/06/segolene-royal-demande-pardon-pour-le-discours-de-dakar-de-nicolas-sarkozy_1177536_823448.html#THYvofPb2Wyf8Er1.99> [Accessed 23 June 2017]

ANON., *The Bible: The English Standard Version* (London: Collins Anglicised ESV Bibles, 2012)

ARENDT, HANNAH, *On Violence* (Orlando FL: Harcourt Books, 1969)

ARMES, ROY, 'From State Production to *Cinéma d'Auteur* in Algeria' in *Film in the Middle East and North Africa: Creative Dissidence*, ed. by Josef Gugler (Austin: University of Texas Press, 2011), 294–306

ARNAUD, DIDIER, and DIDIER PÉRON, 'La France chauffée aux moines', *Libération* (25 September 2010) <http://next.liberation.fr/societe/01012292294-la-france-chauffee-aux-moines> [Accessed 31 July 2013]

AUFFRAY, ALAIN, 'Le refus de lire la lettre de Guy Môquet est incomprehensible: entretien d'Henri Guaino', *Libération* (20 October 2007) <http://www.liberation.fr/jour/2007/10/20/le-refus-de-lire-la-lettre-de-guy-moquet-est-incomprehensible_104309> [Accessed 14 November 2016]

AUSTIN, GUY, 'Drawing Trauma: Visual Testimony in *Caché* and *J'ai 8 ans*', *Screen*, 48:4 (2007), 529–36

——'Representing the Algerian War in Algerian Cinema: *Le Vent des Aurès*', *French Studies*, 61:2 (2007), 182–95

——*Algerian National Cinema* (Manchester: Manchester University Press, 2012)

AZOULAY, PAUL, *La nostalgérie francaise* (Paris: Eric Baschet 1980)

BADER, VEIT, 'The Cultural Conditions of Transnational Citizenship: On the Interpretation of Political and Ethnic Cultures', *Political Theory*, 25:6 (1997), 771–813

BANCEL, NICOLAS, and PASCAL BLANCHARD, 'From Colonial to Postcolonial: Reflections on the Colonial Debate in France', in *Postcolonial Thought in the French-speaking World*, ed. by Charles Forsdick and David Murphy (Liverpool: Liverpool University Press, 2009), 295–305

BANCEL NICOLAS, PASCAL BLANCHARD, and DOMINIC THOMAS, *The Colonial Legacy in France: Fracture, Rupture, and Apartheid* (Indiana: Indiana University Press, 2017)

BARO, ROMAIN, and MICHEL GUERRIN, '"Des hommes et des dieux", quel succès!', *Le Monde* (28 September 2010) <http://www.lemonde.fr/cinema/article/2010/09/28/des-hommes-et-des-dieux-quel-succes_1417054_3476.html#imcgKLkGXC44FrVX.99> [Accessed 23 May 2017]

BAZIN, ANDRÉ, et al., 'Six Characters in Search of Auteurs: A Discussion about the French Cinema (1957)', in *The European Cinema Reader*, ed. by Catherine Fowler (Oxon: Routledge, 2002), 64–72

BEAUGÉ, FLORENCE, *Algérie, une guerre sans gloire: histoire d'une enquête* (Paris: Calmann-Lévy, 2005)

BEAUVOIR, SIMONE DE, and GISÈLE HALIMI, *Djamila Boupacha* (Paris: Gallimard, 1962)

BENGHREBIL, CHAMS, 'La décomposition sociale du djihad dans un quartier populaire d'Alger', *Annuaire de l'Afrique du Nord*, XXXVIII (1999), 137–41

BENKHALED, WALID, 'Algerian Cinema between Commercial and Political Pressures: The Double Distortion', *Journal of African Cinemas*, 8:1 (2016), 87–100

BENSMAÏA, RÉDA, '*La Nouba des Femmes du Mont Chenoua*: Introduction to the Cinematic Fragment', trans. by Jennifer Curtiss Gage, *World Literature Today*, 70 (1996), 877–84

BENTAHAR, ZIAD, 'A voice with an elusive sound: aphasia, diglossia, and arabophone Algeria in Assia Djebar's *The Nouba of the Women of Mount Chenoua*', *The Journal of North African Studies*, 21:3 (2016), 411–32

BEST, VICTORIA, 'Between the Harem and the Battlefield: Domestic Space in the Work of Assia Djebar', *Signs*, 27 (2002), 873–79

BEUGNET, MARTINE, 'Blind spot', *Screen*, 48:2 (2007), 227–31

BHABHA, HOMI K., *The Location of Culture* (London: Routledge, 2009), 145–71

BINION, RUDOLPH, *Past Impersonal* (Illinois: Northern University Press, 2005)

BOUDJEDRA, RACHID, *Naissance du cinéma algérien* (Paris: François Maspéro, 1971)

BOWEN, JOHN R., *Why the French Don't Like Headscarves: Islam, the State, and Public Space*, (Princeton: Princeton University Press, 2007)

BRANCHE, RAPHAËLLE, *La Torture et l'armée pendant la guerre d'Algérie (1954–1962)* (Paris: Gallimard, 2001)

——'Sexual Violence in the Algerian War', in *Brutality and Desire: War and Sexuality in Europe's Twentieth Century*, ed. by Dagmar Herzog (Basingstoke: Palgrave Macmillan, 2009), 247–60

BRITTON, CELIA, 'Broken Images in Resnais's *Muriel*', *French Cultural Studies*, I (1990), 37–46

BROOKER, PETER, 'Key Words in Brecht's Theory and Practice of Theatre', in *The Cambridge Companion to Delacroix*, ed. by Peter Thomson and Glendyr Sacks (Cambridge: Cambridge University Press, 1994)

BRUNET, JEAN-PAUL, *Police contre FLN: le drame d'octobre 1961* (Paris: Flammarion, 1999)

BUDIG-MARKIN, VALÉRIE, 'Writing and Filming the Cries of Silence', *World Literature Today*, 70 (1996), 893–904

BUTLER, JUDITH, *Frames of War*, (London: Verso, 2009)

——Precarious Life (London: Verso, 2006)

CALLE-GRUBER, MIREILLE, Assia Djebar, ou, la résistance de l'écriture: regards d'un écrivain d'Algérie (Paris: Maisonneuve and Larose, 2001)

——Assia Djebar, nomade entre les murs: pour une poétique transfrontalière (Paris: Maisonneuve & Larose, 2005)

CAVARERO, ADRIANA, Horrorism: Naming Contemporary Violence (New York: Columbia University Press, 2009)

CAYROL, JEAN, Muriel (Paris: Éditions du Seuil, 1963)

CELIK, IPEK A., ' "I wanted you to be present": Guilt and the History of Violence in Michael Haneke's Caché', Cinema Journal, 50:1 (2010), 59–80

CHATTERJEE, PARTHA, The Nation and Its Fragments: Colonial and Postcolonial Histories (Princeton: Princeton University Press, 1994)

CHION, MICHEL, 'Without Music: On Caché', in A Companion to Michael Haneke, ed. by Roy Grundmann (Oxford: Wiley-Blackwell, 2010), 161–67

CHUA, LAWRENCE, 'Michael Haneke', BOMB, (Summer 2002) <http://bombsite.com/ issues/80/articles/2489> [Accessed 28 May 2013]

CIXOUS, HÉLÈNE, 'Pieds nus', in Une enfance algérienne, ed. by Leïla Sebbar (Paris: Gallimard, 1997)

——Les rêveries de la femme sauvage: Scènes primitives (Paris: Gallilée, 2000)

CLERC, JEANNE-MARIE, Assia Djebar: Écrire, Transgresser, Résister (Paris: Harmattan, 1997)

COLE, JOSHUA, 'Entering History: The Memory of Police Violence in Paris, October 1961', in Algeria & France, 1800–2000: Identity, Memory, Nostalgia, ed. by Patricia M. E. Lorcin (Syracuse: Syracuse University Press, 2006), 117–34

COLLECTIF RASPOUTEAM, 17.10.61 <http://www.politis.fr/17octobre1961/> [Accessed 14 January 2015]

COOKE, PAUL, and ROB STONE (eds.), Screening European Heritage: Creating and Consuming History on Film (London: Palgrave Macmillan, 2016)

CORREAU, LAURENT, 'Sarkozy a été "victime de son nègre"', RFI (18 September 2008) <http://www1.rfi.fr/actufr/articles/105/article_72481.asp> [Accessed 23 June 2017]

COUSINS, MARK, 'After the end: word of mouth and Caché', Screen, 48:2, 223–26

CROOMBS, MATTHEW, 'Algeria Deferred: The Logic of Trauma in Muriel and Caché', Scope: An Online Journal of Film and Television Studies 16 (2010)

CROWLEY, PATRICK, 'Images of Algeria: Turning and Turning in the Widening Gyre', Expressions maghrébines, 6 (2007), 79–92

DAENINCKX, DIDIER, Meurtres pour mémoire (Paris: Gallimard, 1983)

DAENINCKX, DIDIER, and MAKO, Octobre noir (Paris: AD Libris, 2011)

DERDERIAN, RICHARD L., 'Algeria as a Lieu de Memoire: Ethnic Minority Memory and National Identity in Contemporary France', Radical History Review, 83 (2002), 28–43

DERRIDA, JACQUES, 'Circonfession', in Geoffrey Bennington and Jacques Derrida, Jacques Derrida (Paris: Éditions du Seuil, 1991)

——Le monolinguisme de l'autre (Paris: Galilée, 1996)

——De l'hospitalité (Paris: Calmann-Lévy, 1997)

DI CEGLIE, GIOVANNA, and ANDREA SABBADINI, 'A Camera inside a Monastery: Reflections on Of Gods and Men [Des hommes et des dieux]', The International Journal of Psychoanalysis, 91 (2011), 745–54

DINE, PHILIP, Images of the Algerian War: French Fiction and Film, 1954–1992 (Oxford: Clarendon Press, 1994)

DJEBAR, ASSIA, L'amour, la fantasia: roman (Paris: Lattès, 1985)

——Femmes d'Alger dans leur appartement: nouvelles (Paris: Albin Michel, 2002)

——La Femme sans sépulture (Paris: Albin Michel, 2002)

——'Discours de Mme Assia Djebar', *Le Figaro* (22 June 2006) <http://www.lefigaro.fr/pdf/AssiaDjebar.pdf > [Accessed 10 April 2017]

DONADEY, ANNE, 'Rekindling the Vividness of the Past: Assia Djebar's Films and Fiction', *World Literature Today*, 70 (1996), 885–92

EINAUDI, JEAN-LUC, *La Bataille de Paris, 17 octobre 1961* (Paris: Seuil, 1991)

——*Scènes de la guerre d'Algérie en France* (Paris: le cherche midi, 2009)

ELSAESSER, THOMAS, *European Cinema: Face to Face with Hollywood* (Amsterdam: Amsterdam UP, 2003)

ENTELIS, JOHN P., 'Algeria: Democracy denied, and revived?', *The Journal of North African Studies*, 16:4 (2011), 653–78

EVANS, MARTIN, and JOHN PHILLIPS, *Algeria: Anger of the Dispossessed* (New Haven: Yale University Press, 2007)

EZRA, ELIZABETH & JANE SILLARS, 'Hidden in Plain Sight: Bringing Terror Home', *Screen*, 48:2 (2007), 215–21

FANON, FRANTZ, *Peau noire, masques blancs* (Paris: Seuil, 1952)

——*L'an V de la révolution Algérienne* (Paris: Découverte, [1959] 2001)

——*The Wretched of the Earth*, trans. Constance Farrington (London: Penguin Modern Classics [1967] 2001)

——*Les Damnés de la terre* (Paris: Éditions La Découverte Poche [1961] 2002)

FARMER, ROBERT, 'Marker, Resnais, Varda: Remembering the Left Bank Group', *Senses of Cinema*, 52 (2009) <http://sensesofcinema.com/2009/feature-articles/marker-resnais-varda-remembering-the-left-bank-group/> [Accessed 3 April 2017]

FEVRY, SÉBASTIEN, 'Sepia Cinema in Nicolas Sarkozy's France: Nostalgia and National Identity', *Studies in French Cinema*, 17:1 (2017), 60–74

FITZMAURICE, ANDREW, 'The Genealogy of *Terra Nullius*', *Australian Historical Studies*, 38:129 (2007), 1–15

FLOOD, MARIA, 'Common Vulnerability: Considering Community and its Presentation in Assia Djebar's *La Nouba des femmes du Mont Chenoua* (1978)', *Modern and Contemporary France*, 21:1 (2013), 73–88

——'Politics and the Police: Documenting the 17 October 1961 Massacre', *Contemporary French and Francophone Studies*, 20:4–5 (2016), 599–606

——'Terrorism and Visibility in Algeria's 'Black Decade: *Des hommes et des dieux* (2010)' *French Cultural Studies*, 27:1 (2016), 62–72

——'Brutal Visibility: Framing Majid's Suicide in Michael Haneke's *Caché* (2005)', *Nottingham French Studies*, 56:1 (2017), 82–97

——'Women Resisting Terror: Imaginaries of Violence in Algeria (1966–2002)', *The Journal of North African Studies*, 22:1 (2017), 109–31

FOUCAULT, MICHEL, *Le Corps utopique, les hétérotopies* (Paris: Nouvelles Editions Lignes, 2009)

FREUD, SIGMUND, *The Uncanny* (London: Penguin Books, 2003)

FREY, MATTIAS, 'Haneke's Film Theory and Digital Praxis', in *On Michael Haneke*, ed. by Brian Price and John David Rhodes (Michigan: Wayne State University Press, 2010), 153–66

GALT, ROSALIND, *The New European Cinema: Redrawing the Map* (New York: Columbia University Press, 2006)

GAUCH, SUZANNE, 'Muriel, or the Disappearing Text of the Algerian War', *Esprit Créateur*, 41 (2001), 47–57

GEORGES, CHRISTIAN, 'Résumé — *Des hommes et des dieux*', *Madiana* (2010) <http://www.madiana.ws/pdf/deshommes.pdf> [Accessed 31 July 2013]

GILROY, PAUL, 'Shooting Crabs in a Barrel', *Screen*, 48:2 (2007), 233–35

GOODALL, H.L., JR, PAULINE HOPE CHEONG, KRISTEN FLEISCHER and STEVEN R. CORMAN, 'Rhetorical Charms: The Promise and Pitfalls of Humor and Ridicule as Strategies to Counter Extremist Narratives', *Perspectives on Terrorism*, 6:1 (2012), 70–79

GRACKI, KATHERINE, 'Writing Violence and the Violence of Writing in Assia Djebar's Algerian Quartet', *World Literature Today*, 70 (1996), 835–43

GREENE, NAOMI, *Landscapes of Loss: The National Past in Postwar French Cinema* (Princeton NJ: Princeton University Press, 1999)

GRIGSBY, DARCY GRIMALDO, 'Origins and Colonies: Delacroix's Algerian Harem', in *The Cambridge Companion to Delacroix* ed. by Beth S. Wright (Cambridge: Cambridge University Press, 2001)

HADJ-MOUSSA, RATIBA, 'Marginality and Ordinary Memory: Body Centrality and the Plea for Recognition in Recent Algerian Films', *The Journal of North African Studies*, 13 (2008), 187–99

HANEKE, MICHAEL, 'Violence and the Media', in *A Companion to Michael Haneke*, ed. by Roy Grundmann (Oxford: Wiley-Blackwell, 2010), 575–79

HARBI, MOHAMMED, and GILBERT MEYNIER, *Le FLN, documents et histoire: 1954–1962* (Paris: Fayard, 2004)

HARPHAM, GEOFFREY GALT, *On the Grotesque: Strategies of Contradiction in Art and Literature* (Princeton, NJ: Princeton University Press)

HARRISON, NICHOLAS, *Postcolonial Criticism: History, Theory and the Work of Fiction* (West Sussex: Wiley, 2003)

HAYWARD, SUSAN, *Cinema Studies: The Key Concepts*, 2nd edn (London: Routledge, 2000)

HEYNS, CHRISTOF, *Human Rights Law in Africa: 1999* (The Hague: Kluwer Law International, 2002)

HIDDLESTON, JANE, *Assim Djebar: Out of Algeria* (Liverpool: Liverpool University Press, 2011)

HIGBEE, WILL, 'Locating the Postcolonial in Transnational Cinema: The Place of Algerian Émigré Directors in Contemporary French Film', *Modern and Contemporary France*, 15:1 (2007), 51–64

HIGSON, ANDREW, 'Re-Presenting the National Past: Nostalgia and Pastiche in the Heritage Film', in *Fires were Started: British Cinema and Thatcherism*, ed. by Lester D. Friedman (New York: Wallflower Press, 2006), 91–109

—— 'Nostalgia is not what it used to be: Heritage Films, Nostalgia Websites and Contemporary Consumers', *Consumption Markets & Culture*, 17:2 (2014), 120–42

HORNE, ALISTAIR, *A Savage War of Peace: Algeria 1954–1962* (London: Pan, 2002)

HOUSE, JIM, and NEIL MACMASTER, *Paris 1961: Algerians, State Terror, and Memory* (Oxford: Oxford University Press, 2006)

HUFFER, LYNNE, 'Derrida's Nostalgeria', in *Algeria & France, 1800–2000: Identity, Memory, Nostalgia*, ed. by Patricia M. E. Lorcin (Syracuse: Syracuse University Press, 2006), 228–46

HUUGHE, LAURENCE, *Écrits sous le voile, romancières algériennes francophones, écriture et identité* (Paris: Éditions Publisud, 2001)

IGHILAHRIZ, LOUISETTE, and ANNE NIVAT, *Algérienne* (Paris: Calmann-Lévy, 2001)

IVAKHIV, ADRIAN, 'Cinema of the Not-Yet: The Utopian Promise of Film as Heterotopia', *Journal for the Study of Religion, Nature and Culture*, 5:2 (2011), 186–209

JAUFFRET, JEAN-CHARLES and CHARLES ROBERT AGERON, *Des hommes et des femmes en guerre d'Algérie* (Paris: Autrement, 2003)

JEFFRIES, STUART, 'The Best Exotic Nostalgia Boom: Why Colonial Style is Back', *The Guardian* (19 March 2015) <https://www.theguardian.com/culture/2015/mar/19/the-best-exotic-nostalgia-boom-why-colonial-style-is-back> [Accessed 15 December 2016]

KHANNA, RANJANA, 'From Rue Morgue to Rue des Iris', *Screen*, 48:2 (2007), 237–44

——*Algeria Cuts: Women and Representation, 1830 to the Present* (Redwood City: Stanford University Press, 2008)

KISER, JOHN W., *The Monks of Tibhirine: Faith, Love, and Terror in Algeria* (New York: St. Martin's Griffin, 2002)

——*Passion pour l'Algérie: les moines de Tibhirine*, trans. Henry Quinson (Paris: Nouvelle Cité, 2006)

KLANGWISAN, YAEL, '*Of Gods and Men*: Radical hospitality and the monks of Tibhirine', *Stimulus: The New Zealand Journal of Christian Thought and Practice*, 21:1 (2014), 34–35

KRISTIANASEN, WENDY, 'Truth & Justice after a Brutal Civil War: Algeria: The Women Speak', *Review of African Political Economy*, 33:108 (2006), 346–51

KUNKLE, RYAN, '"We Must Shout the Truth to the Rooftops": Gisèle Halimi, Djamila Boupacha, and Sexual Politics in the Algerian War of Independence', *Iowa Historical Review*, 4:1 (2013), 5–24

LAINE, TARJA, 'Hidden Shame Exposed: *Hidden* and the Spectator', in *The Cinema of Michael Haneke: Europe Utopia*, ed. by Ben McCann and David Sorfa (New York: Wallflower Press, 2011), 247–55

LAZREG, MARNIA, *Torture and the Twilight of Empire: From Algiers to Baghdad* (Princeton: Princeton University Press, 2008)

LE CLÉZIO, MARGUERITE, 'Assia Djebar: écrire dans la langue adverse', *Contemporary French Civilization*, 9 (1985), 230- 231

LEBJAOUI, MOHAMED, *Bataille d'Alger ou bataille d'Algérie?* (Paris: Gallimard, 1972)

LECLÈRE, THIERRY, 'Derniers mois à Tibhirine', *Télérama* (11 September 2010) <http://www.telerama.fr/cinema/derniers-mois-a-tibhirine,59905.php> [Accessed 16 June 2017]

LEGG, STEPHEN, 'Contesting and Surviving Memory: Space, Nation, and Nostalgia in *Les Lieux de Mémoire*', *Environment and Planning D: Society and Space*, 23:4 (2005), 481–504

LEMAIRE, VINCENT, and YANN POTIN, '"Ici on noie les algériens": Fabriques documentaires, avatars politiques et mémoires partagées d'une icône militante (1961–2001)', *Genèses* 49 (2002), 140–62

Le Monde, La Nuit oubliée <http://www.lemonde.fr/societe/visuel/2011/10/17/la-nuit-oubliee_1587567_3224.html> [Accessed 14 January 2015]

LEVY, MARIE-FRANÇOISE, 'Interview: Assia Djebar', *Le Monde* (28–29 May 1978)

LEYRIS, RAPHAËLLE, 'Mort de l'académicienne Assia Djebar', *Le Monde* (7 February 2015) <http://www.lemonde.fr/culture/article/2015/02/07/mort-de-l-academicienne-assia-djebar_4572120_3246.html> [Accessed 26 October 2016]

LLOYD, CATHERINE, 'From Taboo to Transnational Political Issue: Violence against Women in Algeria', *Women's Studies International Forum*, 29:5 (2006), 453–62

LUSTIGER, JEAN-MARIE, 'Entretien', *Le Monde*, no. 15965, Paris (26–27 May 1996)

LYKIDIS, ALEX, 'Multicultural Encounters in Haneke's French-Language Cinema', in *A Companion to Michael Haneke*, ed. by Roy Grundmann (Oxford: Wiley-Blackwell, 2010), 455–76

MacMASTER, NEIL, *Burning the Veil: The Algerian War and the 'Emancipation' of Muslim Women, 1954–62* (Manchester: Manchester University Press, 2009)

MARTIN, FLORENCE, *Screens and Veils: Maghrebi Women's Cinema* (Bloomington: Indiana University Press, 2011)

MASSU, JACQUES, *La Vraie Bataille d'Alger* (Paris: Éditions du Rocher-J.-P. Bertrand, 1997)

McELROY, BERNARD, *Fiction of the Modern Grotesque* (London, The Macmillan Press, 1989)

McGONAGLE, JOSEPH, and EDWARD WELCH, 'Untying the Knot? France and Algeria in Contemporary Visual Culture', *Modern and Contemporary France*, 19:2 (2011), 123–28

McMAHON, LAURA, 'Untimely Resnais: *Muriel*'s Disarticulations of Justice', *Film Philosophy* 20.2–3 (2016), 219–34

MCNEILL, ISABELLE, *Memory and the Moving Image: French Film in the Digital Era* (Edinburgh: Edinburgh University Press, 2010)

MERKEL, IAN, 'Rachid Bouchareb's *Outside the Law*: Aesthetics and Reception in France', *Nka: Journal of Contemporary African Art*, 32 (2013), 62–69

MERNISSI, FATIMA, *Beyond the Veil: Male-female Dynamics in Modern Muslim Society* (Cambridge, MA: Saqi Books, 2003)

MILNE, TOM, '*Muriel ou Le Temps d'un retour*', *Monthly Film Bulletin*, 31:364 (1964), 70–71

MOKNÈCHE, NADIR, 'Nadir Moknèche à Alger', *Le Monde* (1 August 2003) <http://www.liberation.fr/cahier-special/2003/08/01/cette-ville-c-est-la-maman-et-la-putain-nadir-mokneche-a-alger_441196> [Accessed 2 May 2017]

MONACO, JAMES, *Alain Resnais: The Rôle of Imagination* (London: Secker & Warburg, 1978)

MORIN, FABIEN, 'Disparition de l'académicienne Assia Djebar: les hommages se multiplient', *Le Figaro* (7 February 2015) <http://www.lefigaro.fr/livres/2015/02/07/03005-20150207ARTFIG00077-disparition-de-l-academicienne-assia-djebar-les-hommages-se-multiplient.php> [Accessed 26 October 2016]

MORTIMER, MILDRED, 'Assia Djebar's "Algerian Quartet": A Study in Fragmented Autobiography', *Research in African Literatures*, 28 (1997), 102–17

MULVEY, LAURA, 'Visual Pleasure and Narrative Cinema', *Screen*, 16:3 (1975), 6–18

NANCY, JEAN-LUC, *La Communauté Désœuvrée* (Paris: Christian Bourgois Éditeur, 2004)

NICHOLS, BILL, *Introduction to Documentary*, 2nd edn (Bloomington and Indianapolis: Indiana University Press, 2010)

NOOR AL-DEEN, HANA, 'The Evolution of Rai Music', *Journal of Black Studies*, 35:3 (2005), 597–611

NORA, PIERRE, *Les Lieux de mémoire: Vol. 1, La République* (Paris: Gallimard, 1984)

—— *Vol. 2, La Nation* (Paris: Gallimard, 1986)

—— *Vol. 3, Les France* (Paris: Gallimard, 1992)

NOWELL-SMITH, DAVID, 'Of Gods and Humanitarians', *Film Quarterly*, 64 (2011), 59–61

O'GORMAN, KEVIN, 'Jacques Derrida's Philosophy of Hospitality', *Hospitality Review*, 8:4 (2006), 50–57

O'RILEY, MICHAEL F., *Postcolonial Haunting and Victimization: Assia Djebar's New Novels* (Oxford: Peter Lang, 2007)

O'BEIRNE, EMER, 'Veiled Vision: Assia Djebar on Delacroix, Picasso, and the *Femmes D'Alger*', *Romance Studies*, 21:1 (2013), 39–51

O'BRIEN, ALYSSA J., 'Manipulating Visual Pleasure in *Muriel*', *Quarterly Review of Film & Video*, 17 (2000), 49–61

PARKER, MARK, '*The Battle of Algiers (La battaglia di Algeri)*', *Film Quarterly*, 60:4 (2007), 62–66

PASQUALI, ELAINE ANNE, 'Humor: An Antidote for Terrorism', *Journal of Holistic Nursing*, 21:4 (2003), 398–414

PÉJU, PAULETTE, *Ratonnades à Paris, précédé de Les Harkis A Paris* (Paris: La Découverte, 2000)

PÉRON, DIDIER, and BENJAMIN STORA, 'Interview avec Benjamin Stora: Des victimes françaises de l'histoire algérienne', *Libération* (25 September 2010) <http://next.liberation.fr/cinema/2010/09/25/des-victimes-francaises-de-l-histoire-algerienne_681614> [Accessed 31 May 2017]

PETIT, JEAN-FRANÇOIS, '*Des hommes et des dieux*: un phénomène de presse catholique?', *Transversalités*, 2:118 (2011), 123–35

PRÉDAL, RENÉ, *Alain Resnais* (Paris: Minard, 1968)

PRYLUCK, CALVIN, '"Ultimately We Are All Outsiders": The Ethics of Documentary Filming', *Journal of the University Film Association*, 28:1 (1976), 21–29

RANCIÈRE, JACQUES, 'La Cause de l'autre', *Lignes*, 1:30 (1997), 36–49

——*Aux bords du politique* (Paris: Gallimard, 1998)

——*Le destin des images* (Paris: La Fabrique, 2003)

——'Who is the Subject of the Rights of Man?', *South Atlantic Quarterly*, 103: 2/3 (2004), 297–310

——*The Future of the Image*, trans. Gregory Elliott (London: Verso, 2007)

——*Dissensus: On Politics and Aesthetics*, trans. Steven Corcoran (New York: Bloomsbury Academic, 2010)

——*Figures de l'histoire* (Paris: Presses Universitaires de France, 2012)

——*Figures of History*, trans. Julie Rose (Cambridge: Polity Press, 2014)

——'Les idéaux républicains sont devenus des armes de discrimination et de mépris', *L'Obs* (2 April 2015) <http://campvolant.com/2015/04/04/jacques-ranciere-les-ideaux-republicains-sont-devenus-des-armes-de-discrimination-et-de-mepris/> [Accessed 19 May 2015]

RAVITCH, NORMAN, 'Your People, My People; Your God, My God: French and American Troubles Over Citizenship', *The French Review*, 70:4 (1997), 515–27

REJALI, DARIUS, *Torture and Democracy* (Princeton: Princeton Univeristy Press, 2007)

REY, BENOÎT, *Les Égorgeurs* (Paris: Editions de Minuit, 1961)

RINGROSE, PRISCILLA, *Assia Djebar: In Dialogue with Feminisms* (Amsterdam: Rodopi, 2006)

RIVI, LUISA, *European Cinema after 1989: Cultural Identity and Transnational Production* (Basingstoke/New York: Palgrave Macmillan, 2007)

ROSELLO, MIREILLE, *Reparative in Narratives: Works of Mourning in Progress* (Liverpool: Liverpool University Press, 2010)

ROTHBERG, MICHAEL, *Multidirectional Memory: Remembering the Holocaust in the Age of Decolonization* (Stanford: Stanford University Press, 2009)

ROSEN, ELISHEVA, 'L'Étrange séduction du grotesque', in *À la recherche du grotesque* (Colloque international, Institut finlandais, Paris), ed. by Paul Gorcex (Paris: J & S Éditeur, 2003)

ROSENSTONE, ROBERT, *History on Film: Film on History* (London: Routledge, 2006)

ROSS, KRISTIN, *Fast Cars, Clean Bodies: Decolonization and the Reordering of French Culture* (Cambridge, MA: MIT Press, 1996)

ROTMAN, PATRICK and BERTRAND TAVERNIER, *La Guerre sans nom: les appelés d'Algérie (1954–1962)* (Paris: Seuil, 1992)

RUIMY, JORDAN, 'Haneke talks "Happy End"', *The Playlist* (23 May 2017) <http://theplaylist.net/michael-haneke-talks-making-happy-end-wont-explain-film-cannes-20170523/> [Accessed 15 June 2017]

SAÏD, EDWARD, *Orientalism* (London: Penguin Modern Classics [1978] 2003)

SALHI, KAMAL, 'Assia Djebar Speaking: An Interview with Assia Djebar', *International Journal of Francophone Studies*, 2:3 (1999), 168–82

SANSAL, BOULEM, *Poste restante: Alger. Lettre de colère et d'espoir à mes compatriotes* (Paris: Gallimard, 2006)

SARKOZY, NICOLAS, 'Le Discours de Dakar', *Le Monde* (9 November 2007) <http://www.lemonde.fr/afrique/article/2007/11/09/le-discours-de-dakar_976786_3212.html#IzFdCdfucWIKwEwQ.99> [Accessed 2 October 2016]

SARRIS, ANDREW, 'Notes on the "Auteur" Theory in 1962', in *Film Theory and Criticism: Introductory Readings*, ed. by Leo Braudy and Marshell Cohen, 6th edn (Oxford: Oxford University Press, 2004), 400–03

SAXTON, LIBBY, 'Close Encounters with Distant Suffering: Michael Haneke's Disarming Visions', in *Five Directors: Auteurism from Assayas to Ozon*, ed. by Kate Ince (Manchester: Manchester University Press, 2008), 84–111

SCARRY, ELAINE, *The Body in Pain: The Making and Unmaking of the World* (Oxford: Oxford University Press, 1987)

SCHOR, NAOMI, 'The Crisis of French Universalism', *Yale French Studies*, 100 (2001), 43–64

SCOTT, JOAN W., *Gender and the Politics of History* (New York: Columbia University Press, 1988)

SEBBAR, LEILA, *La Seine était rouge* (Paris: Actes Sud, 2009)

SHARPE, MANI, 'Representations of Space in Assia Djebar's *La nouba des femmes du Mont Chenoua*', *Studies in French Cinema*, 13:3 (2013), 215–25

SILVERMAN, MAX, 'Horror and the Everyday in Post-Holocaust France: *Nuit et brouillard* and Concentrationary Art', *French Cultural Studies*, 17:1 (2006), 5–18

——'The Empire Looks Back', *Screen*, 48:2 (2007), 245–49

SLAVIN, DAVID HENRY, *Colonial Cinema and Imperial France, 1919–1939* (Baltimore, MD: The Johns Hopkins University Press, 2001)

SMAIL SALHI, ZAHIA, 'The Algerian Feminist Movement between Nationalism, Patriarchy and Islamism', *Women's Studies International Forum*, 33:2 (2010), 113–24

SMITH, KIMBERLY, 'Mere Nostalgia: Notes on a Progressive Paratheory', *Rhetoric and Public Affairs*, 3:4 (2000), 505–27

SONTAG, SUSAN, *Regarding the Pain of Others* (New York: Farrer, Strauss & Giraux, 2001)

STONE, MARTIN, *The Establishment of Algeria* (London: Hurst & Co., 1997)

STORA, BENJAMIN, *La Gangrène et l'oubli: la mémoire de la guerre d'Algérie en France* (Paris: La Découverte, 1991)

——*La Guerre invisible: Algérie, années 90* (Paris: Presses de Sciences Po, 2001)

——'Entretien avec Nadir Moknèche, réalisateur de "Viva Laldjérie"' (2004), *Dossier de presse: Les Films de Losange* <http://www.filmsdulosange.fr/uploads/presskits/4ae93e0a97 07b0b588761335dcbd5d0ffb756da2.pdf> [Accessed 2 May 2017]

TARR, CARRIE, *Reframing Difference: Beur and Banlieue Filmmaking in France* (Manchester: Manchester University Press, 2005)

TERRIO, SUSAN, 'Crucible of the Millenium? The Clovis Affair in Contemporary France', *Comparative Studies in Society and History*, 41:3 (1999), 438–57

THIBAUD, PAUL, 'Le 17 octobre 1961: Un moment de notre histoire', *Esprit*, 279 (2001), 6–19

THOMPSON, VICTORIA, 'I went Pale with Pleasure', in *Algeria & France, 1800–2000: Identity, Memory, Nostalgia*, ed. by P. M. E. Lorcin (Syracuse: Syracuse University Press, 2006), 18–32

THOMSON, PHILIP, *The Grotesque* (London: Matheur & Co., 1972)

THORPE, VANESSA, 'The Unlikeliest Box-office Hit: a film about doomed French Monks', *The Guardian* (28 November 2010) <http://www.theguardian.com/film/2010/nov/28/ film-french-monks-arthouse-hit> [Accessed 31 July 2013]

THURSTON, ANNE, 'The Eucharist: Passion for Life: — a reflection on "Of Gods and Men"', *The Furrow*, 62:5 (2011), 259–65

TODOROV, TZVETAN, *Nous et les autres* (Paris: Seuil, 1989)

——'Torture in the Algerian War', trans. by Arthur Denner, *South Central Review*, 24 (2007), 18–26

TOWNSHEND, CHARLES, *Terrorism: A Very Short Introduction* (Oxford: Oxford University Press, 2002)

TRANCHANT, MARIE-NOËLLE, '"Des hommes et des dieux": le cinéma en état de grâce', *Le Figaro* (7 September 2010) <http://www.lefigaro.fr/cinema/2010/09/06/03002– 20100906ARTFIG00802-des-hommes-et-des-dieux-le-cinema-en-etat-de-grace.php> [Accessed 31 July 2013]

TURSHEN, MEREDETH, 'Algerian Women in the Liberation Struggle and the Civil War: From Active Participants to Passive Victims?', *Social Research*, 69:3 (2002), 889–911

UNITED NATIONS GENERAL ASSEMBLY (July-August 1998), 'Report of the Panel Appointed by the Secretary General to Gather Information on the Situation in Algeria (Report of Emininet Persons Panel)', April 1999 <http://www.un.org/NewLinks/dpi2007/contents. htm> [Accessed 12 January 2012]

VIDAL-NAQUET, PIERRE, *Les crimes de l'armée française: Algérie, 1954–1962* (Paris: La Découverte, 2001)

VIDAL, BELÉN, *Heritage Film: Nation, Genre and Representation* (New York: Wallflower Press, 2012)

VINCE, NATALYA, *Our Fighting Sisters: Nation, Memory and Gender in Algeria* (Manchester: Manchester University Press, 2015)

WHEATLEY, CATHERINE, *Caché [Hidden]: BFI Film Classics* (London: Palgrave Macmillan, 2011)

WHITTAKER, DAVID J., *The Terrorism Reader,* 3rd edn (London: Routledge, 2003)

WILLIAMS, LINDA, 'Melodrama Revised' in *Refiguring American Film Genres: History and Theory,* ed. Nick Browne (Berkeley: University of California Press, 1998), 42–88

WILSON, EMMA, *Alain Resnais* (Manchester: Manchester University Press, 2006)

WINDHOLZ, ANNE M., 'The Terrible and Sublime Liturgy: Sustaining Mission to the Suffering in Beauvois's *Of Gods and Men*', *New Theology Review,* 26:1 (2013), 63–74

WRIGHT, WENDY M., 'Of Gods and Men (2010)', *Journal of Religion & Film,* 15: 2 (2012)

WRIGHT, PATRICK, *On Living in an Old Country* (London: Verso, 1985)

ZIMRA, CLARISSE, 'Writing Woman: The Novels of Assia Djebar', *SubStance,* 21 (1992) 68–84

FILMOGRAPHY

❖

ADI, YASMINA, *Ici on noie les Algériens* (2011)

ALLOUACHE, MERZAK, *Omar Gatlato*, (1977)

—— *Bab El-Oued City* (1993)

BACHIR-CHOUIKH, YASMINA, *Rachida* (2002)

BEAUVOIS, XAVIER, *Nord* (1991)

—— *N'oublie pas que tu vas mourir* (1995)

—— *Selon Matthieu* (2000)

—— *Le Petit Lieutenant* (2005)

—— *Des hommes et des dieux* (2010)

BENGUIGUI, YAMINA, *Mémoire d'immigrées: les enfants* (1997)

—— *Inch Allah Dimanche* (2001)

BOUCHAREB, RACHID, *Indigènes* (2006)

—— *Hors la loi* (2010)

BOYLE, DANNY, *Slumdog Millionaire* (2008)

BROOKS, PHILIP, and ALAN HAYLING, *Une journée portée disparue: 17 octobre 1961* (1992)

COPPOLA, SOFIA, *Marie Antoinette* (2006)

DENIS, AGNÈS, *La Silence du fleuve* (1991)

DJEBAR, ASSIA, *La Nouba des femmes du Mont Chenoua* (1978)

DUVIVIER, JULIEN, *Pépé le moko* (1937)

FARÈS, TEWFIK, *Les hors la-loi* (1969)

FAUCON, PHILIPPE, *La Trahison* (2006)

GODARD, JEAN-LUC, *Le Petit Soldat* (1963)

GUERDJOU, BOURLEM, *Vivre au paradis* (1998)

HANEKE, MICHAEL, *The Seventh Continent* (1989)

—— *Funny Games* (1998)

—— *Code Inconnu* (2000)

—— *La Pianiste* (2001)

—— *Le Temps du Loup* (2003)

—— *Caché* (2005)

—— *The White Ribbon* (2009)

—— *Amour* (2012)

—— *Happy End* (2017).

HERBIET, LAURENT, *Mon colonel* (2006)

HUSTON, JOHN, *The Dead* (1987)

IVORY, JAMES, *A Room with a View* (1986)

JARMAN, DEREK, *Blue* (1993)

KLOTZ, NICOLAS, *La Blessure* (2004)

KUPFERSTEIN, DANIEL, *17 Octobre 1961: Dissimulation d'un massacre* (2001)

LAKHDAR-HAMINA, MOHAMMED, *Chronique des années de braise* (1974)

—— *Le Vent des Aurès* (1966)

LALLAOUI, MEHDI, *À propos d'Octobre* (2011)
LEAN, DAVID, *A Passage to India* (1984)
LLEDO, JEAN-PIERRE, *Un rêve Algérien* (2003)
MOKNÈCHE, NADIR, *Le Harem de Mme Osmane* (2000)
—— *Viva Laldjérie* (2004)
—— *Délice Paloma* (2007)
—— *Goodbye Morocco* (2013).
MADDEN, JOHN, *The Best Exotic Marigold Hotel* (2011)
PANIJEL, JACQUES, *Octobre à Paris* (1962)
PONTECORVO, GILLO, *Kapò* (1960)
—— *La Bataille d'Alger* (1966)
RESNAIS, ALAIN, *Les Statues meurent aussi* (1953)
—— *Nuit et Brouillard* (1955)
—— *Hiroshima mon amour* (1959)
—— *L'Année dernière à Marienbad* (1961)
—— *Muriel, ou le temps d'un retour* (1963)
ROTMAN, PATRICK, and BERTRAND TAVERNIER, *La Guerre sans nom: les appelés d'Algérie* (1992)
SAHRAOUI, DJAMILA, *Barakat!* (2006)
—— *Yema* (2012)
SPIELBERG, STEVEN, *Saving Private Ryan* (1998)
TASMA, ALAIN, *Nuit noire* (2005)
TOWNSEND, KATE, *We Have Ways of Making You Talk* (2005)

INDEX

❖

17 October 1961 massacre 1, 3–5, 10–16, 20, 24–25, 29, 30, 133

Addi, Lahouari 83, 106
Adi, Yasmina 1, 14
Alger: Etude 21
Algerian Civil War 2, 75–76, 81–88, 101, 104, 106–09, 114–15, 134, 136
Algerian War 2, 35, 37–40, 50–52, 58, 60–61, 134
Alleg, Henri 5, 7 n. 8, 41
Allouache, Merzak 84, 101 n. 27
Alloula, Malek 40
Amour 11
L'Année dernière à Marienbad 51
L'An V de la révolution algérienne 61
Arendt, Hannah 85
Austin, Guy 4, 12, 65
auteur 11

Bab El-Oued City 84
Bachir-Chouikh, Yamina 76, 114–15
Bancel, Nicolas 113, 136
Barakat! 84, 115
Barratier, Christophe 110
La Bataille d'Alger 3–4, 37, 41–42, 52, 61, 92, 115
La Bataille de Paris 13, 37
Bazin, André 36
Beaugé, Florence 38, 39
Beauvoir, Simone de 38, 50
Beauvois, Xavier 2, 104–05, 108, 123–25
Benkhaled, Walid 95
Bensmaïa, Réda 60
The Best Exotic Marigold Hotel 114
Bhabha, Homi K. 129 n. 36
La Blessure 56 n. 68
Biyouna 81, 89–90
Blanchard, Pascal 113, 136
Blue 56 n. 68
Bouchareb, Rachid 3, 14
Boudjedra, Rachid 41, 67
Boumediène, Houari 61, 82
Boupacha, Djamila 5, 38–39, 50, 66
Boyle, Danny 114
Branche, Raphaëlle 38–40
Brecht, Bertolt 42
Brillat-Savarin, Jean Anthelme 17
Britton, Celia 50

Brunet, Jean-Paul 13, 108
Butler, Judith 52–53, 134

Caché 2, 4–5, 10–12, 16–31, 108, 133–34, 136
Cardinal Lustiger 108, 126
Cavarero, Adriana 86–87
Cayrol, Jean 36, 42–43, 45, 50
censorship 4, 32, 52, 133
Chaix, Roger 15, 24
Chatterjee, Partha 62
Chion, Michel 27
Chirac, Jacques 3, 108
Christianity 110–11, 114, 116, 121, 123–27, 135
Les Choristes 110
Chronique des années de braise 65
cinéma de l'urgence 2, 84–85
cinéma djidid 66
cinéma moudjahid 2, 65–66
Cixous, Hélène 117
Code Inconnu 11
Cole, Joshua 12
Conrad, Joseph 21
Crowley, Patrick 93

Daeninckx, Didier 14
Les Damnés de la terre 21
The Dead 124
Delacroix, Eugène 40
Délice Paloma 93
Derderian, Richard 5
Derrida, Jacques 117–19, 127
Des hommes et des dieux 2, 5, 6, 84–85, 104–27, 133, 135–36
Dine, Philip 117
Dissimulation d'un massacre 14
Djebar, Assia 2, 5, 6, 58–77, 81, 134, 136
  Le Blanc de l'Algérie 59
  and *francophonie* 75–77, 136
  Femmes d'Alger dans leur appartment 59, 64, 74, 77
  La Femme sans sépulture 59, 68, 74
  Loin de Médine 59
  Vaste est la prison 59
Donadey, Anne 60, 73
Duvivier, Julien 21

Les Egorgeurs 21
Einaudi, Jean-Luc 5, 12–13, 108

Elsaesser, Thomas 11, 94
Evans, Martin 107–08
Ezra, Elizabeth 12, 16

Fanon, Frantz 21, 41, 61, 68, 115
Farès, Tewfik 65
Farmer, Robert 36
Faucon, Philippe 36
Fevry, Sébastien 110
Feydeau, Ernest 21
Les Filles du feu 21
Flaubert, Gustave 21
Flood, Maria 12, 32 n. 29, 60
Foucault, Michel 96–97, 99–100, 133
French New Wave 2, 36
Front de Libération Nationale 10, 12–15, 37, 61, 66–67, 83, 92

Gauch, Suzanne 47
Gilroy, Paul 12, 25, 114
Godard, Jean-Luc 36, 41
Goodbye Morocco 93
Grimaldo Grigsby, Darcy 40
grotesque 12, 25–31, 134
Guerdjou, Bourlem 14
La Guerre des Boutons 110

Hadj-Moussa, Ratiba 92, 96, 100
Halimi, Gisèle 38
Haneke, Michael 2, 5, 10–12, 14, 16–31, 35, 105, 133–34
Happy End 30–31
Harbi, Mohammed 61
Le Harem de Mme Osmane 93, 100
Harrison, Nicholas 74–75
Hayward, Susan 122
The Heart of Darkness 21
Herbiet, Laurent 36, 116
heritage film 106, 109–10, 120
heterotopia 96–100, 133, 135
Hiddleston, Jane 71, 72
Higbee, Will 4
Higson, Andrew 106, 109–10
Hiroshima mon amour 33 n. 42, 36, 58
Hollande, François 59
Horne, Alistair 39
Hors la loi 3, 4, 14, 127
Les hors-la-loi 65
House, Jim 12
Huston, John 124
Huffer, Lynne 118, 127

Ici on noie les Algériens 1, 14
Indigènes 3, 4
Ivory, James 110

Jarman, Derek 56 n. 68
Jeunet, Jean-Pierre 110
Joyce, James 124

Kagan, Elie 16
Khanna, Ranjana 11, 21, 70
Kiser, John 107
Klotz, Nicolas 56 n. 68
Kunkle, Ryan 40
Kupferstein, Daniel 14

Lakhdar-Hamina, Mohammed 65, 92
Lakhous, Amara 75
Lazreg, Marnia 39, 66
Lean, David 110, 114
Les Lieux de mémoire 5
Lledo, Jean-Pierre 37
Un long dimanche de fiançailles 110
Lonsdale, Michael 104, 108, 131 n. 70

Macmaster, Neil 12
Madden, Joan 114
Malle, Louis 47
Marie Antoinette 105
Marker, Chris 36
McElroy, Bernard 25, 26, 29
McGonagle, Joseph 6
McNeill, Isabelle 12, 32 n. 30
Meurtres pour mémoire 14
Meynier, Gilbert 61
mission civilisatrice 116, 136
Moknèche, Nadir 2, 6, 81–83, 85, 87–88, 90, 92–96, 98, 100
Mon colonel 36, 41, 116, 118
Mortimer, Mildred 61
Mulvey, Laura 62
Muriel, ou le temps d'un retour 2–5, 35–37, 41–54, 58, 60, 108, 134, 136

N'oublie pas que tu vas mourir 105
Nancy, Jean-Luc 65
Nerval, Gérard de 21
Nichols, Bill 72
Nora, Pierre 5
Nord 105
nostalgia 109–14, 117–18, 136
La Nouba des femmes du Mont Chenoua 2, 5, 58–77, 134–36
nouvelle vague see French New Wave
Nowell-Smith, Geoffrey 121–22
Nuit et Brouillard 36, 42–43
Nuit noire 14

O'Brien, Alyssa 44
Octobre à Paris 16, 32 n. 29, 52
Omar Gatlato 101 n. 27

Panijel, Jacques 16, 32 n. 29
Papon, Maurice 12, 13, 16
A Passage to India 110, 114
Pépé le moko 21
Le Petit Lieutenant 105
Le Petit Nicolas 110
Le Petit Soldat 41, 52
Phillips, John 107–08
La Pianiste 11
pied–noir 109, 116–17
Pontecorvo, Gillo 3, 37, 42, 92
Pryluck, Calvin 71

Quinson, Henri 107–09

Rachida 76–77, 115
raï 98
Rancière, Jacques 6, 14–15, 25, 28, 30, 125, 133
Rejali, Darius 41–42, 51
Resnais, Alain 2, 5, 35–37, 41–54, 58, 134
Un rêve algérien 37, 41
Rey, Benoît 21
Robbe–Grillet, Alain 36, 51
A Room with a View 110
Rosello, Mireille 4, 14
Rosenstone, Robert 2, 3, 105–06
Rothberg, Michael 4
Rotman, Patrick 5, 39

Sagan, Françoise 59
Sahraoui, Djamila 84, 115
Saïd, Edward 130 n. 57
Sansal, Boualem 98
Sarkozy, Nicolas 119–20
Sarris, Andrew 11
Saving Private Ryan 3
Scarry, Elaine 49–51, 134
Schor, Naomi 120
Sebbar, Leïla 14
La Seine était rouge 14
Selon Matthieu 105
Sharpe, Mani 4, 60

Sillars, Jane 12, 16
Silverman, Max 12, 21, 43
Slumdog Millionaire 114
Smail Salhi, Zahia 61, 88
Sontag, Susan 28, 53, 70, 134
Sophia Coppola 105
Spielberg, Steven 3
Les Statues meurent aussi 36
Stora, Benjamin 6, 83–85, 93, 106, 108

Tarr, Carrie 4
Tasma, Alain 14
Tavernier, Bernard 5, 39
Le Temps du Loup 11
Texier, Jean 1
The Family Code 62, 88
Third Cinema 3
Thomas, François 47
Tirard, Laurent 110
Todorov, Tzvetan 38, 51, 76
torture 5, 37–40, 50–52, 134
Townshend, Charles 86
La Trahison 36, 41

uncanny 11, 21, 27
universalism 6, 120–21, 123–27, 133, 136

Varda, Agnès 36
Le Vent des Aurès 92
Vidal, Bélen 110, 112
Vince, Natalya 78 n. 10
Viva Laldjérie 2, 5–6, 81–83, 85–100, 104, 133–36
Vivre au paradis 14
Voyage en Orient 21

Welch, Edward 6
Wheatley, Catherine 11
The White Ribbon 105
Wilson, Emma 50–51

Yema 84, 115